Approaching
Authority

Approaching Authority

Transpersonal Gestures in the Poetry of Yeats, Eliot, and Williams

Anthony Flinn

Lewisburg
Bucknell University Press
London: Associated University Presses

Associated University Presses
440 Forsgate Drive
Cranbury, NJ 08512

Associated University Presses
16 Barter Street
London WC1A 2AH, England

Associated University Presses
P.O. Box 338, Port Credit
Mississauga, Ontario
Canada L5G 4L8

The paper used in this publication meets the requirements of the American National Standard for Permanence of Paper for Printed Library Materials Z39.48–1984.

Library of Congress Cataloging-in-Publication Data

Flinn, Anthony, 1954–
    Approaching authority : transpersonal gestures in the poetry of Yeats, Eliot, and Williams / Anthony Flinn.
        p.   cm.
    Includes bibliographical references and index.
    ISBN 0-8387-5340-X (alk. paper)
    1. American poetry—20th century—History and criticism.
2. Yeats, W. B. (William Butler), 1865–1939. Tower.   3. Eliot, T. S. (Thomas Stearns), 1888–1965. Four quartets.   4. Williams, William Carlos, 1883–1963. Paterson.   5. Modernism literature—United States.   6. Modernism (Literature)—Ireland.   7. Authority in literature.   I. Title.
PS310.M57F58   1997
821'.91209—dc21   96-52060
                                                                    CIP

PRINTED IN THE UNITED STATES OF AMERICA

Contents

Acknowledgments

In this book I argue that the pursuit of cultural authority is, at bottom, an effort to redeem the self from disorienting, vertiginous isolation. The more conspicuous the pursuit, like writing a book, for example, the greater the danger to the integrity of the self. For this reason, acknowledgments are especially important, for they remind us that writing a book is not so solitary as it seems, except perhaps in the literal sense. Those who, however distantly, stood by as I wrote remain vital presences in my thinking.

Most prominently, these include Malcolm Griffith, Jacob Korg, and Robert Abrams, from the University of Washington; but most especially Charles Altieri, whose arduous acumen is approached only by his generosity, an attribute he is, of course, too generous to acknowledge. I would also like to thank Michael Cavanagh, long of Grinnell College, who early on refused to discourage me.

I must also thank Paul Metzner for his predatory editorial eye on this manuscript, and further thank the anonymous reviewers of Bucknell University Press for their astute and supportive comments, as well as the editorial and production staff at Associated University Presses for their professionalism and patience.

Finally, I dedicate these pages with gratitude to my wife, Tama, who has ever been with me—here, now, always.

Excerpts from W. B. Yeats's "The Tower" are reprinted by permission of Simon and Schuster and A P Watt Ltd., on behalf of Michael Yeats.

Excerpts from T. S. Eliot's *Four Quartets* are reprinted by permission of Harcourt Brace & Company and Faber and Faber Ltd.

Excerpts from William Carlos Williams's *Paterson,* copyright © 1946, 1948, 1949, 1951, are reprinted by permission of New Directions Publishing Corporation.

Jack Gilbert's poem, "They Call It Attempted Suicide," is reprinted by permission of the author.

Approaching
Authority

1
Introduction: Temporal and Atemporal Authority

Cervantes smiled Spain's chivalry away;
A single laugh demolished the right arm
Of his own country;—seldom since that day
Has Spain had heroes. While Romance could charm,
The World gave ground before her bright array;
And therefore have his volumes done such harm,
That all their glory, as a composition,
Was dearly purchased by his land's perdition.
—*Don Juan,* Canto 13, 11

This book traces the efforts of three modernist poets to craft and secure a voice of cultural authority. I have three purposes in this study: to describe the peculiarly modernist features of their quest for authority, to propose an approach for analyzing the authority's source and scope, and to demonstrate how the poetic strategies for crafting a voice of cultural authority disclose the pervading cultural assumptions with which poets must negotiate.

For the purposes of this study, I define "cultural authority" as a structure of beliefs, attitudes, and values used to interpret experience. A poetic "voice" of cultural authority, then, articulates its interpretive structure in order to describe and evaluate the conditions of perceived reality. It not only measures the "is" of experience against the "ought" of authority, but it can shape what constitutes the "is" of experience. Importantly, this voice—the text—is not the source of the authority, but rather its mediator, situated between internalized cultural principles and the individual consciousness in the act of perception. The relationship between the cultural authority and the mediating voice, however, is not a static one. The two are continuously engaged in a dialectic of mutual revision: as poetic speakers interpret and grant meaning to experience according to the ordering forces of their cultural authorities, the validity of those authorities is tested, and in times of crisis, challenged. For to serve as a means of interpretation and thus as a cultural authority, the prevailing structure of beliefs about the conditions of reality must seem to be authentic, that is, inductively derived from an empirically determined, though dynamic, sense of actuality. The extent to which a cultural authority fails the authenticity test that each poet implicitly puts to it is the extent to which the authority is revised or replaced. However, the challenge is not one-sided. The greater the poet's desire to challenge, revise, or dismantle a cultural authority—thereby reshaping the audience's interpretations of experience—the greater the poet's struggle to achieve mediating status. It is this tension within the effort to establish and then mediate a cultural authority that this book explores.

The above quotation from *Don Juan* suggests something of my focus; there exist few statements in Western literature that so explicitly address the authority of language to compose—and impose—structures of belief. A more recent statement, however, can help clarify that focus by foregrounding the interplay among poetic authority, the authenticity of poetic language, and the speaker's situation between the reader and the kind of authority the speaker professes:

> My brother's girlfriend was not prepared for how much blood
> splashed out. He got home in time, but was angry
> about the mess she had made of his room. I stood behind,
> watching them turn it into something manageable. Thinking
> how frightening it must have been before things had names.
> We say *peony* and make a flower out of that slow writhing.
> Deal with the horror of recurrence by calling it
> a million years. The death everywhere is no trouble
> once you see it as nature, landscape, or botany.
>
> (Gilbert, 53)

This poem quickly and simply introduces the expanse of my critical concerns. First, it explains the basis for poetic authority: that language, by mediating reality, has the fundamental role in authorizing our understanding of it. Second, given language's potency, the poet raises the question of its authenticity, implicitly demanding that language serve as a transparent medium for expressing experience rather than as an ideological tool. Third, the particular authority the poem draws upon is the concept of a fundamental, *a priori* version of reality that can be experienced directly when not ob-

scured or distorted by language. Of course, expressing in language
an assault on language's authenticity necessarily invites that same
assault. A poem's authority, and thus its value as a poem, can
survive only to the extent that we can accept the speaker as a
mediator; we must be convinced of the poet's disinterest.

It is because this speaker's disinterestedness is problematic that
the poem above is archetypal for my purposes. The speaker is an
explicitly marginal figure, remaining outside the action to situate
himself between it and the audience, to mediate our understanding
of the experiences he describes. His authority to mediate depends
on the authenticity of his language and on his self-staging as a
disinterested character. The poem, in turn, through the speaker's
mediating position, draws authority from the conception that language is authentic only when it can evoke rather than contain experience. As a mediator the speaker strives to become an avenue
toward, not the source of, the conception's authority. What makes
the speaker's situation engagingly ambiguous, however, is not the
inauthenticity of the authority the speaker mediates but the kind
of gestures he makes to demonstrate privileged access to a "truly
represented" reality. Setting "peony" against "slow writhing" dramatizes the contrast between generalizing language that names ar-
bitrarily and categorically, and particularizing language that almost
suggests self-authorizing expression of the thing itself. Thus "slow
writhing" seems more authentic than "peony" because it evokes a
unique experience of apprehending the flower in its essence as a
living thing. Moreover, the speaker's presence fades from focus,
joining the readers marveling at the "slow writhing." The conflu-
ence of these two conditions, authenticity and the speaker's detachment, enhances the speaker's authority. The "horror of
recurrence," however, marks a shift in the speaker's self-staging
and a challenge to his authority. It expresses a partisan reaction
to the expanse of a million years and therefore an intrusion into
the readers' experience of the expanse of time. The stronger the
speaker's reaction, the less (apparently) unmediated is the readers'
access to the experience. What finally sustains his authority to
mediate, though, in the face of his briefly partisan voice, is the
suspicion of language the poem generates, a suspicion serving as
the interpretive structure for which the speaker is merely the expression, not the source.

Though faced with similar issues, the modernist poetic speaker's
ability to mediate is made considerably more problematic because
of the prevailing sense of crisis: a new self-consciousness arising
from the felt distinction between an interpretive structure itself

and *belief* in the interpretive structure. Put another way, it is the distinction between the unconscious acceptance of a particular cultural authority and the self-conscious, willed, and thus skeptical commitment to its authenticity: the conviction that culturally authorized language can usefully represent experience versus the uneasy sense that the language replaces experience. Because the moderns lived in the latter, uneasy state of mind, a nostalgia for the former drove them, warily, to create or resuscitate the former and so restore the ground of human measure, the means of self-evaluation. In modernist poetry, I will argue, this effort is essentially a circular attempt, on the one hand, to establish the authenticity of an unarticulated cultural authority, and on the other, simultaneously to use that same authority to interpret contemporary experience. Naturally, such efforts to escape self-consciousness, when necessarily acknowledged as such, breed further self-consciousness. As I discuss below, this essentially neurotic condition forces the question of whether the individual reflecting consciousness is be of any cultural consequence.

One of my central premises about modernism is that there is a frustrating weight of history tied to the heels of all individual creative effort, so that one of the few claims that apologists for modernism can make for its originality is that beneath its rebellious rhetoric lies the nearly paralyzing belief that consequential individualizing gestures can no longer be authorized. What is new is the lack of possibility for the new, as well as the corresponding desire for the new.[1] Within this constricting circle of self-consciousness lies the primary project of the poets I consider here: the need to confront and transcend self-conscious examination of the mind, thus permitting identification of (and with) authorities that might enrich the modern identity. The poems of my primary figures here—Yeats, Eliot, and Williams—describe the mind's attempts at self-objectification, at removing its unauthorized presence from the mediating center of perception and replacing it with what I call a "transpersonal" one: an extension of the private self into the voice, or voices, of an entire culture.[2]

C. K. Stead's *The New Poetic* situates this modernist crisis of authority at a particular cultural source. He describes the prevailing voices of English poetry prior to the First World War as outwardly directed, seeking to please a self-satisfied, jingoistic audience that wanted only its own unexamined prejudices to be reinforced in print. Though Stead does not refer to it as such, this public, and the reviewers of periodicals like *Atheneum* and *The Daily Telegraph* who guided public taste, were the temporal arbiters of poetry's cultural authority. In concert they compelled obedience to the reviewers' dictates, possessing the standards, however vaguely articulated, by which poetry was judged and values were formed. If we accept Stead's examples as typical, the poetry endorsed by this authority is self-congratulatory in its civic-mindedness, and it presumes a unity of values, morality, and aspirations among readers whom the poet could shield from unsettling emotions.

In the relationship between reader and reviewer, Stead identifies two interlocking authorities that project a third to sustain them. The reviewers were the temporal figures in authority, yet their authority was granted and sustained by the tastes of the reading public. However, though the reviewers based their evaluations on what would be well received, the public was dependent upon the reviewers to instruct them in what they ought to receive well (Stead, 46). It is therefore the interplay between reader and reviewer that projects a structure of beliefs used to interpret contemporary experience.

This enclosed system of cultural authority was overthrown, I argue, because it failed two interrelated tests for authenticity: its description of contemporary reality lost its sense of authenticity, and it failed to project atemporal values grounded in authentic experience. Thus the "ought" that the authority exhorted did not correspond to the "is" of experience, as represented in the popular poetry. Put another way, because its descriptions did not seem to be derived from the felt realities of experience, the authority's terms for evaluating human action seemed ungrounded, unjustified. The atemporal beliefs authorizing this verse—patriotism, virginity, bourgeois prosperity, military glory—lost their credibility when felt to be a facade papering over a reality considerably less glossy and secure. Thus, the verse attacked by the new poetic crumbles when poked; its fictiveness is exposed, so the loss of the verse's credibility becomes an equivalent loss of authority. Literature then could not thrill, inspire, or bind a community if its assertions lived only in what is perceived to be fantasy; it could entertain but not be taken seriously, having no authority to reveal features of reality. As a result, this inauthentic public verse tried to survive solely on its own claims to authority, isolated in the incestuous play among reviewers, readers, and poets (Stead, 61–62). The literature, consequently, became inbred and repetitious, without the vitality of authenticity to restore its authority. What authorizes, then, must at least appear to dwell beyond the closed system of temporal authority and its subjects, and within that system there must dwell a faith in, first, the temporal authority's contact with atemporal values, and second, in its responsiveness to the demands of authenticity.[3]

These basic claims about the structure of poetic authority lead to two questions: what kind of atemporal values invest the new poetic with legitimate claims to the throne offered by public demand, and why should we examine these journalistic quarrels in terms of authority rather than by Stead's rhetorical model?[4] As for the latter question, these quarrels between the bourgeois press and the avant garde were struggles for control over poetic and cultural values; over the authority to state what poetry is and what it is for; over what ought to seize, engage, and inspire; and over conceptions of what constitutes the mind. As for the authority investing the new poetic, there was none, of course. Authority, temporal or atemporal, is present only where it is felt, and it exists only to the degree that it compels a specified or projected line of thought. I do not mean to imply, though, that all authorities are at bottom fictions—their basis in reality is of no concern to my purposes here. The issue, rather, is that when an authority is perceived to be fictional, serving interests other than the culture's need to understand and enhance itself, it is no longer an authority. The authorities that Sir Henry Newbolt and T. S. Eliot appealed to in their poetry are neither real nor unreal, but the fact that Eliot bears greater cultural weight than Newbolt suggests that the authority Eliot draws upon has been more convincingly mediated by his poetic speakers.[5]

But we need to look further at precisely which authority was overthrowing which, and if indeed it does make sense to speak of a modernist authority supplanting that of the bourgeois public. The temporal authority wielded by the new poet/critics like Eliot and Pound was contingent upon the belief that no attentive mind could locate value in either the sprawl of the contemporary world or in the efforts of the lone, idiosyncratic individual. Statements by such figures as Yeats, Eliot, Pound, and Hulme, expressing a sense of their Western civilization's diminished capacities and failed constructions, are well known; however extensive their differences, these poets all founded their aesthetics on the view that history is not progressive and that the modern mind is broken from any imaginary or real culture that might have granted the individual more than animal being.

The authority sustaining these poet/critics, though, is double-edged, both a negating and an affirming presence. First, to dislodge the hold of bourgeois complacence, they can point to the vanity of human efforts in the midst of the ugliness of contemporary existence, but doing so invokes no new authority to replace it. The new interpretive structure becomes an affirming presence—and thus an authority—when it can convincingly revitalize a set of values and a way of interpreting the world that justifies the mind's presence in it. It is a primary contention in modernist poetry that "true" authority resides in high culture, that is, in atemporal values lodged in the greatest works of artistic and religious thought, values that must be recovered and reintroduced into the twentieth century and acknowledged as enduring and necessary, thus atemporal.[6] These implicitly admonitory values were a means of ordering the disruptive forces damaging the fabric of society and the life of the mind, a means of controlling these forces by apprehending and containing them within mythic structures.

Explaining the modernist tendency toward political conservatism and autocracy, Charles Altieri sees in these poets the intention to put

> the burden on the individual to reconcile himself to collective myths and authorities, myths and authorities, one might add, which depend on the poet's custodial function and his powers to remake what was vital in the culture and has gone dead. (*Enlarging the Temple*, 42.)

For certain of these poets, civilization depends on individual submission to the authority of a collective, one in which individuals are not to help to shape except by this submission. Absolute authority lies absolutely outside the individual. What is more to my purpose here, however, is the strength that temporal authority, represented by the poetic speaker, must assert in order to make convincing the atemporal culture authorizing it. Within that requirement is the despairing consciousness that the poets' authorizing, atemporal ground is principally the invention of desire and thus continually suspect.[7] Furthermore, the negating force of self-consciousness, which is the inevitable companion to assertions of atemporal authority, works to repel what these poets would attract, that is, a cultural order authorized and sustained by ideas of the sacred.

As proof of the value of the cultural ideals they wished to restore to contemporary society, modernist poets have to display the relative inaccessibility of these ideals to the common mind. This inaccessibility reinforces the view that cultural values cannot originate from a structure collectively conceived by the masses. Consequently, the poetic act thrusts the speaker between the reader and the ideals imaged in the poem to maintain the speaker's control over their articulation and to preserve them from a cheapening in democratic hands that would reductively distort and disperse them. But given their premise that, in Hulme's words, the individual is a "puny, finite creature" except in submission to a higher order, these poets could not dramatize themselves as mediating figures—their egos had to absent themselves from any embodiment of atemporal authority, lest they too shrink into the puny irrelevance of the modern mind. Yet without the authority to mediate hieratically, however, projecting at least the mystery of atemporal and possibly sacred authority, they cannot make the authority convincing, nor even disclose its existence. In short, to negate a contemporary authority necessarily presumes access to another authority, but to claim further that the blessings and knowledge of that authority, and thus a sustaining participation in it, are not available to the undisciplined, uninitiated mind, inevitably negates the force of the original negation and puts the entire revolution in jeopardy.

But before outlining the modernist solutions to this apparently crippling paradox, I must set forth the theoretical position on authority that I am using to structure both my use of this term and the complex strategies Yeats, Eliot, Williams, and others use to invoke an atemporal authority successfully without letting it collapse into solipsistic invention. I have so far distinguished between temporal and atemporal authority, but as we shall see, that distinction alone is insufficient. My use of the concept will focus on its power to direct thinking, on how authority serves as a way of knowing. In this analysis I do not diverge from the more common political sense but instead argue that it is this very use that permits the political connotations.

II

Any act of thinking invokes an authority of some kind, a system of beliefs, whether abstractly conceived, instinctively felt, or invested in a human or an institution. A self-conscious utterance makes an even deeper commitment to authority, being more stable. John Guillory, in his study of Miltonic and Spenserian authority, takes as his premise that "Authority encloses any discourse whatever within its brackets of common perception and value; it is the court of final appeal whose existence is presupposed by every utterance" (vii). Except in the case of conflicting authorities, in which case their status as authorities is in doubt, authority by definition must go unexamined by those subject to it for any shared understanding—and thus contact—to exist between individuals. More precisely, three related conditions presuppose and support authority's presence: a shared set of assumptions and values, which grants the individual membership in a community; a coherent set of means to interpret experience; and a generally held belief that the individual in some way participates in the shape authority takes, drawing the sustenance of purpose and identity from it and upholding it in return.

Though it may seem odd to speak of authority as communal, cooperative, and reciprocating considering its more widely held connotations of tyranny and coercion, any conflict in meaning results from a confusion between definitions of power and authority. These three conditions must be met to some degree, or authority falls to the random forces of chaos, and in political terms, to the exercise of power. Authority lives in the belief that it arises from the legitimacy of the natural order. Without that belief, hierarchies are imposed and maintained by force. These conditions imply further that no authority is ever a static, inflexible presence; we might usefully liken it to a polar electric field, each pole exerting an attraction on the human consciousness suspended between.[8] This polar tension takes many forms, but it can be reduced conceptually to an eternal conflict between two radically opposing perspectives of where authority is and ought to be centered—in the fluctuating judgments of the individual ego or in the somewhat more rigid collective body of received tradition, or Logos.[9] I speak of a "tension" between the two because neither pole or perspective by itself is sufficient to maintain the three communal conditions; both tend to deny the idea of participation and would impose interpretive values rather than allow them to emerge dialectically. Consequently, authority exists dynamically, an interpenetrating, mutually dependent relation between collective and private spheres.

In differing degrees, ego-centered and Logos-centered authorities partake of the following qualities: source, founder, sustainer of values and identity; a transcendent, atemporal measure of human aspirations and accomplishments; the problematic agent displacing a temporal or atemporal authority; a temporal mediator between a transcendent order and a contemporary chaos; and a pressure for closure, for that that seals off alternative ways of knowing and determines the indeterminate. These qualities represent opposing positions on the magnetic field in which our intellectual and emotional disarray is suspended. Because these qualities are clustered at ego-centered and Logos-centered poles, they are interdependent, impossible to discuss out of the context of the other. The first qualities I examine are in the conflict at the Logos-centered pole: authority as source and measure versus authority as closure.

Hannah Arendt, in her famous essay, "What is Authority," locates Western ideas of what I call Logos-centered authority in Greek and Roman social ideals (91–141). In a discussion of Plato's *Republic*, she points to the philosopher's experience of encountering transcendent ideas outside the cave and then returning to the cave to bring back expressions of those ideas to serve as "transcending measurements and rules" (127). These rules, without compelling obedience, implicitly acknowledge that earthly life and the individual could not provide their own terms of value, that for a nation's or an individual's actions to be judged, a perspective beyond the temporal and partisan was necessary. The Romans adopted this platonic idea as measure of human value but transferred it from a transcendent, incorporeal realm to the past, to the sacred moment when Rome was founded.

The political consequences of this transferral are considerable. First, though the founding is sacred and unrepeatable, it brings the possibilities of human endeavor closer to that which measures them. Second, it strengthens the individual's sense of identity with the larger community and the union of his private interests with the community's. Third, the combined effect of these first two consequences ensures that the community considers its purpose to be the fulfillment of the cultural possibilities latent in the sacred origin. Ideally, such a society balances atemporal traces of and temporal pretensions to authority because they are mutually dependent: the atemporal, sacred past must rely on what is passing and to come for its latent implications to be realized, and its temporal representatives depend on it for direction and authorization, acknowledging their own contingency. Thus, the actions of these temporal representatives are more than hieratic mediation and less than pretensions to Satanic self-authorization.

The Utopian desirability of such an organic interplay between individual and authority is apparent. It is a Unity of Culture granting value both to self and state, with no existential anxiety about identity, value, or purpose, presupposing an interpenetration of the ideal and the real, the imaginary and the empirical. In such a culture, the poet takes the happy role of the speaker for the culture's destiny who imaginatively brings the past into the future, whose gift it is to see with special clarity the culture as a whole rather than just the parts grasped by other individuals. In their hieratic capacity, poets do not merely mediate but are themselves inescapably among the makers of the atemporal authority their poetry evokes.[10]

Modern Western cultures have diverged and fallen away from this Roman ideal that unifies Logos-centered and ego-centered authority, thus spawning opposing urges to restore some version of it. John Guillory describes Milton's efforts to recover a version of that ideal by displacing the Renaissance tradition of secular literature and restoring the Logos-centered authority, the sacred, to poetry (3–35). In poetry of the early Renaissance, the imagination is only an image-making faculty, a "messenger" transferring an image from the sense to the reason, from perception to judgment. But imagination "usurps" authority from reason when it alters its message to a fiction "which it has invented out of nothing and which has no origin but itself. The mind discovers itself as origin, capable of a kind of self-begetting" (13). This action of the imagination is indeed usurpation. It displaces what truly ought to authorize it— both in the sense of giving permission and creating—and sets itself up as the authority, the legitimate source and arbitrator of value, for its own images. This usurpation disrupts the Logos-centered field of authority, and even though it does not thrust new truth claims upon the audience, it is dangerous because it damages the balance of the mind, dividing united faculties instead of insuring their harmonious interaction under the natural authority of reason. But worst of all, the usurpation of the image-making faculty diminishes poetic authority to a trafficking "in airy nothings," cutting off the poet from access to the divine and thus to cultural consequence. Unless the poet's imagination is mimetic, transferring from apprehension to reason the word of God undistorted (and by extension, from God to humanity), attempts at sacred poetry must be at best ridiculous, and at worst blasphemous.

Restoring the sacred poem to literary tradition, a task that Guillory sees as the essential Miltonic purpose, demands inspiration, "visitations upon us of powers outside of ourselves, not the workings of our own minds" (6). For the poet to claim successfully that the divine can be returned to poetry and Logos-centered authority restored, then inspiration, as Guillory argues, must be literal rather than founded on the groundlessness of figurative language. The literalness of this inspiration, to be convincing as the conveyor of the divine word, must presuppose among the poet's audience a set of shared assumptions about the nature of the divine so that the text forms what is unformed and latent in the general mind. Also, literal inspiration depends upon the surrender of the poet's ego to the Logos. In more metaphysical terms, "the imaginative act is initiated by the opening of an absence, by emptying the present of sensation so that the emptiness may be filled with the image" (21). Such an action removes the ego from its presence in the moment and returns it to the capacity of messenger, no longer its own agent. Yet this is a willed submission, a point beyond which "each choice dissolves into the inevitability of the already chosen; no choice is successful except the emptying of the will before God" (18).

What are the consequences of this submission for the Logos-centered poet's temporal authority? In Milton's case, Guillory does not suppose the ego annihilated but merely refocused, reinvested with a larger purpose. The desire to surrender one's private imaginative life is, paradoxically, a claim to authority because it drains authority from a current set of assumptions into another, reorienting an audience's sense of where authority lies and setting the poet up as a mediator with access to atemporal authority. Mediation, then, presupposes disordered relations between authority and its subjects. Consequently, it sets in relation, orders and organizes, proposing not a gesture in solitude but a public revolution in ways of thinking, for mediation implies both an audience—authority's subjects—and the presence of the Logos. But the position of the mediators is always unstable simply because they choose to mediate, making presumption a sin difficult to evade. The office of mediator must define the temporal figures occupying it rather than the reverse, yet because these figures must also justify their place in the office over their competitors, their success requires their own continued presence.[11]

This balance between the ego's presence and absence in mediation requires that mediators both usurp and identify with authority, justifying their act by identifying with another, preferably prior temporal authority, so that the claims of the ego become indistinguishable from those of the Logos.[12] But even in Milton's time, when we imagine relations between authorities and subjects to have been at least a trifle less disintegrated than now, mediators' balance was inherently unstable because the set of assumptions their audience shared was not and could not be so unified. Had their been such a unity, of course, Milton's poem would have had no purpose; authority need not be asserted where it is already felt. Consequently, aware that a mediator's authority is more a claim than a possession, Logos-centered poets like Milton must continually redefine and reexamine their authority to mediate.

A third examination of authority from the Logos-centered position is David Bell's *Power, Influence, and Authority,* which distinguishes between these three eponymous terms in a way I use to clarify the relations between reader, mediating poetic speaker, and atemporal authority. Bell's book also explores, in ways especially useful to descriptions of the Logos-centered perspective, the psychological artifices maintaining authority, the criteria for submission to authority, the reasons for crises in temporal authority, and, like Arendt's views on Roman authority, the utopian project of Logos-centered authority.

Bell distinguishes power from influence and authority by defining it as an understood, implied, or declared ability to manipulate circumstances affecting another's well-being (17–26). Power is inherently illegitimate: its subject audience is offered certain progressively unpleasant alternatives in order to compel a particular response. The demands of muggers, for example, are not endorsed by either explicit or implicit moral codes shared by the victim; they exact obedience only by their ability to cause pain. Influence, on the other hand, is exerted by mediating figures who manipulate behavior not by the power to alter another's circumstances but by the ability to alter perceptions of those circumstances. By predicting the outcome of different alternatives, figures of influence can direct the way their listeners see and evaluate. A weather forecaster, a pollster, a scientist, and as I shall argue, a poetic speaker, have "influence"; their success is measured not in the obedience they exact but in how convincingly they read the world. Though Bell is anxious to insist that the figure of influence does not possess authority, he admits that this figure is considered "an authority," possessing access to without being the source of authority—the rain will come whether or not the weather forecaster predicts it. Using Bell's terms, then, influence is that capacity possessed by the Logos-centered mediating poet. This poet is equivalent to what I have been calling temporal authority, which from a Logos-centered position provides access to its atemporal foundation. From this position the poet sees but does not create.

How, then, does Bell define authority? It is with this term that the political connotations must be revised and overcome. If power coerces, and influence counsels or instructs, then authority commands. The first two imply the presence of alternatives, while the third leaves only a course of action and is otherwise distinct from the two related terms in that it incorporates them. But a figure of authority does not exercise power or display information, though perhaps possessing both. Authority is maintained solely by being acknowledged as authority by those subject to it. Thus, a challenge to political authority, at least, is a usurpation of it, reducing it to power. For example, to law-abiding citizens, the police are to be obeyed because of their authority as representatives of a code whose legitimacy the citizens have internalized—and thus accepted as authority. Criminals, those who do not acknowledge the code's legitimacy, obey or disobey according to their perceptions of the police's power. To extend Bell's definition, we may conclude that because authority exists by being internalized in its subjects, what defines it is less a controlling than a shaping force, directing and defining the relations between individual and society. Thus, we are characterized and defined by the authorities we acknowledge.

Seeing the predominant characteristic of authority to be the shaping of the mind's sense of itself and the world, the mind's way of knowing, the relationship between a poem's cultural authority and the reader becomes clearer. First, if we define culture as the set of values, moral assumptions, traditions, laws, aspirations, and ideals a society possesses, we can think of culture as possessing authority. And as we have seen, authority and coercion cannot coexist; we can therefore set aside authority's conventional political connotations.[13] Yet there is no such thing as a unified culture because all cultures at least to some degree are composed of different authorities warring for supremacy over the mind's perceptual categories. Authorities speak through poetry, among other media, existing as a set of claims or projections, references to atemporal authorities that come into being as felt—and hence authentic—presences to the extent that they accord with or echo prior structures already internalized by the audience. Without reference to a prior authority, poetry is either unintelligible, preposterous, or both. This is not to say, though, that poetry must recite truths universally acknowledged; rather, good poetry augments, complicates, and enriches the audience's internalized beliefs. Poetry extends what authorizes it, just as the Roman Empire was to extend what its founders envisioned. This view of poetry as the voice of cultural authority can help explain the revolution of English modernism Stead describes in *The New Poetic:* Logos-centered authority must extend itself as an expanding spiral, not circle back in repetition. The poet, authority's mediator, a figure of influence, must remain safely inside the invisible scope of expanding authority, staying between the collapsing circle of repetition and the aimless peregrinations of anarchy.

We need to look now at Bell's explanation of what draws the individual into the sway of authority to be united with a common purpose directed by temporal authority. Discovering these causes should help explain what sustenance a culture provides an individual and what the consequences are in the perceived absence of an authorizing culture. Bell presents two possible sets of criteria necessary for a submission to authority (67).[14] The first set presumes a Logos-centered authority sustained by three conditions: individuals must see some identity of interest between themselves and the authority; they must acknowledge the authority's greater competence in decision-making; and they must presume that the authority can decide, judge, or initiate action more readily than they could if left to themselves. These three criteria suggest that the persuasiveness of authority bears an inverse relation to individuals' ability or desire to conduct their affairs in solitude. The more unified a culture, the more individuals tend to characterize themselves as interlocking parts of a whole than as self-determining, self-defining beings. The stronger one's sense of belonging to a culture, the more the subjective world is externalized and invested in that culture, which is regarded as a larger, more inclusive selfhood.

The second set of criteria is also founded on acceptance of the greater powers of Logos-centered authority, but these criteria are oppositions similar to the poles of Logos-centered and ego-centered authority. The first is "identification," the surrender of private purposes for the benefits of organization, and the second is an inversion, "adaptation," which is an acceptance of an authority to bring it closer to one's private purposes. The primary difference between the two sets of criteria is in the implied conceptions of the individual, in which self-realization occurs by either submission or domination. More interesting, however, is the similarity of these apparently opposing criteria: from either perspective, the individual has neither consequence nor even identity except in relation to authority, to a structure of beliefs complicating themselves into a culture.

But what founds such a structure? What legitimizes the hierarchies and terms of value shaping a culture and determining how and where the mind can locate a sustaining strength it does not possess alone? Though he does not use these terms, Bell distinguishes between Logos-centered authority and the temporal figure invested with it, arguing that the source of all authority is located outside and prior to any human pretensions to it, in what Max Weber calls "credenda" (45–47). He names three mutually involved types of credenda that authorize temporal authority and seal the seams of culture: charismatic, traditional, and rational/legal. Charismatic authority arises during revolutions, crises caused by a culture's inability to increase and complicate itself, that is, to grant those subject to authority a sense of participation in it. In such crises a charismatic figure emerges, invested with authority because of qualities established as charismatic prior to the figure's possession of them. As a temporal being, then, the charismatic figure remains essentially a mediator who must conform to the demands of the office and answer to charismatic credenda, the subjects' expectations. Because these expectations antedate and grant form to the charismatic figure, any attempt to violate or alter those credenda weakens temporal authority. There is, however, a dynamic tension between charisma and role, alternately compelling a redefinition of the role or a dilution of authority. It might be more accurate to say, then, that the charismatic figure embodies or incarnates authority, serving as a cultural symbol rather than a source, whether for a Logos-centered or ego-centered authority.

The credenda of tradition locate authority more explicitly beyond the temporal charismatic figure, appealing to whatever has always existed or reviving ancient standards. Though these credenda could buttress either Logos-centered or ego-centered authority, depending upon which tradition is being championed, they typically emerge in an anxious, contracting gesture, returning culture to previous limits or directions. In contrast, the credenda of rational/legal authority provide for the most flexible culture because of the dialectical structure of its beliefs, a tension between seeing the good as whatever is most efficient and whatever is constitutionally established. These credenda permit stability as well as change, which occurs principally through the exertions of individuals acting through ego-centered authority—"adapting," to use Galbraith's term, the forces of the collective to suit private purposes. The credenda of rational/legal authority, most prevalent in modern times, encourage the most stability because they allow the greatest degree of mutual involvement between public and private realms. However, because the rational/legal culture is inherently flexible and dynamic, its subjects tend to suffer a nostalgic longing for the comfortable fixities of an abandoned tradition or for the myth of autonomy incarnated in the charismatic figure.

A primary purpose of Bell's book is to define authority as a set of beliefs originating as a condition rather than as a consequence of human consciousness, thus removing it from the unsafe hands of human design. At the same time, Bell wishes to show authority to be inherently legitimate, that is, in accord with human wishes. This apparent contradiction leads Bell to posit in neo-Hegelian terms the ideal State, in which the distinction between authority and the individuals subject to it breaks down (52). The first stage of this process is "submission," a childish kind of obedience generated in a psychological state beneath even the Hegelian Stoic Consciousness, in which the individuals' self-knowledge comes only from their limited range of responses to authority's commands. The second stage is "accountability," when individuals recognize that temporal figures of authority form a conventional structure answering a collective need. They know themselves as parts of a social structure maintained by legitimate powers beyond individual control. In the third, participatory stage, corresponding to Hegel's Rational consciousness, individuals acknowledge their role in the creation and maintenance of authority, realizing that it exists through their own will. The distinction between inner and outer, private and public, ego-centered and Logos-centered authority at first appears to fade here, but it is finally the outer, the Logos-centered authority that prevails at this stage. The inner is turned inside out to reveal its identity with the collective will. Authority is dispersed, of course, made collective, but Bell's utopia is a proletarian state rather than a tribe of heroes and giants such as Yeats or William Morris imagined.

To conclude this examination of Logos-centered authority as a source of human value and a measure of human mediation, we must look at Bell's distinction between descending and ascending authority (49). This opposition will further complicate the Logos-centered position and outline the modernist perspective of authority: a despairing doubt in the possibility of any version of either Logos-centered or ego-centered authority.

Briefly, descending authority originates in God—as an atemporal presence or through a temporal mediator—and moves down a hierarchy to manipulate and direct its subjects below. Ascending authority is the democratic ideal, the will of the people being delivered up for expression by an elected representative. But what is most peculiar about this distinction is that, except as a superficial description of certain political systems, it does not exist as an accurate account of the distribution of authority. Instead, as I have argued thus far, authority is more properly regarded as a continual conflict between ascending and descending powers to establish one's legitimate supremacy over the other. Furthermore, this conflict can never be resolved because each camp must rely upon the other for its legitimacy: descending authority must be maintained by popular belief, and the ascending authority of popular will needs a locus outside of itself to serve as an image or mirror of its substance, a locus necessary for it to know itself as authority. Thus, neither camp is self-authorizing, and both can claim authority only

in opposition to the other. Authority as source is continually eva-
sive, existing in the flux of conflict.[15]

I have so far examined atemporal and temporal authority from
the Logos-centered perspective, seeing the atemporal as a source
and measure and the temporal as the mediating representative. I
will now examine both authorities from the ego-centered position,
which locates authority's function as source and measure in the
ego to reveal it as the realization of the divine in the human. The
relevant theoretical treatments of the ego-centered perspective are
in the work of Richard Sennett, David Simpson, and Edward Said,
each betraying a different degree of suspicion for ego-centered
claims.

Without derogation, Sennett can be called a radical, or naive,
advocate of ego-centered authority. He does not distinguish between power and authority, and neither does he accept the existence of an atemporal presence as a source of human self-
knowledge. Instead, he reduces the idea of authority to the capacity
to punish, and what is more subtle, to the manipulation of individuals' self-regard in order to keep them in subjection. Authority
as external source and measure of identity does not exist in his
conception; what Bell calls "power" and "influence" Sennett collapses as "authority." Sennett attempts to drain any sense of the
sacred or autonomous from temporal figures of authority and then,
in turn, to demonstrate the ego's authority to determine and identify itself on its own terms, to be, in effect, self-authorizing. As
one might expect, his analysis reveals that the authority exerted by
temporal figures is illegitimate and illusory, based on the subject's
mistaken belief that the authority figure is both autonomous and
vested with the best interests and concerns of the subject. In short,
the subject feels contained by the authority figure, existing only as
a smaller element of a larger structure. The authority figure therefore holds the subject's self-regard on a leash. Sennett points out
that this belief is an implicit, unspoken contract between authority
and subject, the terms of which demand that the authority stabilize
the subject's uneasy sense of identity, providing the comfort of a
measure, and that the subject in return grant the authority figure
the prestige of autonomy. The very fact of this contract, however,
proves the illegitimacy of such claims to authority and autonomy
because this relationship implies mutual dependence. Those in authority lack the moral entitlement as well as the psychological sufficiency for their pretensions; they wield authority not for the well-
being of society or an individual but on behalf of their own self-

regard. Ironically, their pretense to authority demonstrates need and thus a lack of autonomy.

In Sennett's argument, authority and autonomy are properly found in the ego, to be awakened and confronted in progressive stages of self-consciousness. Adapting Hegel's Master/Slave structure, Sennett traces the ego's liberating discovery of its capacity for self-authorization through stoicism, skepticism, the unhappy consciousness, and rational consciousness (128–29). Stoics accept the authority of the master in spite of their discomfort, believing in their master's superiority, with no terms for challenging it. Skeptics remain submissive but live a secret life of disbelief in their master's authority; in Bell's terms, skeptics see the master's power rather than the master's authority. They therefore do not see themselves as inherently subject, yet they still lack the means or the measure to reevaluate themselves. The unhappy consciousness perceives a pattern in this skepticism, realizing that the master/slave relationship is of the self's own creation, constituting that self as a divided consciousness, a contradiction. This "consciousness of self as a duality," though, paralyzes the self in subjective isolation. If rational consciousness is achieved, however, "the unhappy schism each person feels in himself he also sees in others." As a result, the rational consciousness has externalized and thus objectified the subjective conflict of a divided consciousness, an action that both abolishes hierarchical distinctions between individuals and frees consciousness to realign its actions and identity according to its own purposes, since it need no longer struggle with others or itself. Identity is no longer determined by a relationship with another, leaving only the ego as a measure of its own value. However, the rational consciousness is not a solipsistic ego, for it sees itself in others and so sees its purposes as equivalent and cooperative.

Sennett argues that any legitimate idea of divinity—an energy that brings the mind from a sense of incompleteness and absence to completeness and presence—is latent in the ego. Yet as I suggest above, according to Sennett's interpretation, rational consciousness discovers itself in others, so that it still knows itself by its contact with other selves. Thus, the self's authority for claiming a liberation is still not internally derived but externally measured by a relation to others. Sennett cannot verify, therefore, that the authority of the rational consciousness's self-conception is any more ontologically true than the master's view of the slave, or the slave's of the master.

The furthest one can safely go toward establishing an ego-centered authority is to portray the ego as vital evidence of divinity, a position Wordsworth takes in *The Prelude,* as I show in the next chapter. With this evidence, the individual ego achieves a sense of wholeness, locating its place in the act of being human. It is in this human sympathy that Sennett finally locates "authority," though he cannot use the term because of his restricted meaning and his need to locate powers of determinacy—authority—in the ego. But the mediator of ego-centered authority depends on a reference to a greater authority that at the same time does not force a distinction between the infinite presence and its finite manifestation in the individual. The authority of this mediator can then, as Sennett does, presuppose the ego's capacity for self-renewal and growth, for self-authorization.

Sennett tries to demystify temporal authority, which he could do simply by revealing its temporality, but he must then remystify it in translation to a spirit of cooperative human sympathy, a move that on one side democratizes authority by removing the mediator, but on the other restricts the ego to action in concert with others. From this latter perspective, the ego would not be self-determining at all, but bound to submit to an all-inclusive, prior concept of human identity. Ideas of individual will and self-authorization would thereby lose all meaning in the loss of discrimination between previously separate selves, throwing the ego back into a Logos-centered universe. The ego cannot both make itself and know itself as self-making.

David Simpson, in *Irony and Authority in Romantic Poetry,* adopts the ego-centered perspective to challenge Logos-centered claims. But such a challenge, he realizes, also undermines the ego's own claims to authority. He defines authority as determinacy, the power to locate and fix textual meaning, and he draws an analogy between the poet's confrontation with experience and the reader's confrontation with the Romantic poem. These confrontations can be seen as a circle around which consciousness chases meaning that, once apprehended, must be distrusted because it could not have been formulated without an ordering principle prior to and not derived from the experience. Meaning does not inhere in an object but is applied to it as a place is made for the object in a preconceived system of thought. But for Simpson, acknowledging that our epistemological principles are arbitrary does not bring us any closer to the "true" meaning that convention leads us to seek in a poem, because "we can never see it [the ordering principle] from a critical distance" (ix). Any model of reading or knowing begs the question of its authority, and any answer to such a question begs another. Thus, all preconceptions are unverifiable, lacking authority. As Simpson continually declares, there is no place to stand outside the hermeneutic circle, no way to show the filial link between interpretation and reality.

With this theoretical framework, itself a model of reading, Simpson claims that in Romantic poetry at least, meaning is indeterminate. The Romantics deliberately subvert readers' attempts to fix on a single voice to speak a poem's meaning. As an opening example, Simpson presents a reading of "Ode on a Grecian Urn" to show how different layers of commentary—distinguished by perceived excesses of poeticized language, ironic qualifications of remembered epiphanies, unsatisfactory resolutions of lyric tension, and the readers' own examination of their preconceptions—are structurally determined to conflict, thwarting the rise of any one layer to the authoritative realm of "meta-commentary," or "actual" meaning. This structural resistance to determinacy Simpson calls "English Romantic Irony," which

> broadly put, consists in the studied avoidance on the artist's part of determinate meanings, even at such times as he might wish to encourage his reader to *produce* such meanings for himself; it involves the refusal of closure, the incorporation of any potentially available "meta-comment" within the primary language of the text, the provision of linguistic sign which moves towards or verges upon a "free" status, and the consequent raising to self-consciousness of the authoritarian element of discourse, as it affects both the author-reader relation and the intentional manipulation, from both sides, of the material through which they communicate. . . . Romantic poetry, in general, seems to refuse this stability [caused by a desired formal balance of internal pressures] by insisting upon a context which is at least in part always forcefully and evidently outside or beyond the poem. This externality provides a posited but unsupplied content which in turn creates a necessary indeterminacy, one which keeps us reading. (190)

More briefly, because this structural indeterminacy frustrates attempts to locate a conclusive position, the text points beyond itself to the absent source of meta-commentary—the authority—it is presumably the text's purpose to evoke. The text deconstructs itself by emphasizing the absence of determining authority. But this refusal of determinacy creates the opposite impulse, a continued pursuit of determinacy that justifies the presence of the text and the act of reading.

For Simpson, Romantic irony defers and distances authority, the source and arbiter of meaning, which in the poetic utterance is based upon the convention of the stable self. The Romantic self,

Simpson argues, is "unfixed" because "the world is a text, but no longer in the sense that it is the book of God; the act of reading is one of imaginative self-confrontation, setting up a framework of interdetermination from which there is no escape" (180). Conscious of interdetermination, the reader/poet can never be sure to what extent the text/world shapes perceptions and to what extent the mind's preconceptions shape them. The world's indeterminacy presumes the poet/reader's. Poets, examining their conflicting responses to a landscape, for example, wonder and doubt whether a coherent meaning can be drawn from the scene and then objectively defended, whether a divine purpose can emerge from contemplative contact with the natural world, whether indeed one's responses are not the idlest of fantasies. So, too, the reader wonders which of the voices in the text can authorize meaning, and further, how many of them originated in or were distorted by the very privacy of reading. The reader must, therefore, lose all conviction in reading's authority to locate meaning. The self, the mind, is therefore unfixed because it must perpetually vacillate in its sense of what constitutes it. Consequently, Simpson explains, "we are left with no 'author' in the affirmative sense" (191).

Simpson's argument makes suspect any claims to either Logos-centered or ego-centered authority, to even the possibility of finding any final basis for our assumptions about the world. This position, however, presents two serious problems for itself. First, the authority of his theoretical framework relies on what it deconstructs. He is sawing off the branch he stands on, since any utterance presumes a reference to an authority dwelling in assumptions shared by speaker and audience. Second, Simpson does not account for the mind's need to locate authority, a need that reveals a more stable identity than he is willing to grant the self. Solving these problems finally requires him to come to a tentative resting place near an ego-centered authority.

With his first problem, it is to Simpson's credit that he acknowledges the fallacy inherent to his book's very presence: he wonders how he can "make a case for the historical origins or presence of the syndrome of the hermeneutic circle without falling into the traps which the syndrome itself sets up," but this admission does not check his critical efforts. He sidesteps the consequences of his admission by calling his situation a "true paradox" instead of a contradiction, implying that he can do what he has just claimed is impossible, which is to step outside the hermeneutic circle. To support his claim for paradox, he challenges his reader to "test out his suspicions of (or agreement with) this preselection against his own 'readings,'" presuming that a consensus will validate Simpson's historical method, as if an aggregate of united opinions carries an authority that contact with the text does not (x). But even if Simpson's readers were to echo his reading, all he would prove, of course, is that his readers either already share or have been persuaded to share his preconceptions, not that those preconceptions elude the hermeneutic circle. On the other hand, even if his readers reject his position, his claim for the antiauthoritarianism of Romantic poetry would not be invalidated but would only suggest that it is eccentric and unconvincing. The difficulty Simpson is left with, then, even as he begins, is the absence of his own authority, a fact that is poignantly ironic in light of his thesis that the Romantic purpose is to throw into question "preconceptions" of the normative, "belief in a general nature."

If the Romantics intend to overturn attempts to codify the inchoate and solidify the uncertainties, insisting, as Simpson claims, that such questions are not to be answered by imposition from without but by personal searching within, as readers search their responses to the text, then these poets are locating authority in the self and then doubting the self's legitimacy. In other words, with the world as their text, they, like Simpson, are trying to escape the hermeneutic circle and are self-consciously aware of the impossibility of doing so. As Simpson's argument implies, their texts can assert the self's heroic necessity to break free from preconceptions of itself, relying for the legitimacy of this enterprise on preconceptions of poetry as the publication of private thoughts. This effort presupposes that the value of the poetic text is to investigate and comprehend the self in the world, a purpose that further presumes the inherent value of the self, pointing to the self as its own authority because it rejects all Logos-centered authority. But Simpson's project is not so fortunate; he preserves an antiauthoritarian selfhood for the Romantics, but the hermeneutic circle still cuts away the ground of his argument.[16]

Simpson's second problem with deconstructed authority is that authorizing voices cannot vanish from between text and reader. There are essentially three reasons for their relentless presence. First, Simpson points to the "paradox" that "the text must try to remain both open and closed; capable of being filled out by the reader's active response, and yet capable of controlling that response within limits in some sense foreseen by the author" (148). The poet must authorize the perceived lack of determining authority so that the reader must simultaneously see and not see this controlling presence. Second, Simpson admits that certain Romantics, notably Wordsworth, have a lingering faith in the determinate ego as a center of knowing. Simpson justifies Keats's attack on Wordsworth's "egotistical sublime," restating it as

> the intrusive and reductive, intentional aspect of perception which is presented as a necessary concomitant to description and communication. The eye uses one object to reduce the whole scheme to order, and then builds its own identity upon the dismissal of that object. . . . What the poet is really doing is establishing his empire over the field of vision, constituting himself at the expense of the world which makes him possible. . . . (136)

Perception itself, at least for Wordsworth, is necessarily intentional and self-constituting, and thus the stabilizing activity of a single authorizing voice. The very notion of the "stable" self thus becomes unstable; the self is not fixed, static, or inert, but it maintains a form of being as a perceiving, experiencing, and reflecting presence.

The third reason why an authorizing voice cannot vanish or be too dispersed for recovery by the act of reading is that the Romantic poetic experience cannot be presented except through a mediating consciousness. Simpson struggles against the idea of poetry as a mediating utterance by drawing on Derrida's notion of difference, explaining that the Romantic "commitment to language only dramatises the inability to express; utterance articulates absence, experience which can be 'spoken around' but never contained" (196). Still, it is easy enough to acknowledge this—that reflection does not recover sensation but only establishes its absence—and nonetheless point out that the very anxiety at the ego's inevitable disunity posits a mediating consciousness, a self-conscious entity watching itself search for a restorative, centering position and not finding it. This entity is an unfixed but ego-centered authorizing voice that directs and observes the conflict between the opposing and equally necessary impulses to ironic dispersal and lyric unity of personality. In the uncertainties of identity, the Romantic poet must begin and end the search for authority with the perceiving self-conscious ego, continually rediscovering limits, gaps, and transformations.

To conclude this analysis of Simpson's version of Romantic authority and to distinguish between the Romantic and modernist quests for determinacy and stable identity, we need to examine the shades of meaning in "authoritarian" and "authority." When Simpson asserts that the Romantic poem is antiauthoritarian, he means that it resists the formulation of a meta-commentary that would impose a fixed meaning. However, given the weight of its connotations, authoritarian suggests an unreasonable restriction of autonomy and freedom, meaning therefore that the Romantic text is under pressure to liberate itself. Regardless of whether or not Simpson's theory of reading is verifiable, his traditional conclusion about the liberating energies of Romantic poetry depends on a specific historical context to which the poets saw themselves subject: an excessively rationalist, Logos-centered authority that is illegitimate because it is derived from outside the poets' experience. This authority is alien to the fertile and complex imagination it seeks to dominate, rather than its source. The urge toward the ego's liberation from the rationalist confines is, in effect, an appeal to an authority that displaces a previous ordering principle. Logically, though a challenge to authority can be "antiauthoritarian," it cannot be antiauthority; challenges imply the need for a substitute authority rather than for none at all. However, as I will elaborate further, the modernist position is at the opposite pole, operating in a perceived vacuum of authority rather than under overly determinate pressure. Of course, there can be no social condition without at least claims to authority, but the sensation of the modern mind is of a prevailing absence, a vacuum into which rush chaos and moral instability and spiritual decay. In this abandonment by a sustaining atemporal presence, the ego is "puny and finite," as T. E. Hulme declares in his famous assault on Romanticism. In this cultural crisis, alignment with an external, that is, Logos-centered, authority may have seemed the only way of achieving an identity that possesses value. This alignment requires not the erasure of the ego but rather the ego's reorientation, no longer venturing inward to examine and evaluate its own substance but outward to realize its diminished place in a larger order.

Edward Said's *Beginnings* provides a theoretical structure for understanding the process compelling modernist thought to reject the ego as a self-authorizing force and to make new claims for Logos-centered authority. Said describes claims to authority as a series of oppositions analogous to those between ego-centered and Logos-centered authority. The foundation for these oppositions is the one between "beginning" and "origin." Though Said is understandably reluctant to force apart words generally thought synonymous, very early in his book he uses "*beginnings* as having the more active meaning, and *origin* the more passive one" (6). Said clarifies this distinction much later when he says "we generally locate origins before beginnings, since the Origin is a latent state from which the beginnings of an action move forward; retrospectively considered, then, the Origin is a condition or state that permits beginnings" (316). Still later, he explains that the "state of mind that is concerned with origins is, I have said, theological. By contrast, and this is the shift, beginnings are eminently secular, or gentile, continuing activities" (372–73). Origin and beginning are thus analogous but not synonymous: beginnings are attempts to either displace or—what is arguably the same action—restore an Origin. In my analogous terms, a beginning makes a claim for self-inauguration, for ego-centered authority, while an Origin is the Logos-centered authority the mediating poet points to as its source.

Said treats authority as a beginning trying to assert itself as an origin but doomed to self-conscious awareness of the inherent fictiveness of these pretensions to self-origination. His model sets up the following theory of narrative fiction. By definition, the novel displays warring assertions of authority—claims for the ability to inaugurate and order a world and the self's place in it, claims opposed by an uneasy awareness of a prior originating authority that renders all ego-centered gestures illusory. The author, disclosed in the text's assertions of authority, inevitably must come to recognize that "Man is never the author, never the beginning of what he does, no matter how willfully intended his program may be. . . . Authority . . . permanently resides outside man" (133). The text, then, is the field where these counterforces combat each other, with temporal poetic authority forever sliding under the wheels of a self-conscious awareness of a prior, atemporal origin.

Said's definition of authority is both complex and coherent, but finally insufficient, I think, for the fullest, most productive extension of the word's meanings. He in effect builds authority as a straw man, reducing the term to the individual ego's will to power and then burdening it with impossible demands. Where I unfold the term into a conflict between Logos and ego, Said restricts his concerns to the one function I call "displacement" by appeal to ego-centered authority. Acknowledging the cumbersomeness of "authority" as a critical term, Said sees a "constellation of linked meanings" that compose the word, from the common lexical sense of "power to enforce obedience" to "a connection as well with *author*—that is, a person who originates or gives existence to something." Said grounds his definition on four assumptions:

(1) that of the power of an individual to initiate, institute, establish—in short, to begin; (2) that this power and its product are an increase over what had been there previously; (3) that the individual wielding

> this power controls its issue and what is derived therefrom; (4) that authority maintains the continuity of its course. (83)

In the apparent expansiveness of his definition, Said puts enormous pressure on the individual author so that, as we shall see shortly, all attempts at fulfilling the terms of his authority result in a contraction of the ego's capacity to act, to begin. If, as Simpson argues, the English Romantics successfully burst the bonds of conventional ideas about the self, thus expanding—if destabilizing—the self's spiritual possibilities and displacing a prior authority, then we see in Said's theory of modernism the opposite. The net of prior authority is cast over the ego's self-inaugurating projects, constricting the ego until its consequence vanishes.

But we have to examine Said's critical framework more closely to see precisely how an author undertakes a beginning and how, as a beginning, it must be undermined. And though it is not Said's focus, we must first of all presume that the very need to begin, cutting oneself off from origins, implies the absence of an atemporal cultural authority that sustains, directs, and identifies. Bluntly put, the modern ego despairs at being an inert product of a culture and so itself wishes to reverse the flow of energy, to become a producer.[17] What interferes with the author's authority to produce is "molestation," which thrusts between author and the authorized "a consciousness of one's duplicity, one's confinement to a fictive, scriptive realm" (84). Molestation, then, is the realization that the self's authority proves illusory when measured against reality, that sphere external to the author that exerts pressure but is not subject to a reciprocating pressure. Because of molestation, authority by Said's definition must be accompanied by an awareness of its limits, the fact that its claims are suspect; the beginning's necessary fictiveness places it in a secondary relation to the originating authority of reality, a prior origin that the fictive beginning cannot reach and so cannot challenge. "To use words is to substitute them for something else—call it reality, historical truth, or a kernel of actuality. . . . The difficulty of this method is that it does not imitate nature, but displaces it" (66). Therefore language, the vestments of authority, paradoxically hides, or veils, what it is supposed to express. If this deconstruction is a legitimate account of the workings of language and the mind, then language cannot begin, and beginnings can have no authority.

Said's series of oppositions defining the author's quest for authority unfold further through an improvised history in which he sets the "dynastic" against the "fraternal" and "story" against "construction," oppositions that both justify the need for modernist art and display its power to begin and thus replace prior cultural authorities. Briefly, a story is dynastic, implying a genealogy, continuous along a linear path of development and pointing to its origin, an established genre repeating and extending itself in stories (79–188). The parts of a story, too, form a narrative, a series whose elements bear a linear, progressive relation to each other, subordinate to and defining the whole, each element situated by filial relation. A story does not "begin" but extends from and repeats or revises its origin, while a "construction" does begin, and its relation to prior texts is adjacent, "fraternal." Construction also contains an embedded analogy to a nonrepresentational form, like a building, a structure designed according to abstract, purely functional specifications, a structure whose parts are without meaning except when combined—in a nonlinear relation—according to the unique requirements of the particular whole. A construction points not to a history of prior forms but to its own uniqueness and purpose. Finally, in the absence of linear progression, either narrative or historical, the construction is to be apprehended not in a progressive accumulation of parts but as a whole, simultaneously.

Yet by distinguishing the linear, traditional, genealogical text from the nonlinear, nontraditional text, Said is ultimately subject to the molesting influence of their fictionality, thus finally evaporating modernists' opportunities to authorize their own aesthetic activities. The distinctions are derived from verbal constructions rather than from the texts they purport to describe. Specifically, the metaphorical label "construction," which is Said's term, or even "composition," one more frequently used by modern poets to describe their own work, could quite comfortably be applied to any text, regardless of period or the historical presuppositions directing the reader's field of interpretations.[18] Also, any modernist construction must still be genealogically derived: simply by attempting to displace an origin with itself as an autonomous beginning declares a relation, if only a bastard one, to a prior form.

Still, a construction need not inevitably be forced into identity with its predecessors as another pale repetition, and neither is it necessarily latent in its origin. What is of special interest to me here is that Said's dichotomy is from the modernist perspective, the modernists' view of themselves and their situation, as well as the view of those wishing to champion the originality of modern art. But what distinguishes the modern period from what came before, what testifies to the newness of its art, is the very desperation of that need to distinguish itself as a period, a self-generated and isolated historical moment.

Evidence of the consciousness of those problems and of the attempt to solve them lies in the trumpeting of impersonality, a surrender of the private self to a cultural icon, as a necessary criterion of modern art.[19] Impersonality could almost serve as an emblem for modernity, in that it implies the irrelevance of the private voice, an identity indistinguishable from others in the multitude. Impersonality, though, also suggests the isolation of one personality from another, the sense that the perceiving subject is the only animate being in existence. Art rendered impersonally thus serves at least two purposes. First, it overcomes the problem of the individual voice's irrelevance by echoing the ego's sense of general anonymity. Second, it accords with and perpetuates the view that modern life is disordered and directionless, and that cultural intelligibility and coherence therefore require a unifying, ordering symbol. Such claims for impersonality reach for Logos-centered authority to be made temporally present by the mediation of art. The poet assumes the role of cultural prophet or even savior, claiming the authority to restore value and cultural identity to a lost people. Because the absence of all forms of authority is so powerfully felt, the poet, in the guise of an impersonal nonpresence, occupies the vacuum of temporal authority.

But pretensions to an authority through impersonality are undermined by Said's central distinction between "contingent" and "absolute" authority, which exposes the inevitable gap between claim and possession. Authors have only contingent authority because they can only "initiate or build structures whose absolute authority is radically nil, but whose contingent authority is a quite satisfactory alternative to the absolute truth" (86). Authors can have no absolute authority not only because their words are "substitutions" for immediate contact with experience or the sacred, thus disrupting that contact, but because their very existence as distinct, secondary egos means that they can have no radical access to their Origin, absolute authority. To possess such access they would have to be identical to that from which by definition they are distinct. Furthermore, if we adapt Said's formulation slightly, an author's authority is contingent upon concealing that the supposedly impersonal text stands between the reader and absolute authority. The text must seem to stand in place of absolute authority, and this effect can only be managed if a textual voice conceals the artifice and intentionality, the hand of its author's private self, and seems to work as a way of seeing rather than as a thing seen. The periodic displacement of the mediating speaker—like Milton's invoking speaker disappearing into the narrative—is the principal means toward this effect.

But the very problem demanding this kind of concealment prevents such a solution. Only an acknowledged Logos-centered authority could grant the poet the contingent, temporal authority to present a text as a window to the absolute. Were it actually possible to conceal language that creates distance from an originating presence, it would not be necessary. In addition, as Said insists, the contingent author's power is ultimately illusory and insufficient because of the necessity to speak. Presumably Said means here that speech is a display of incompleteness, painful consciousness of the division between self and other, a division that utterance, ironically, attempts to overcome. But absolute authority, the source of "truth," "has no need of words" (86). It can be distinguished from the gestures of its contingent counterpart because it is utterly without gesture; it is silent, self-contained, autonomous. And contingent authority is just that, contingent, upon an absolute source. The beginning can never begin, be authorized, without reference to a prior authority as a context and ground.

The modernist text is therefore pursuing an impersonality belied by the fact of pursuit. That the poet "must labour to be beautiful" supposes an ego's need to flee egoism, and the need denies the ego's escape, forcing failure upon all authoritative gestures the poet makes to transcend finitude and contingency. Yet the poet's contingent authority preserves a credibility by admitting the priority of an absolute authority. Poetic speakers are at their most authoritative when they most vigorously undermine their own pretensions to authority; they are closest to perceiving the truth when they lament their distance from it. And in projecting the boundaries of absolute authority's absence, which is what poetic lamentation of finitude accomplishes, the poets locate themselves in a hieratic mediating function between the reader and absolute authority. Thus, it is only by confessed failure that poets can maneuver themselves into a position of authority, for these confessions authorize—permit and sustain—images of anxiety and longing. Though not the source or cause of the pain, poetic speakers can present themselves as arbiters of how that pain is to be expressed and perceived, thus authorizing the shape of the readers' culture.

III

But what form, then, can modern poetry take? What voice or voices can it be allowed? The mind, taking internal or external measure of its value, sensing its inadequacy to projected ideals, is unable to find authority for those ideals because they are not culturally shared. They must inhabit a Logos-centered authority, which cannot exist except in the mind's desire for one that can affirm the mind's value. One possibility lies in the meditative poem, a form presenting with detachment an apparent variety of perspectives, or rather, presenting challenges to the single perspective. In the meditative poem, "the soul or mind engages in acts of interior dramatization . . . a man projects a self upon a mental stage, and there comes to understand that self in the light of a divine presence" (Martz iv). These acts of interior dramatization are self-conscious examinations of the self, presented in a tension between lyricism and irony. Each position the poetic speaker takes is brought into question and revealed as a self-deceptive posture either by metamorphosis of the speaker or by self-conscious reflection on these positions. Unexamined lyricism makes an untenable claim for ego-centered authority, asserting greater power and vision for an individual mind than the reader can easily grant. The goal of meditation is to bring the mind, and so the reader as well, to a place of self-knowledge. Such a place is necessarily inhabited by Logos-centered authority, without which the mind has no means of determining identity, value, or purpose.

The problem for meditative speakers is threefold. First, they must confront their insufficiency and aloneness, that they are divided, with crippling consequences, from the sustenance of a vitality that both exceeds and precedes them. This confrontation makes them aware of all that they are not, causing them to project imaginatively what they ought to be to become sufficient and to end desire. Second, they must demonstrate that the source of their projected ideal does not spring from their own fancies but from an external source that, theoretically at least, is also available to the readers. Such a demonstration requires that they overcome the paralysis caused by ironic attacks on lyricism. Third, they must persuade the reader that this source is an authority, so that they can speak from it and address the readers' unarticulated psychic suffering.

Solving this threefold problem to establish the poet as a mediating authority requires that the poetic speaker be transported from the finite ego to a mediating voice detached from the historical moment and from the particular concerns of unique selfhood.[20] This movement, which I call "transpersonality," can be conceived of as a redistribution of selfhood from the focus of the ego to the broader range of the objects the speaker sees and imagines, establishing at a point of climax a new relation to those objects in a way that secures the speaker's temporal authority. This new relation compels the objects in the poetic field into the speaker's service and the reader into the charismatic field of poetic vision to determine, disrupt, expand, or distort purely conventional relations between self and object, making elastic the referentiality of word to thing. If the speaker as a finite ego is at first alienated from the object of contemplation, the successful conclusion of the poem is the result of transpersonality, which both frees the speaker's self-conceptions from a sense of insufficiency and arranges the contemplated world in a way that declares the speaker's new status as a mediator for atemporal authority. In short, transpersonality transforms the speaker's voice from a personal to a textual identity. By this latter term I mean the achievement of two conditions: first, the loss of self-consciousness in the shift of imaginative attention from self to world; and second, the blurring of boundaries between the speaker and imaginative projections of atemporal authority.[21] The act of reading, when the speaker has a purely textual identity, submits the reader to at least a trial acceptance of both the poet's authority to mediate and that authority the poet mediates.

I must make an important qualification here, however. Textual identity can only be approached, never achieved; transpersonality can never fully release the speaker from finitude and self-consciousness, for two reasons. First, the complete absence of a finite speaker is silence, and thus oblivion. Second, however transparent the speaker becomes, the reader does not lose awareness of the fact that utterance presupposes a unique perspective, never the totality of possible perspectives.[22] Transpersonality brings poetic speakers to the edge of authority and oblivion but then pulls them back, so that the reader glimpses and shares in the mingling of desire and dread aroused by the images of union the speakers present. These feelings emerge because of the presence of atemporal authority, which is manifested by the speakers' declared or displayed inability to assume that voice of authority on their own. Mystification of authority, rather than successful elevation of the speaker, is thus the actual and necessary result of the speaker's transpersonality.[23] Only failure grants the poet authority. And the readers, to the degree that they are moved, accept and thus increase the authority exerted in the poem by assenting to its arbitration of values.

In the succeeding chapters I study the efforts of specific poets to secure the presence of atemporal authority. In chapter two I examine Milton's invocative voice as the archetypal temporal authority mediating for the atemporal, the divine. His particular difficulty is less the credibility of the authority he wishes to mediate than his own credibility as a mediator. To fulfill this role he must simultaneously absent himself and yet still demonstrate his singular fitness for the task. In the second part of the chapter I discuss the Wordsworthian ego of *The Prelude.* Wordsworth's problem of authority is how to justify himself as a center of perception. Without the solid comfort of a Logos-centered authority, he tries to establish the ego-centered authority of the Imagination, simultaneously portraying it as an Other and as grounded in his own being.

The next three chapters are devoted to close analysis of "The Tower," *Four Quartets,* and *Paterson.* In "The Tower," the speaker tries to recover the ego-centered authority of an archetypal bard. He does so by internalizing the objective world and transforming it into a series of images, allowing him to assert an authority over it on the grounds that it is only the imaginative world that survives and has value. In *Four Quartets* the speaker struggles both to remain passive and to assert the redemptive power of the Logos-centered authority the poem summons. His transpersonality is a contraction into impersonal rhythm and image, showing that Eliot is "more concerned with the object of belief than with his own feelings in regard to it" (Dembo, 200). But this contraction is not easily achieved; the finite speaker that periodically emerges is implicitly chastised by the poem's form because of his—and the reader's—inability to empty the mind of ego. In *Paterson,* there is a struggle to achieve a suspension between Logos and ego.[24] Where Williams is successful, his poetry manifests the "co-extension" of the mind and the world in which no ideal order is abstracted and removed from human reach, and no ego swells to occupy and direct human perceptions and purposes. Instead, the issue of authority vanishes because there is no idea of a directing center or mediation from one realm to another. Rather, the radical source of value is in the vitality stirred by contact between imagination and world, seer and seen.

2

The Poles of Poetic Authority: Logos and Ego in *Paradise Lost* and *The Prelude*

In the Eastern porch of Satans Univers Milton stood & said

Satan! my Spectre! I know my power thee to annihilate
And be a greater in thy place, & be thy Tabernacle
A covering for thee to do thy will, till one greater comes
And smites me as I smote thee & and becomes my covering.
Such are the Laws of thy false Heavns! but Laws of Eternity
Are not such: know thou: I come to Self Annihilation
Such are the Laws of Eternity that each shall mutually
Annihilate himself for others good, as I for thee.
                    —Blake's *Milton*, Book 2

I have three purposes in bringing Milton and Wordsworth into this discussion of modernist poetic authority. First, like the modernist poets, Milton and Wordsworth wrote during times of extraordinary challenge to political, social, and moral authorities, and consequently had to respond to those challenges, struggling to reanchor their cultures in values that would extend beyond their own times. Second, by straying from the modern period I can more readily identify the ahistorical problems of speaker authority and thus by contrast suggest what is peculiarly modern about the efforts of Yeats, Eliot, and Williams. Third, my reason for focusing on Milton and Wordsworth, as opposed to, say, Spenser and Shelley, or Pope and Keats, is that more than any other major British or American premodern poets they mark the outside limits of what can be claimed for Logos-centered and ego-centered authorities and for the mind's access to them. That is, their claims for the level of access to the authorities they mediate, as well as for the sway those authorities hold over the way the mind experiences and evaluates the world, conspicuously exceed those of other poets in the Anglo-American tradition. And not only do the speakers of *Paradise Lost* and *The Prelude* serve as archetypal mediators of Logos-centered and ego-centered authority respectively, but each one explicitly counters the opposing position, showing it to be ungrounded, a manifestation of desire rather than reality. Milton's speaker unveils the inauthenticity of that quintessential ego-centered authority, Satan, while conversely, Wordsworth's speaker dismisses as inauthentic the received, book-ridden images of Fancy.

What links these separate purposes of mine is that the very reason they are archetypal speakers distinguishes them from modernist speakers. Their claims promise—or at least project—the possibility of redemption from puny mortality; Milton identifies a redemptive response to Satanic despair, and Wordsworth illuminates a sublime release from wearying, inauthentic structures of thought. These speakers are distinguished from their modernist counterparts by the authorities they represent, authorities more strongly felt, more nourishing to the cultures in which and to which they speak. The sense of cultural community and individual value their authorities offer are far greater and come at less cost than anything extended by the modernists I examine here. Though Milton's and Wordsworth's speakers both take only tentative mediating positions, and though both are circumscribed by anxiety, it is to a lesser degree than for the modernists, and their aims are far grander, indicating a greater confidence that their contemporary cultural authorities were more firmly held and more generally acknowledged. The modern poets cannot make the absolute claims that Milton and Wordsworth can; terms for human value lack content when there is no strong cultural authority to generate and nourish them. But by contrasting the modern and the premodern I am not proposing that the moderns achieved less but that in their particular effort to identify and mediate cultural authority, theirs was the greater burden.

Regardless of the era or the authority being mediated, a poetic speaker sails between the Scylla of banal mortality and the Charybdis of oblivious divinity. In *Paradise Lost,* the Miltonic speaker must keep the Logos of inspiration unreachably divine yet still accessible to the worthy, identifying himself as the archetypal mediator of the Logos yet without making that effort explicit, for such an effort would be proof of desire. On the other hand, in *The Prelude,* the speaker must prove that the Imagination is fundamentally divine, demonstrating both its otherness and that he is himself its source. He must therefore mediate an aspect of his own selfhood. To do so, he extends the Imagination to the general mind of the archetypal Poet, deferring contact with the Imagination to remembered past moments and anticipated moments of the future. When Milton and Wordsworth succeed, projecting the authority of the ego or the Logos, their speakers are transpersonalized into textual voices, their private identities dispersed among the images expressing that authority.

The speaker's object in the invocation passages of *Paradise Lost* is to establish and sustain his position as a mediator for Logos-centered authority, a mediator through whom God speaks. Yet because of his expansive claims for the narrative's source, this ostensibly anti-Satanic position constantly threatens to invert itself, to be disclosed as self-generated and thus Satanic. To succeed as a necessary alternative to Satan, the speaker must enact the undoing of his own ego, replacing it with a voice of textual authority, that is, a voice raised from the partiality and limited perspective of the ego to "click into an eternal pattern" (Kerrigan, 227). Only in so doing can he justify the movement from invocation to narrative.[1] What grants this movement its fundamental authenticity is the speaker's claim that no language can emerge to define divine purpose unless it comes from beyond him, from the Logos. Furthermore, if indeed the speaker does become the mediating vessel of a divine voice, that result is not dependent on any special attributes of the speaker—such as a larger mind or more expansive imagination—and no special glory or redemption is conferred on the speaker for having served in this capacity. He is neither transformed nor enlightened, and the contents of his mind are of interest to us only in that they emphasize their own irrelevance.

In this section of the chapter, I will first delineate the speaker's necessary situation between the moral and the divine world and explain how he stages his right to this position. Next, in the context of Stanley Fish's reader-based formulation in *Surprised by Sin,* I briefly discuss the Satanic pitfalls Fish creates for the speaker by accepting as given his authority to mediate the Logos. I devote the remainder of the section to a close reading of the four invocation passages. As I shall show, the speaker does not simply move but progresses from one invocation to the next; each one is buttressed by the presumption that preceding books were divinely inspired. But less assertively, the repeated invocations point to the need for the ego's continued submission; there is no still point of achievement, and each invocation is a necessary reassertion of authority. His use of the epic tradition also helps establish and strengthen his mediating authority. In each invocation he grounds his poetic venture in the classical tradition but finally dismisses his classical counterparts as misdirected failures. In this way, his poetic efforts take on the grandeur and cultural authority of the events he alludes to yet without being merely imitative or absorbed by them.

But the speaker's most powerful rhetorical gesture is in the transpersonal movement from invocation to narrative. Each invocation, even, more guardedly, the one in Book IX, ends with a plea for inspiration, a plea immediately followed by the return of the narrative. If indeed the "human request and the divine response give prophetic authority to the verse of the poem" (Kerrigan, 141), it is because the resumption of the narrative is credible only if it is preceded by an unanswered prayer. The speaker cannot know himself in the act of receiving inspiration; he can only be transpersonalized, like the bird, into pure voice.

But even the act of prayer must be properly staged. That is, the speaker must locate himself between the fallen and unfallen worlds, a placement that allows him to partake of both. Putting this situation in terms of identity, Anne Ferry calls it Milton's "double nature," that of the "blind bard (bird) and fallen man, mortal and inspired" (87). Ferry's formulation is useful here because it describes the linguistic trappings necessary for a mediator of Miltonic Logos-centered authority. What defines his mortality is desire, expressed in each invocation's statements of need, where Milton draws a line between mortal and divine abilities. The speaker desires supernatural vision and answerable style, but in his refusal of personal agency he demonstrates that neither one can descend through an effort of personal will. What links him to the promise of inspiration is faith—a subrational expectation of divine inspiration. Faith alone permits the erasure of ego, an emptying of those qualities the speaker examines in moments of self-consciousness.

The doubt implicit in desire is both rhetorically and logically essential; it is evidence of self-consciousness, which the speaker, being fallen, must display. In *Surprised by Sin,* Stanley Fish disregards the issue of self-consciousness by presuming the speaker's authority rather than treating the text as a struggle to attain it. If Fish's argument held, the speaker's credibility would be irrevocably undermined. For Fish, the text situates the reader at the receiving end of chastising self-examination: "We shall learn Milton's lesson," Fish explains, "only if we enter the poem on his terms" (46). Given this rhetorical staging, we can either ignore Milton's lessons, identifying ourselves as rebellious children, or learn, becoming submissive disciples. In either case, we automatically submit to the text's authority to define us according to our response to it. Fish assumes that the speaker—the text's voice—is Milton, a stable, didactic presence, and that the reader, not the speaker, is the locus of the poem.

The problem with Fish's formulation is that the authority of this didactic presence is far more problematic than Fish allows. The textual authority of the narrator is grounded in the uneasy meditative voice of the invocational passages, a voice that must mediate between divine and fallen.[2] Without such a mediator explicitly lodged in the poem, only the reader, an otherwise ego-centered Satanic presence, is left to mediate. More important, this essential mediator cannot spring perfectly formed from the forehead of God, as Fish would have Milton be. Instead, he must be both fallen and self-consciously aware of his fallenness. One cannot be other than fallen, and a lack of self-consciousness describes either an angelic or Satanic mind, neither of which could stand as a bridge between fallen and divine, ego and Logos. Redemption comes through a loss of self-consciousness, but only by an emptying of the ego; giving up the self frees the mind from the sense of Otherness. Gabriel and Abdiel, for instance, are free from self-consciousness because there is no distinction between their wills and God's. Conversely, Satan is not free of self-consciousness but merely evades it, blotting out the expanse of divine will by cloaking himself in his own desire.

To illuminate the path to redemption, the speaker must first be able to speak from that place that the soul must leave, to dramatize the pain of fallenness.[3] Without the speaker's self-consciousness and doubt, which locate him among the fallen, the idea of inspiration would be meaningless; there would be neither need nor reason for inspiration. Nor would there be anything to instruct, for there would be no one from among the fallen to demonstrate how to surrender the self in favor of divine will. This fact of self-consciousness, the evidence of our fallen condition, is the spiritual impediment requiring the poem. Hence it is the speaker's passage into mediating authority rather than the reader's moral enlightenment that is necessarily the fundamental issue in the poem. Were it a simple and automatic movement from self-consciousness to inspiration, to the realm where Fish accepts it as given that the Miltonic speaker resides, the poem would have nothing to prove except its inauthenticity, collapsing from internal contradictions. The path to God and right reason cannot begin with Abdiel and Gabriel but only with the invocations of the Logos-centered speaker, who must stage the dissolution of his self-consciousness in the will of God.

In the first invocation, the speaker sets forth the conditions under which inspiration is necessary, displacing the focus from his fitness as a mediator to the greatness of the argument:

> Of Man's First Disobedience, and the Fruit
> Of that Forbidden Tree, whose mortal taste
> Brought Death into the World, and all our woe,
> With loss of Eden, till one greater Man
> Restore us, and regain the blissful Seat,
> Sing Heav'nly Muse, that on the secret top
> Of Oreb, or of Sinai, didst inspire
> That Shepherd, who first taught the chosen Seed,
>   . . . I thence
> Invoke thy aid to my advent'rous Song,
> That with no middle flight intends to soar
> Above the Aonian Mount, while it pursues
> Things unattempted yet in Prose or Rhyme.
>
> (I, 1–16)

Here he displaces the focus from self to Spirit. Any uncertainty the speaker may profess about his abilities serves less to raise doubts in the reader than to emphasize the divine majesty of his purpose:

> And chiefly Thou, O Spirit, that dost prefer
> Before all Temples th'upright heart and pure,
> Instruct me, for Thou know'st; Thou from the first
> Wast present, and with mighty wings outspread
> Dove-like satst brooding on the vast Abyss
> and mad'st it pregnant
>
> (I, 17–22)

The lines that follow, "What in me is dark / Illumine, what is low, raise and support," express not the difficulty of preparing him for his prophetic role but simply the need for prophetic vision. His epigrammatic injunction presents his fitness as a fact almost algebraically inevitable, an event requiring only the logic of its form to resolve it rather than any wrenching effort of the soul. Yet at the same time, he does not possess the inspiration during this or any of the other invocations; their presence in the poem proves inspiration's absence. By not explicitly claiming to be inspired, the speaker manages to leave the issue in question, unresolved, yet without raising the question and forcing a resolution.

Here, as in each of the other invocations, the speaker displaces questions about his fitness by partially identifying with his classical predecessors; he cloaks himself in their cultural authority so that the reader cannot easily dismiss him without dismissing the epic tradition. Yet identification with this tradition is not enough. The speaker must exceed his predecessors, display "Things unattempted yet in Prose or Rhyme." This apparent arrogance can go unchallenged, however, because he displaces his epic agency to his "Song," which is grammatically and thus ontologically separate. Even the grandiosity of "I may assert Eternal Providence / And justify the ways of God to men" is muted by his dependence on illumination by the Muse, an illumination by no means made certain.[4] Nowhere does the speaker make declarative assertions of authority or lay claim to greater than mortal abilities. Instead, he sidesteps the pedestal by displacing his identity into Song and by keeping his claims contingent upon inspiration.

The speaker's path to mediation of Logos-centered authority is further complicated in Book III, where his efforts to dramatize his struggle for inspiration—and its accompanying authority—are more evident. Instead of the trumpet blare of Book I, Book III begins with a humble, flute-like apostrophe that displays the problem the speaker wishes to overcome, a lack of vision, a sense of his own frailty in the face of his task's immensity. This change in posture does not diminish our regard for him, but instead forces us to look to the new subject, the realm of Heaven, as the cause. He stages himself as one acted upon rather than the agent of image-making, so we look elsewhere for that agency, finding it in an unnameable divine presence, or rather, in the desire to subordinate itself to that presence. By the end of the invocation, having surrendered the authority of the ego, the speaker has acquired the authority to mediate the Logos.

The speaker's search for the right name shows the distance between the mortal and the divine. The mortal, fallen mind must delineate and thus limit the divine in order to make it present, while the divine by definition is ineffable and irreducible. That very search provides his solution; attributes rather than a name emerge, displaying the cosmic, prophetic perspective of one disengaged from ego-centered concerns:

> Hail holy Light, offspring of Heav'n first born,
> Or of th'Eternal Coeternal beam
> May I express thee unblam'd? since God is Light,
> And never but in unapproached Light
> Dwelt from Eternity, dwelt then in thee,
> Bright effluence of bright essence increate.

> Whose Fountain who shall tell? before the Sun,
> Before the Heavens thou wert, and at the voice
> Of God, as with a Mantle didst invest
> The rising world of waters dark and deep,
> Won from the void and formless infinite.
>
> (III, 1–12)

By this attribution he reproduces, if not a divine Presence, at least the confounded sensations of encountering it.[5] Thus, achieving credibility as a witness is the first necessary step toward mediation. Without explicitly lecturing the reader or making claims to greater visionary powers, he mediates this Presence and implicitly instructs us how to regard it. Because the search for a name is dramatized by apostrophe, the speaker appears to have no rhetorical stake in his success, no apparent audience over whom to hold sway. Consequently, he does hold sway over his audience, which to read the drama must identify with his role in it. There is little ironic room for the reader to stand in; the speaker's own self-diminution in the face of his project anticipates challenges by the reader.

He portrays himself as isolated and abandoned, thus countering Satan's professions of independence by inverting them:

> thee I revisit safe,
> and feel thy sovran vital Lamp; but thou
> Revisit'st not these eyes, that roll in vain
> To find thy piercing ray, and find no dawn;
> So thick a drop serene hath quencht thir Orbs,
> Or dim suffusion veil'd.
>
> (III, 21–26)

He requires Light in Book III, not merely instruction, meaning that the fact of his darkness has figurative consequences. Because of that isolation he can speak as an "extraordinary minister," suffering like the rest of the world but removed from their "unreflective commonness" (Kerrigan, 179). His isolation in blindness is a figure for emptiness and absence, pointing to the need for inspiration and distilling our sense of the speaker's suffering. He speaks from a position of great and guiltless loss, but presents himself as merely an example rather than individuating himself. Consequently, without insisting on his right to do so, he can nonetheless stand between Logos and audience, overcoming the tension between his two roles as hieratic mediator and helpless supplicant. And because he is distanced from the audience, his authority is enhanced by the resulting attraction of autonomy, a freedom from worldly concerns. At the same time, however, he has staged himself as a figure passive and pliant before God. His blindness removes the world from him, leaving a vacuum that only the presence of God can fill. The speaker's implicit claim, of course, is that having been stripped of worldly vision, he is now, by force of natural balance, entitled to celestial vision. Yet the speaker masterfully evades this Satanic trap, this reconstruction of the universe to suit personal will, by presenting only his desire, not its anticipated consequence:

> Yet not the more
> Cease I to wander where the Muses haunt
> Clear Spring, or shady Grove, or Sunny Hill,
> Smit with the love of sacred Song; but chief
> Thee Sion and the flow'ry Brooks beneath
> That wash thy hallow'd feet, and warbling flow,
> Nightly I visit
>
> (III, 26–32)

The equation of worldly and celestial vision is made only by the textual voice, while the speaker secures his authority to mediate by refusing to extend the limits of ego.

The effect the speaker is striving for is *kenosis,* or willed will-lessness, a state he achieves at the center of the invocation (Guillory, 6):

> Then feed on thoughts, that voluntary move
> Harmonious numbers; as the wakeful Bird
> Sings darkling, and in shadiest Covert hid
> Tunes her nocturnal Note.
>
> (III, 37–40)

Vanishing grammatically and reappearing as a "wakeful Bird," he is transformed into a kenotic figure for inspiration.[6] With the speaker apparently gone, we are left with an image of pure medium, a projection of the speaker that temporarily replaces him.[7] This image serves both to seal off the reader's understanding of the kenotic purpose—dispelling the aura of a complaining old man—and to make real the possibility of mediation.[8]

However, the speaker returns, again to describe his loss and to propose once more that the absence of earthly vision should bring a countering celestial vision:

>   Thus with the Year
> Seasons return, but not to me returns
> Day, or the sweet approach of Ev'n or Morn. . . .
> So much the rather thou Celestial Light
> Shine inward, and the mind through all her powers
> Irradiate, there plant eyes, all mist from thence
> Purge and disperse, that I may see and tell
> Of things invisible to mortal sight.
>
>   (III, 40–55)

The easier course rhetorically would have been for the speaker to begin the narrative immediately following the "wakeful Bird" passage. But his reemergence serves his purpose better, demonstrating the impossibility of sustained inspiration and consequently reaffirming the distance between mortal and divine. Moreover, had the grace of the Muse brought him a permanent change in status, he would have lost contact with his audience and thus the ability to mediate. Because inspiration can only be given, never achieved, and certainly never willed, only a failure to sustain inspiration can demonstrate the true condition of the soul. As a result of that failure, the inspiration that presumably returns has a greater sense of authenticity. To recover from that failure and rise once more toward inspiration, he makes the equation between kinds of visions more explicit, but still it remains without agency: we do not know who would "rather," or rather, we do not know that the "Celestial Light" would not prefer to grant him vision. As the invocation ends, the speaker remains uncertain, as he properly should be, imprisoned as he is in supplicatory self-consciousness. Yet the reader can be more certain. The integrity of the speaker's identity—established by conventional expectations—encourages the view that the narrative's return is due to the Muse's.

In the invocation of Book VII, the speaker once again finds the Muse unnameable, but he reasserts his authority by four additional means: maintaining his active passivity, presupposing the Muse's presence in his Song, identifying with and overcoming the pagan tradition, and confining his readership to "a fit audience, though few," a group defined by its willingness to acknowledge his mediating authority. With the weight of six books behind him, the speaker claims that he has indeed "drawn Empyreal Air," but having achieved this height he qualifies his status considerably. The "Air" has received her "temp'ring," her accommodation of the Word to mortal ears; that he admits to having "presum'd" implies an unease born of a laudable self-consciousness, making credible the claim that he has indeed seen what he says. He is at least assuming the correct posture, which grants the rhetorical equivalent of credibility:

> Up led by thee
> Into the Heav'n of Heav'ns I have presum'd,
> An Earthly Guest, and drawn Empyreal Air,
> Thy temp'ring; with like safety guided down
> Return me to my Native Element:

The allusion to Bellerophon points to his prevalent use of the ancients' heroic tradition. He first identifies himself with a heroic figure and then supersedes it:

> Lest from this flying Steed unrein'd (as once
> *Bellerophon,* though from a lower Clime)
> Dismounted, on th'Alexian Field I fall
> Erroneous there to wander and forlorn.
>
> (VII, 12–20)

Even as he appropriates the magic and greatness of Bellerophon's exploits, the speaker asks for help in avoiding his errors. Such a request strengthens his position in two ways. First, it presupposes that his deeds are already equivalent or analogous to Bellerophon's. Second, that he asks for help rather than asserting a freedom from error sustains the moral authority of passive waiting and colors it with a heroic aspect. The speaker further supersedes his predecessors by taking on the attributes of Orpheus:

> But drive far off the barbarous dissonance
> Of *Bacchus* and his Revellers, the Race
> Of that wild Rout that tore the *Thracian* Bard
> In *Rhodope,* where Woods and Rocks had Ears
> To rapture, till the savage clamor drown'd
> Both Harp and Voice; nor could the Muse defend
> Her Son. So fail not thou, who thee implores:
> For thou art Heavn'ly, shee an empty dream.
>
> (VII, 32–39)

Most important among these attributes is that they implicitly name him "another" first poet, an originator, the great precedent for all future poets. And having identified him as a poet of Orphic power, we are drawn into the great pathos of longing that through this transpersonality becomes heroic. Finally, because the speaker is not a pagan, he emerges as Orpheus's moral superior.

The seeming arrogance in these lines is tempered, however, by the fact that their claims emerge as the quiet consequence of unarguable positions. Clearly, no good Christian can argue that Orpheus's theology was true, and it is not arrogant of the speaker to imply with aesthetic grace that he has been treated shabbily. Furthermore, his prophetic status is not innate but dependent upon the grace of the Muse. The speaker has nimbly vanished, too, from the Orpheus references, so that any parallels between the poets comes from the textual voice, to be assembled by the reader. Lastly, as with the end to the Book III invocation, his parting plea to the Muse extends his necessary uncertainty about his ability to mediate. With that plea, of course, the narrative resumes.

Book IX's invocation begins with confident presumption of the authority to mediate the Fall, but once again it is a final uncertainty—though never doubt—that sustains the speaker's authority to mediate. Presuming a history of inspiration, he refers to the Muse as his "Celestial Patroness," and explicitly articulates the posture of Christian heroism, a posture he identifies with his own efforts. For the first time, he claims, however briefly, complete control over the tone and direction of the narrative: "I now must change / Those notes to Tragic; foul distrust, and breach / Disloyal on the part of Man," (IX 5–7). But however secure his mediating role has become, the need remains for further inspiration, a prize that according to his own terms must be withheld unless he can unself-consciously stage himself as a fulfillment of heroic passivity. The aspect of dependence created by these requirements makes the tension of uncertainty both inevitable and necessary:

> If answerable style I can obtain
> Of my Celestial Patroness, who deigns
> Her nightly visitation unimplor'd
> And dictates to me slumb'ring, or inspires
> Easy my unpremeditated Verse
>
> (IX 20–24)

But it is an uncertainty that is formalized, no longer felt; it is an uncertainty without the reflexive anxiety of Book III, which by contrast seems self-regarding. Here, though the speaker may be uncertain whether he will obtain a style equal to his subject, his confidence that the divine Muse speaks to him, serving as the source of his narrative, contradicts and overcomes his uncertainty. This tenuous positioning between certainty and uncertainty lets him retain his display of passivity before divine will while at the same time keeping secure his position as a mediator. He grants himself just enough doubt to be humbly worthy, yet not enough to chip at his prophet's pedestal. The proper place for doubt is in his mind, not in the reader's.

The speaker clears a space for Christian heroism by raising images of conventional heroism, emptying them from the heroic mold, and then occupying their space by default. In other words, he appropriates the authority of the classical tradition without burdening himself with its liabilities, in fact, emphasizing those liabilities in order to demonstrate his superiority. He is, he says,

> Not sedulous by Nature to indite
> Wars, hitherto the only Argument
> Heroic deem'd, chief maistry to dissect
> With long and tedious havoc fabl'd Knights
> In Battles feign'd; the better fortitude
> Of Patience and Heroic Martyrdom
> Unsung; or to describe Races and Games,
> Or tilting Furniture, emblazon'd Shields
> Impreses quaint, Caparisons and Steeds;
> Bases and tinsel Trappings, gorgeous Knights
> At Joust and Tournament; then marshall'd Feast
> Serv'd up in Hall with Sewers, and Seneschals;
> The skill of Artifice or Office mean,
> Not that which justly gives Heroic name
> To Person or to Poem. Mee of these
> Nor skill'd nor studious, higher Argument
> Remains

(IX 27–43)

With this catalog of knights and knightly trappings, he shifts his discourse to an epic plane, compelling us to read his "Argument" in epic terms, in the same martial context that he explicitly rejects. With the epic as the only medium through which we can understand his poem, and with that medium at best only an analog and at worst a corruption, the speaker's efforts take on the grandeur of the epic but remain *sui generis,* in a place infinitely loftier. Had the speaker said his poem was part of the epic tradition, he would be judged on those terms, as an imitator rather than a mediator. But because he draws on the emotive power of the epic genre without being circumscribed by it, the terms we are left with to judge his efforts are his alone.

It is only a short leap from singularity to divinity of purpose. What takes him that short distance is the image of "Patience and

Heroic Martyrdom / Unsung," which, thrust starkly into the midst of the epic catalog, stands apart from it in abstract inertness; its syntactic detachment expresses its moral distinctness. The images of the loyal angels and the speaker's account of his own plight in earlier invocations rush to occupy with concreteness the abstract structure of this "Martyrdom," and once again it is the speaker's language rather than his explicit intentions that buttresses his authority to mediate. Our own inferences—which create this textual voice—rather than the speaker's claims are what grant him the right to continue his narrative.

The parting lines of this invocation force similar inferences about his moral legitimacy; the speaker simultaneously expresses both humble uncertainty about and unshakable confidence in his inspiration:

> higher Argument
> Remains, sufficient of itself to raise
> That name, unless an age too late, or cold
> Climate, or Years damp my intended wing
> Deprest; and much they may, if all be mine,
> Not Hers who brings it nightly to my Ear.
>
> (IX 42–47)

Even as he holds forth the possibility that he alone rather than divine inspiration is the source of his poem, he withdraws it in the abrupt reversal of the last line. Does this withdrawal succeed? As in Book III, he has staged himself as a reduced figure stripped of worldly power, so that his efforts are utterly without meaning unless they are inspired. The chief reason we are led to believe in their divinity is that no greater degree of certainty can inflate the speaker's consequence; he is distinguished from the rest of humankind by his miserable isolation, not by his mediation. Whether lost in error or raised by divine inspiration, as an ego he has nothing to gain from either eventuality. He thereby performs a miracle of rhetoric: sustaining the necessary posture of doubt without enduring the debilitating consequences of uncertainty. This combination of a collapsed ego, doubt in self-worth, and unrelenting faith forge at least a provisional shield against the Satanic ego.

In *The Prelude,* the speaker's efforts to justify the ego-centered authority of the Imagination confront him with the paradoxical challenge of constituting the Imagination as an Other, requiring mediation, yet at the same time demonstrating that he is the source of the Imagination, that it arises from within him. On the one hand, it is only as an Other that the Imagination can escape a field of perception that is idiosyncratic and partial, in both senses of the word. But conversely, unless the Imagination resides in the ego, the poetic speaker can make no claim for its authenticity, its contact with the inner and outer worlds it must mediate. To elude the rhetorical collapse this paradox presents, the speaker transpersonalizes himself into three elements: a younger, more naive self, Nature, and an imaginative faculty invested with divinity. Thus detached, the speaker mediates rather than participating in the growth of a poet's mind. When at the end of *The Prelude* the speaker has annexed the sublimity of Nature to express the divinity of the Imagination, the claims he makes for how beautiful the mind of man becomes are nearly tenable because in spite of the use of first person, the narrative tracks the progress of a mind different from the speaker's.

To speak with the necessary authenticity, he must show that he is simultaneously part of both the audience and the authority he mediates. But the speaker's distinctness from both Imagination and audience demonstrates a consciousness of the problems binding anyone who speaks for ego-centered authority. The poem's title announces the enormous scope of Wordsworthian poetic desire, but at the same time it holds forth a darker alternative, the counterposition that the self-conscious subject is not adequate to respond to his own imaginative nature. The subject cannot authorize itself, cannot finally collect the fragments of identity scattered into past moments, because the necessary mastery of self-consciousness would bring only silence, shutting off his access to the imaginative powers of the ego. The unmediated relationship to Nature that would result would make him Nature's object instead of his own. Thus, by treating the Imagination as an Other, he can draw on its authority because, lying only within, it is unchallengeable. At the same time, as an Other it retains sufficient mystery to prevent him from exerting it consciously or peeling back the obscuring layer of sublimation. The ego-centered authority of the Imagination, by definition a force transcending individual desire, can never act in the present; it can only be remembered from the past or projected into the future. Thus, all the speaker can produce is a prelude: a summing up of events to the ever-shifting present moment.

Essential to the mystery of the Imagination is the naiveté of the speaker's younger self. By presenting the younger self's strawman arguments on behalf of Fancy, the speaker can undermine them ironically to clear space for the force of Imagination. As a result, the speaker can remember epiphanic moments of rapture without insisting on their authority, reducing the degree of irony he is subject to. Through this distance from both Fancy and his younger self, he accomplishes three essential projects: he demonstrates the poet's "growth of mind," distinguishes Imagination from pedestrian consciousness, and displaces himself from the center of poetic creation, sparing himself the entire burden of arguing for the Imagination's authority. In doing so, he characterizes himself as a passive observer acted upon by the Imagination, even though it partially constitutes his own identity. The speaker is thus delegating authority, locating the will "outside" the conscious, rational mind. This delegation directly feeds the Imagination's mystery and authority, the mist surrounding the younger self as the Imagination continually eludes his conscious control. That continually deferred presence is what makes it require the speaker's mediation, yet the speaker's ability to mediate is continually being countered because his access to his imaginative faculty is continually being denied. When the Imagination is shown to be inaccessible—not to the speaker but to his earlier self—it is that self rather than the speaker whom we are led to question, and against whom irony is vented. The speaker's self-division removes him from the creative authority of the Imagination, liberating him from charges that he has usurped authority. Separated from the speaker by time and self-consciousness, the Imagination can remain analogous to or even identified with the divine. Of course, in its status as a faculty of the speaker's ego, the Imagination can never actually be separate from the mind except when staged as such. Consequently, the speaker's own authority to mediate depends upon his failure to know his Imagination and exert it at the same time. As we see by Book XIV, which proposes a future union between speaker and Imagination, a far greater authority is drawn from Imagination's distance than if it had been lodged within the speaker's own self-conscious gestures. Because the speaker is logically identical to his Imagination but rhetorically separate, he manages to speak authoritatively from both the transcendent realm and the realm of stumbling, self-conscious finitude.

In this next part of the chapter, I explore the progress of the speaker's younger self by examining the passages describing his relationship to Nature and his ascents of Mont Blanc and Mt. Snowdon. In these passages, I focus on the younger self's progress from Fancy to Imagination, from inauthentic Logos-centered categories derived from his reading to an understanding—in the terms

Nature provides—of the unconscious, ego-centered Imagination. The younger self is at first utterly confident in his mediation of Nature, free of any suspicion that Fancy, which structures his reading of Nature, is inauthentic. In a second phase, he is paralyzed by the discovery that Fancy is inadequate to identify and mediate sensations of the sublime. A third phase, which is projected rather than achieved, brings the understanding that the natural sublime serves to express the divine power of the Imagination. Being simultaneously divine and ego-centered, the Imagination can neither be mastered by nor distinguished from the self, thereby validating the speaker's claims as a mediator of ego-centered authority.

The speaker's claims for the Imagination begin and end with Nature's role, which is to reveal itself as an expression of his own creative will. Nature alone provides the vocabulary of the sublime, with which he can articulate the mind's grandeur to itself. According to the speaker's construction, Nature not only teaches but displays a parental sympathy:[9]

                                                        Was

> it for this
> That one, the fairest of all rivers, loved
> To blend his murmurs with my nurse's song,
> And, from his alder shades and rocky falls,
> And from his fords and shallows, sent a voice
> That flowed along my dreams? For this, didst thou,
> O Derwent! winding among grassy holms
> Where I was looking on, a babe in arms,
> Make ceaseless music that composed my thoughts
> To more than infant softness, giving me
> Amid the fretful dwellings of mankind
> A foretaste, a dim earnest, of the calm
> That Nature breathes among the hills and groves.

                                          (I 269–81)

This passage establishes the speaker as a poet and figure of consequence, elevating him by both his admission of failure and his presumed alliance with the forces of Nature. To claim he has squandered Nature's generosity is to presume that he has until now been Nature's beneficiary, that Nature is both conscious and generous, and that the reader sympathetically shares this reading of Nature. Characterizing Nature by premise rather than direct statement, the speaker releases the role of Nature from the realm of argument.

The speaker also gains rhetorical ground when he puts his younger self at an ironic distance. In the Simplon Pass section of Book VI, the speaker emphasizes the breach between expectation and fulfillment:

> That very day,
> From a bare ridge we also first beheld
> Unveiled the summit of Mont Blanc, and grieved
> To have a soulless image on the eye
> That had usurped upon a living thought
> What never more could be.
>
> (VI 523–28)

The image of the summit is "soulless," the thing itself unmolested by the Imagination, overwhelming the conscious mind before it can interpret the message the eye brings to the mind. The thing itself usurps and by implication kills the "living" thought, the younger self's preconceived meaning of the summit as a symbol of beatification. The irony is vented against that younger self, for the mind that generates epistemological categories should not be in competition with its objects—or so Nature has taught. Had the younger self not set himself in conflict, he would not have read soullessness into the summit. The younger self errs in not acknowledging that his mental structures are not inadequate to identify, or identify with, the sublime. His mind is at that point only equipped to mediate gentler surroundings, those more submissive to preconception:

> The wondrous Vale
> Of Chamouny stretched far below, and soon
> With its dumb cataracts and streams of ice,
> A motionless array of mighty waves,
> Five rivers broad and vast, made rich amends,
> And reconciled us to realities;
>
> (VI 528–33)

The speaker transfers a scene to us directly because the "wondrous Vale" is beneath the younger self and his companion; it can be subdued. The scene does not threaten the speaker's acts of mediation, and so the adjectives recounting his response to the scene— "wondrous," "mighty," "rich"—are kept to a minimum, allowing most of the details to emerge relatively unmolested. Still, the scene is not presented to display Nature but to show the younger self's response to it, the way he mediates it as a scene designed for his own pleasure. It is an evasion of Nature, not a participation in it.

In these two passages the younger self is caught in a loop of self-consciousness, passing from where speech begins at the "soulless" summit, the first astonished contact between mind and thing, to where speech finally overcomes the object and replaces it, at the "wondrous Vale." From that point he approaches silence once again; equipped with Fancy alone, his mind turns in on itself without drawing on the authority of the imaginative vision, nearing self-annihilation by blocking from consciousness his thought's object. His release from the loop of self-consciousness can come only from movement along a continuum leading from Logos-centered to ego-centered authority, from book-ridden Fancy to an Imagination located in objectified creative faculties. But from the beginning the younger self rejects the Other as the source of its interpretive authority and self-knowledge: confronting the soulless summit, the mind feels itself alien to it, conscious only of that alienation. Because his predetermined categories are his only way of knowing, when the younger self encounters a phenomenon that transcends them, he cannot really see it. The summit is soulless, devoid of evidence that it participates in the divine, because the younger self cannot find in the summit an echo of his own identity. For the divine to be known and made present to the ego, it must be on the ego's terms, through sensations of a transpersonal extension of selfhood into Nature.

Having been "reconciled to realities" amid less sublime surroundings, the younger self annexes its objects by constructing readings of them: "While Winter like a well-tamed lion walks, / Descending from the mountain to make sport / Among the cottages by beds of flowers" (VI 538–40). Our perception of these natural elements are authorized not by their inherent qualities but by the Fancy of the younger self. The fact that the speaker uses simile rather than metaphor counters Fancy's authority, suggesting, as the following lines emphasize, that the meaning he drew came from his own mind:

> Whate'er in this wide circuit we beheld,
> Or heard, was fitted to our unripe state
> Of intellect and heart. With such a book
> Before our eyes, we could not choose but read
> Lessons of genuine brotherhood, the plain
> And universal reason of mankind,
> The truths of young and old.

(VI 541–47)

The younger self's distance along the continuum toward pure mind leaves the speaker in an opposing ironic position, recounting not the experience of Nature but the experience of a response to Nature. He mediates the younger self's experience with a thick layer of irony yet still evades the determinate stance of ridicule. For instance, "was fitted" is in the passive voice, making the agent of the action indeterminate. Either Nature fits itself to "our unripe state," willingly submitting to the mind's humanistic categories, or the mind fits Nature to those categories. In either case, Nature submits to the mind, the "wide circuit" contracting to accommodate an "unripe state." That contraction and the new lyrical focus away from Nature both reflect ironically on a younger mind congratulating itself rather than learning from the new forms Nature provides.

The speaker's ironic stance becomes clearer as he comments on the younger self's means of interpretation:

>   Nor, side by side
> Pacing, two social pilgrims, or alone
> Each with his humor, could we fail to abound
> In dreams and fictions pensively composed:
> Dejections taken up for pleasure's sake,
> And gilded sympathies, the willow wreath,
> And sober posies of funeral flowers,
> Gathered among those solitudes sublime
> From formal gardens of the lady Sorrow,
> Did sweeten many a meditative hour.
>
>   (547–56)

For the younger self, Nature existed only to fuel emotionally satisfying "dreams and fictions." However benignly, the speaker distances his younger self, aware that the inwardness and the passivity—"we could not choose but read"—must surely be anti-creative, no matter how pleasing. They join in a fundamentally inauthentic attempt at ego-centered authority, for they do not enlarge the mind, engage it in its surroundings, or generate a new understanding of either Nature or the mind. Even though in the poem as a whole the speaker examines the contents of his own mind rather than the contents of Nature, by deriding, however gently, a younger self for such a flagrant display of self-approval, he in effect constructs excesses of the straw authority of Fancy that, once trampled, leaves room for the Imagination, an authentic ego-centered authority.[10]

The climactic lines that follow counter the shallow, self-conscious artifice with the unembraceable expanse of the Imagination: "Yet still in me with those soft luxuries / Mixed something of stern mood, an under-thirst / Of vigor seldom utterly allayed" (557–61). The speaker has now strengthened his younger self's position, for what did "sweeten many a meditative hour" is now dismissed as "soft luxuries," demonstrating a more clear-eyed willingness to address the discomforts of self-consciousness.[11] Moreover, the presence of an "under-thirst of vigor" implies a yearning for unintimidated contact with the sublime, a contact that would verify the great wells of being, the ego-centered authority of the Imagination. However, the authentication of that authority seems to demand the impossible: that the speaker overcome the Otherness of the Imagination—and thus his own self-consciousness—yet know himself as having overcome it. Since the mind cannot be simultaneously active and reflective, unself-conscious and self-conscious, the speaker must mediate these moments of integration. The Imagination's agency can only be reflected upon as part of the past or desired for the future.

But at this point in the growth of a poet's mind, when the pilgrims inadvertently cross the Alps, the emergence of the Imagination brings on paralysis rather than poetic authority. Once more, mental categories are unable to accommodate or overcome natural phenomena. But these failed attempts become meaningful for the speaker precisely because they are failures, disrupting categorical expectations and thereby paralyzing the conscious mind—"the light of sense"—and permitting unmediated contact with Nature. Yet that contact is never felt, because for Wordsworth it is not the poet's mission to mediate Nature but to use it as a way to mediate the Imagination. Because the younger self has not yet acknowledged this mission, the Imagination, "that awful Power," arises to usurp both the "light of sense" and the priority of the natural object. This alienated creative faculty emerges in prearticulate expression of the mind's correspondence to Nature.

Beneath the speaker's account of this usurpation is the implicit argument that the fully grown poetic mind, which the younger self does not possess, is not only capable of apprehending the sublime but is in turn enlarged and made great by it. Sensations of the sublime emerge in the dynamic disproportion between an awesome natural phenomenon and the dwarfed mental category struggling to encompass it. Elation, or heightened consciousness, comes when the mind is released from mediation by category to achieve immediate contact with the phenomenon and "becomes aware of the sublimity of its own being" (Monk 8).[12] The mind can then draw emotional power from an unconscious identification with natural power, for the prior selfhood drops away when its relational categories collapse. It is in this equation between natural and emotional power that the Imagination emerges. But this power and elation is denied to the pilgrims because they remain bound by a preconception without a natural correlative, arising as it does from book-stricken enthusiasm for revolutionary man rather than from an understanding of the mind's place in Nature. Centering their expectations in the abstract ideal of Divine Man, and presuming that Nature's purpose is to submit herself as a source of images for that ideal, the young pilgrims would necessarily resist a natural sublime, in the face of which their ideals and their very identities, which are grounded on these expectations, would evaporate. The extraordinary irony, which is disclosed at the poem's end, is that the speaker reaches a conclusion essentially identical to the preconceptions of his younger self. The difference is in the means: to grant authority to the Imagination, the speaker must dislodge the creative faculties from the rational ones controlled by conscious desire. He must therefore distinguish his divine man from his younger self's, and show that the later vision of Book XIV is an earned one.

The youthful preconceptions of Divine Man are inauthentic and self-deceiving. Though the speaker insists that it was love of Nature urging him to cross the Alps, his younger self was clearly moved by a countering urge as well, a love of the abstractions feeding a revolutionary zeal that finally overcomes the stated love of Nature:

> But Nature then was sovereign in my mind,
> And mighty forms, seizing a youthful fancy,
> Had given charter to irregular hopes.
> In any age of uneventful calm
> Among the nations, surely would my heart
> Have been possessed by similar desire;
> But Europe at that time was thrilled with joy,
> France standing on the top of golden hours,
> And human nature seeming born again.

(VI 333–41)

Given its placement in this passage and the little space left to Nature, it is clearly the mind's status rather than Nature's that preoccupied the younger self. The speaker discredits the younger self's enthusiasms further, emphasizing their pastness. His "youthful fancy" was impulsive, his hopes "irregular." And while he savors the memory of "golden hours," he floats above it, realizing that human nature was only "seeming" to be "born again."

There are two rhetorical consequences for the authority of the Imagination, and thus for the speaker's ability to mediate it. First, the stated love of Nature is countered, perhaps contradicted, by a love of revolutionary ideals that celebrate the creative powers of the mind. Second, the speaker sustains his ambiguous relationship to his younger self, simultaneously endorsing and detaching himself. This ambiguity is important because it permits the implicit claim that the younger self is capable of growing beyond Fancy into the poetic voice of the speaker, and it clears the way to demonstrate the nature of and necessity for the Imagination.

Blocked from immediate experience by the expectations woven in his now-paralyzed mind, the younger self makes contact at last with an Other, one adequate to his desire and rising necessarily from within:[13]

> Imagination—here the Power so called
> Through sad incompetence of human speech,
> That awful Power rose from the mind's abyss
> Like an unfathered vapour that enwraps
> At once, some lonely traveller. I was lost;
> Halted without an effort to break through

(VI 592–97)

The prospect of Mont Blanc here is in excess of the mind's ability to categorize it, so a void is left in perception; the younger self is thrust back into self-consciousness, facing a sublimity that diminishes rather than expanding or releasing his mind because he refuses to allow the authority of his preconceived structures to be usurped. Apparently in conflict with Nature, the younger self is actually in conflict with his own mind, his rational consciousness finally defeated by his creative faculty of Imagination. The speaker, with the authority of distance, detachment, and experience, displays the proper posture toward the Imagination. He does so by transpersonality, beginning as a fragment of an ego addressing his conscious soul and ending it as a godlike figure distributing his excess to a barren world:[14]

> But to my conscious soul I now can say—
> 'I recognize thy glory': in such strength
> Of usurpation, when the light of sense
> Goes out, but with a flash that has revealed

The invisible world, doth greatness make abode,
There harbours, whether we be young or old.
Our destiny, our being's heart and home,
Is with infinitude, and only there;
With hope it is, hope that can never die,
Effort, and expectation, and desire,
And something evermore about to be.
Under such banners militant, the soul
Seeks for no trophies, struggles for no spoils
That may attest her prowess, blest in thoughts
That are their own perfection and reward,
Strong in herself and in beatitude
That hides her, like the mighty flood of Nile
Poured from his fount of Abyssinian clouds
To fertilize the whole Egyptian plain.

(VI 598–616)

The proper posture, he tells us, is to surrender the rational faculty, the "Light of sense," to accept the "usurpation" of the Imagination. Yet even though such a surrender seems to demand a loss of self-consciousness, if the invisible world is revealed thereby, then there still remains an experiencing subject to be distinguished from the objective world. But because the experiencing subject has grammatically vanished as the mediator, all focus shifts to the activity of the Imagination, just as it does when the Imagination prevails over the rational mind.

The disappearance of the speaker and the focus on the Imagination has principally two consequences in solidifying speaker authority. First, by disappearing, the speaker is no longer a self-conscious witness to the actions of his Imagination and so can speak from the hieratic position of the text itself, a position as self-sufficient as the state he describes. Second, that the speaker focuses on the Imagination as an activity—it is in the "strength of usurpation" that "greatness" abides—and that it serves as "our being's heart and home" reinforce both the authority of the ego as an integrated set of faculties and, paradoxically, the otherness of the Imagination. Both reinforcements justify the speaker's implied claim to mediating authority. Such is the rhetorical success of this paradoxical balancing that the mind seems to maintain a subordinate relationship to its sublimated faculties without seeming to be subject to the deceptions of solipsism. Furthermore, the mind is located in "infinitude," which allows the aura of transcendence hovering about that word to attach itself, in turn, to the mind. Yet this infinitude refers to the potential in human longing, in "hope that can never die, / Effort, and expectation, and desire." In short, the only infinitude the poetic mind must apprehend or compete with is the infinitude of human desire, the only universe the poetic mind. With this claim for infinitude he has shown the way out of the loop running between Fancy and self-conscious paralysis.

But the speaker does not rest in beatitude above the Egyptian plain. His epiphanic reflection fades into the narrative, which resumes at the peasant's disappointing news. The text itself, by juxtaposing lyrical meditation with narrative, wields the authority of metacommentary, which here tempers the glory of the Imagination by denying closure to the preceding lines. I say tempers rather than undercuts because the narrative does nothing to contradict the Imagination's authority, only to shift its status to one of possibility, a flashing moment that the conscious mind can neither create nor sustain. Consequently, once more the speaker both collapses our suspicions about his claims to agency and inflates the mystery and authority of the Imagination as well as the significance of his position as mediator.

In the vision from the summit of Mt. Snowdon and the reflective passage following it, Wordsworth unites the speaker and the younger self as he solidifies the Poet's authority. With the ascent of Mt. Snowdon, the speaker can assume a fuller mediating control over the Imagination and consequently has greater latitude with otherwise intractable natural forms. But before he can finally exert that control he must continue to obscure his agency behind the younger self's apparent passivity. Climbing to see the sunrise from the summit, the younger self witnesses a sudden vision:

> For instantly a light upon the turf
> Fell like a flash, and lo! as I looked up,
> The Moon hung naked in a firmament
> Of azure without cloud, and at my feet
> Rested a silent sea of hoary mist.
>
> (XIV 38–42)

He is passive before this phenomenon, making no claims to have usurped the tyranny of the eye with a beauty imaginatively composed. Still, the vision is mediated; the moon is "majestic," "sovereign;" the ocean "lay / All meek and silent." Also, from the top of Mt. Snowdon, the younger self is situated to share the moon's perspective without having to claim a similar majesty. The speaker's crowning rhetorical feat comes through the pressure for meaning exerted on the vision by the expository interpretation following it. This exposition argues that Nature and mind exert "mutual domination" over each other, that neither alone is the source of reality's forms and values. However, this claim is belied by both the vision and the contents of the very exposition predicating it, for both display the mind's mediating mastery over its perceptions. Though Nature provides the object of perception, the mind still provides the object's meaning, without which the object can take no form.

The contents of the vision serve less as evidence of divinity glowing through the surface of Nature than as a trope, an "emblem of a mind / That feeds upon infinity, that broods / Over the dark abyss" (70–72). That is, Nature is there to show the mind's supremacy over it, not the mind's place in it. Thus, the speaker does not present the image for its own sake but to display the mind's ego-centered authority to re-create what perception only mediates. In the vision, Nature, as the lower world, is subordinated to and categorized by the mind, expressing the mind's majesty and authority. Also, the very presence of exposition asserts the priority of mental structures over natural forms and the importance of a mediator in authorizing the meaning of natural phenomena. The vision, in fact, contradicts the view that mind and Nature are "mutually dominating." Though the speaker apparently refers to the entire scene as "the type / Of a majestic intellect," clearly the moon is a figure for the mind. The vision focuses on the moon's pictorial glory and sovereign vantage point rather than any participatory role. The moon is the source of the scene's visionary quality; everything else, with certain notable exceptions, stands in a "meek and silent" relation to it. The "ethereal vault," a figure for the divine, is not diminished by the moon's "clear presence," but neither does it have any strong visionary or thematic role here except as a frame for the moon's majesty. The moon does, admittedly, stand between the heavens and the oceanic earth, but it does not draw sustenance from either one, instead hanging there independently, serving none but the self-fulfilling purpose of giving off its creative glow of being.

Nature's response, "the roar of waters, torrents, streams / Innumerable, roaring with one voice," suggests a counter or challenge to the moon's usurping majesty, but it is an inconclusive, ambiguous one. Because the voice is "felt by the starry heavens," we might read this line as divine acknowledgement of Nature's self-sufficiency, a reaffirmation of Nature's existence apart from changing perceptions of it. Yet within the vision passage it is finally unclear what influence the voice exerts on the moon/Imagination. We must go to the interpreting exposition to be told that the moon's relationship to the rift in the clouds is equivalent to the mind feeding upon infinity. However, the moon trope itself utterly refuses to support such a meaning, which only arises from mental structures grounded on the mind's own authority. As a result, instead of a "mutual domination," what we are finally left with is a reflexivity: the ego examining its own creations and seeing that they are good:

> They [higher minds] from their native selves can send abroad
> Kindred mutations; for themselves create
> A like existence; and whene'er it dawns
> Created for them, catch it, or are caught
> By its inevitable mastery,
> Like angels stopped upon the wing by sound
> Of harmony from Heaven's remotest spheres.
>
> (XIV 93–99)

Higher minds converse with and respond to their own products. Mind and Nature here are running parallel, analogous courses, each exerting "mutual domination" over their own creations, each independent of the other. Consequently, higher minds exist in self-contained, exclusive realms, appearing to authorize themselves, in fact, because the line between creator and creation blurs. Whether they catch or are caught by the "inevitable mastery" of their "like existence" is irrelevant—this mutual pursuit is fundamentally an act of self-expression and self-appreciation, an act of remaking subject into object and then back into subject again. The angels' simile seems to reintroduce passivity, awe, and a subordinate relationship to the Logos, but it actually reinterprets the seraphic identity Milton prescribes. The "sound of harmony" is the sound of the angels themselves in their angelic motions. Thus, listening "stopped upon the wing," they live in a moment of self-consciousness brought out of themselves by their own creative genius. Of course, the angels' origin is divine, but their listening is not reverent acknowledgement of their lesser relation to God but an ecstatic realization that they are identical to their divine source. Their beatitude is their own in a world composed solely of their beatitude.

The ascent of Mt. Snowdon and the expository passage following it express the essence and essential paradox of ego-centered authority. The creative mind comes to itself in moments of self-consciousness, moments when it knows itself simultaneously as subject and object, liberated by a divine origin, not determined by it. The creative mind in contact with itself—rational self-consciousness united with the Imagination—by definition displays and exerts a divine authority. The transcendent is then located in the revelation of these heightened moments of self-consciousness, moments generated as the mind shapes its perceptions. Worshipping the self in this kind of manifestation, as the speaker does here, becomes the same as worshipping the creating Imagination of God.

Yet the speaker ultimately slips down from this extravagant height, not ironically, as in the earlier passages, but to elude the vulnerable fixity of his transcendent repose: "Oh! who is he that hath his whole life long / Preserved, enlarged, this freedom in himself?" (XIV 130–31). By withdrawing he returns with a certain humility to his earthbound audience, admitting his fallenness yet at the same time challenging his reader to name a creature more fit than he: "Where is the favoured being who hath held / That course unchecked, unerring, and untired, / In one perpetual progress smooth and bright?" (XIV 133–35).[15] His humility becomes archetypal, positioning him, as younger self and speaker blend into one, to step into the role of poet he has created for himself. The speaker's poetic stance at the end is both lordly and generous, beckoning the reader to see himself through the transcendent eyes of a self-creator.

3

The Archetype of Failure: Ego-centered Authority in "The Tower"

Glendower: I can call spirits from the vasty deep.
Hotspur: Why, so can I, or so can any man.
              But do they come when you do call for them?
                                                    —*1 Henry IV*

With these blanketing clouds there will be a warm dell above Ticknock, where I can do nothing until it is time to fall down on Dundrum and give Yeats the Governor-General's invitation. Will he accept it? Of course not, at first; but a little strategy, a little strategy. I have already in my mind a little scheme to endow him with the necessary distinction. He must be made to see that he has an opportunity to take up the position which he likes beyond all others; the position from which he can both dominate and endow.
                                    —Oliver St. John Gogarty
                                    As I Was Going Down Sackville Street

Having presented the meditative speakers of *Paradise Lost* and *The Prelude* as examples of Logos-centered and ego-centered mediators respectively, in this chapter I will focus on the example of Yeats's "The Tower" to illustrate the challenges peculiar to modern poetry that a poet must address when speaking from an ego-centered authority. The example of Yeats is significant because it presents the purest successful form of ego-centered authority in either the English or the American modern tradition. Yeats's quest to establish the authority of the mind's imaginative faculties is particularly urgent in "The Tower," displaying most clearly the speaker's process of transpersonality, departing from the mortal and finite to speak from archetypal permanence.[1]

The core of ego-centered transpersonality emerges from the speaker's primary purpose in "The Tower": to certify the primacy of the imagination, the world subjectively conceived, over the actual, the objective world prior to its handling by the imagination. But the poetic authority of the text as a mediator depends, paradoxically, on the speaker's failure to install himself unselfconsciously into an archetypal role. The speaker accepts his failure to extend his imaginative powers and his cultural authority beyond the range of his mortality.[2] The character of this acceptance establishes a model of how the mind can pad the impact of circumstantial reality and thus diminish its consequence. This model, the Yeatsian archetype, exerts authority: it is an interpretive structure, a means by which we can measure our own actions. The speaker mediates rather than originates the authority of the model because the model exists prior to its appearance in "The Tower." Without the speaker's failure to transform the actual world, he would have no cultural authority in the actual world, for the modern reality is defined by its indifference to the exertions of the individual mind.[3] A successful speaker must dissolve in his own idiosyncratic vision, and thus fail. Apparent failure becomes actual success, and despite the modernist premise that "the world stays" even under the pressure of the imagination, the world does not stay. When the mind apprehends the world differently, the world changes because its significance to the mind changes. The mind tampers not with facts but with how they are read; the world is not our authority for claims we make about it, but our interpretive structures are, and they originate in the ego. These structures take on cultural authority to the extent that they shape a culture's thinking. The cultural authority of "The Tower" cannot be empirically measured, of course, and the poem mediates rather than originates its model, but we still read with admiration the speaker's indifference to parting from consciousness, so perhaps Yeats's implication is justified: the mind can create a world that will insure that mind's significance.

The speaker of "The Tower" begins by characterizing himself as fragmented, broken, reality's fool, but ends by having presided over his own funeral, having seen to it that his self-created identity persists on his terms, though not in his hands. He instructs us how to read him, demonstrating why he as a poet is the authority for the world he and the reader perceive.[4] The first section sets up the speaker's complaint, portraying him as beaten and vulnerable and finite, but also as separate from the fragment of self that is perishable, ephemeral:

> What shall I do with this absurdity—
> O heart, O troubled heart—this caricature,

> Decrepit age that has been tied to me
> As to a dog's tail?
> Never had I more
> Excited, passionate, fantastical
> Imagination, nor an ear and eye
> That more expected the impossible—

We note first that his aged body is not the voice's source. The speaker is thus already detached from the center of suffering. The body has withered into an object, "this absurdity," while his identity strives to detach itself from the rot of circumstances, in effect forcing a transpersonal distance.[5] He is dislodging himself from the merely physical simply by lamenting his link to it.[6]

Distinguishing the imaginative from the mortal self is his first transpersonal gesture, and tied to that gesture is his complaint that old age is somehow dragging down the flights of his imagination.[7] When critics summarize the opening complaint, they typical refer to this passage from *Per Amica Silentia Lunae* as an explanation:[8]

> A poet, when he is growing old, will ask himself if he cannot keep his mask and his vision without new bitterness, new disappointment. Could he if he would, knowing how frail his vigour from youth up, copy Landor who lived loving and hating ridiculous and unconquered, into extreme old age, all lost but the favor of his Muses? . . .
>
> Surely, he may think, now that I have found vision and mask I need not suffer any longer. He will buy perhaps some small old house, where, like Ariosto, he can dig his garden, and think that in the return of birds and leaves, or moon and sun, and in the evening flight of the rooks he may discover rhythm and pattern like those in sleep and so never awake out of vision. Then he will remember Wordsworth withering into eighty years, honoured and empty-witted, and climb to some waste room and find, forgotten there by youth, some bitter crust. (342)

But this passage has typically been misread. It does not lay out a dichotomy between old age and poetic vigor, claiming the former saps the latter; instead, it mocks that claim. The poet who pursues Landor's and Ariosto's example does so to escape suffering, not to sustain vision and mask for their own sake. But such liberation as Ariosto had is neither available nor desirable. According to this passage, he lived in ungrounded fantasy, free from suffering because free from self-consciousness. The alternative to this slumbering vision is not Wordsworth's poetic vacancy but the inevitable bitter crust: self-conscious knowledge of limitations and mortality and pain. Yet that crust, as we shall see, is a kind of food nonetheless, the compensation for warring against foreknown failure.

Old age, therefore, does not restrain the imagination's exertions. Rather, it may even inflame them: the eye and the imagination are more passionate than ever, and Yeats's vision of interdependent contraries prescribes for the antithetical man that where loss is most keenly felt, a mask and opposite are projected by the imagination (*A Vision* 140–45).[9] The actual problem of the opening complaint, then, is different from the stated one. The actual issue here is how to avoid the suffering of old age, not whether old age silences the muse. Thus, the choice in the following passage is not between imaginative pursuits that the speaker has lost the capacity for and philosophical pursuits he must resort to, but between failed or successful means of distraction from suffering:

> It seems that I must bid the Muse go pack,
> Choose Plato and Plotinus for a friend
> Until imagination, ear and eye,
> Can be content with argument and deal
> In abstract things; or be derided by
> A sort of battered kettle at the heel.

Thus, though the speaker has prepared for transpersonality by loosening his mind from its mortal coil, he still has a distance to travel before he can recover the imagination's purpose in remaking the world, the ego's purpose in authorizing his given reality. Chasing a release from suffering is both a false and inadequate resolution. First, the very presence of the speaking voice demonstrates that he need not and does not intend to bid the Muse go pack. Second, continuing to speak only proves that pursuing abstract forms as a distraction from the actual and sensual drains no venom from the speaker's psychic wound. Pursuit of abstract forms is both an escape and a self-denial. Worse, it is the death of desire and thus of being.[10]

The second part of "The Tower" returns the speaker to a kind of human form: "I pace upon the battlements and stare / On the foundations of a house." Many textual features, however, keep him in a suspended state between self and soul. First, the prosody has become more formal: the verse is rhyming, stanzaic, and metrically more consistent than the first part, qualities reinforcing the magisterial, ceremonial sense of the diction. Pacing on battlements and staring in a proprietary way on the landscape are gestures rooting him in the great tradition of battlement pacers, of vigorous but meditative martial figures, to make a "connection with the general mind and present himself as an artifice" (Langbaum 185). Moreover, the comparative formality of the second part makes the first seem by contrast a spontaneous, unself-conscious outburst, expressing a want and finitude he must abandon in favor of aestheticized being, a pattern of permanence.[11]

But the authority over the landscape the speaker pretends to comes from the dual quality of the experience he draws on: the summoned spirits exist simultaneously in the subjective and objective world.[12] Even the historical figures—Mrs. French, Raftery, Mary Hynes, and the "ancient bankrupt master of this house"—are "images and memories," not idle impressions floating in his mind alone. He does not say whose images and memories they are because they exist independently of anyone's perception of them; their objective authenticity is his premise, not what he seeks to prove.[13] What he does intend to show is how the empirical world, recorded historically, takes on significant form only when dislodged from petty circumstance and reshaped by the mind into meaningful events. To demonstrate how such a transformation works, the speaker erases the distinction between inner and outer reality, the merely inner becoming as empirically palpable as the outer because both are presented in the same terms. Characters from both the imagination and historical reality exist in the poem as figures touched by the regenerative power of passionate imagination. Subjective and objective figures thus become generically equivalent. In the world of the poem, Red Hanrahan has the same ontological status as Mrs. French, who in turn has the same historical actuality as Lord Nelson or Woodrow Wilson. Consequently, Red Hanrahan is to exist, or have existed, in the reader's consciousness just as these latter figures do.[14] From this new relationship between fact and fiction, the speaker can imply that every thing of value exists only in its fabulation. Such an implication grants him nearly infinite scope in his poetic authority to claim that the imagination, exercised by the ego, brings forth the only significant reality.[15] It is with the sixth stanza, the announcement that "I myself created Hanrahan," that the mediating speaker of ego-centered authority has swollen to crowd out any world existing apart from his imaginative perceptions. All that is is because the speaker perceives it so.

The growth of the speaker is the exercise of his transpersonality, in which he annexes objective reality for his own purposes, and in his droll detachment he teaches a disregard for things in their thingness, celebrating instead not only the imagination's power to remake but also a willingness to forgo contact with the material world. This detachment is most evident in the second stanza:

> Beyond that ridge lived Mrs. French, and once
> When every silver candlestick or sconce
> Lit up the dark mahogany and the wine,
> A serving man, that could divine
> That most respected lady's every wish,
> Ran and with the garden shears
> Clipped an insolent farmer's ears
> And brought them in a little covered dish.

We receive a double shock here, first at the ear clipping and second at the speaker's attitude toward it. The stanza describes a version of Unity of Culture, presumably existing when aristocratic will and action were identical, when mental and physical gesture were one. The speaker's account emphasizes the ceremony of the event and a certain adroit justice displayed—the farmer was insolent, after all, and since the clipping was done with mere garden shears rather than a more martial implement, the effect is more comic than tragic; the farmer's indignity is bloodless. By denying the horror of the clipping, the speaker is in effect taunting the reader into the same droll appreciation of the event, to see it as aesthetic rather than historical, subject to artistic rather than moral criteria. Aesthetically transformed in the poem, the clipping incident is as formally complete as its rhyme scheme, existing in the mind as an isolated motion of desire, with no prior cause and no nasty consequences.

The mind has two sources of control over the incident. First, its formal integrity makes it easily apprehensible by the mind and thus easier to fit into a pattern of meaning the mind has itself constructed. Second, the speaker's version of the event has the authenticity of historical fact; however, because this version is simultaneously an art object, the incident as a series of raw facts is subordinated to its fabulation. In fact, except as a tale the incident cannot persist beyond the brief circumstances of its occurrence. The mind's fabulations are what give it being. And because the speaker mediates rather than originates the event, he is not surrendering to solipsism in the telling. The incident exists not as a product of his consciousness but as a feature of it. Finally, because fact achieves form only in the telling, because poesis brings events into public consciousness, such fabulations as the speaker's become models for identifying and interpreting events the mind sets in parallel with them. They authorize the meaning of those events that are measured against them.

But the next stanzas show an ironic self-consciousness about

the disrupting and reshaping of historical reality, as if by mocking
both the reality and the fabulation he need not seem to surrender
passively to the former nor naively and self-servingly to the latter.
At first he seems unmoved by either one:

> Some few remembered still when I was young
> A peasant girl commended by a song,
> Who'd lived somewhere upon that rocky place,
> And praised the colour of her face,

and the cause of this apparent indifference is the mind's inevitable
distance from barren historical fact. Given this distance, the consequences of song, of artistic remaking of reality, must be that the
mind is not only granted contact with reality but able to improve
it. Raftery

> had the greater joy in praising her,
> Remembering that, if walked she there,
> Farmers jostled at the fair
> So great a glory did the song confer.

A miracle occurs here that, significantly, the speaker does not create but dispassionately reports. Only through Raftery's song does
Mary Hynes become a woman so beautiful she can only be described by the stir she causes (Jeffares 260–63). The Mary Hynes
who made the farmers jostle each other had sprung full grown from
Raftery's wild brain, making him the author of not only the song
but the new reality of archetypal beauty, the only Mary Hynes of
consequence. He has made her "matter" in both senses of the
word.

But the speaker has not put quite enough distance between his
body and his imagining ego, has not fully formed that ego yet, and
so cannot yet commit his uncertain passions to it. He maintains
his ironic separation from it in the stanza following:

> And certain men, being maddened by those rhymes,
> Or else by toasting her a score of times,
> Rose from the table and declared it right
> To test their fancy by their sight;
> But they mistook the brightness of the moon
> For the prosaic light of day—
> Music had driven their wits astray—
> And one was drowned in the great bog of Cloone.

Again the droll tone sounds here. First, not pinning the cause of the madness conclusively to either art or drunkenness mocks art's claim; he is tainting art by association with delirium. Second, he seems to be accepting Plato's argument that poetry leads to error and insanity, that it lies. The speaker is dramatizing the conflict between the real and the imagined, thus arguing by implication that poetic models authorize our interpretations of the world. Ego-centered poetic authority possesses and displays its own authenticity, for if it were dependent on the endorsement of a poet, it would by definition lose authenticity. The ego's authority must seem to be displayed in the circumstances of an unalterable reality.

Behind the apparent conflict between imagination and the objective world for control of human perception, there is a brilliantly begged question: by locating the dispute between drunkenness and poetry, the speaker can still let stand as his premise the belief that poetry possesses the power to change our perceptions of the objective world. And because this begged question is only implied, embedded, it is not immediately subject to challenge. Because it is not the focus of overt assertion, it is less vulnerable.

Grounded on his unstated but established premise, he can now move forward to make himself an archetype, or at least argue for its possibility:

> Strange, but the man who made the song was blind;
> Yet now I have considered it, I find
> That nothing strange; the tragedy began
> With Homer that was a blind man,
> And Helen has all living hearts betrayed.

With this passage, the speaker has returned the reverie to his own mind. It is a pivotal passage, where his contemplation shifts from outer to inner landscape, a move justified by the implied priority of imagination over the objective world. The sense of spontaneous thought here strengthens the effect of discovery as opposed to calculated argument or self-conscious performance. His meditation moves of its own accord, revealing truth to him, rather than a premeditation revealing truth to us. His particular role as mediator grants him no special status at this point, though what his mediation reveals does: the implied connection the reader is asked to make between the unnamed Raftery and Homer cements the poet's pedestal. According to the Yeatsian logic here, there is a tradition of such relationships as the one between Raftery and Mary Hynes. Therefore, because blind Raftery created the perception of Mary

Hynes's beauty and thus the beauty itself, then Homer, also blind, created Helen's beauty. By a similar extension, Raftery and Irish poets in general, because of their roots in time and empirical reality, take on Homer's power with his authority by joining his tradition, even, perhaps, by absorbing Homer into theirs.

With the speaker's turn inward at this point in the poem, his tone loses its amused detachment. Now that he has established poetry's authority, he faces with some ambivalence the question of its legitimacy, its value, its dangers—issues he must examine to demonstrate conclusively the primacy of the imagination. The focus of this ambivalence is "tragedy," a word that neatly encapsulates the history of Western self-consciousness.[16] "Tragedy" carries with it a great weight of pain, coupled as it is with the betrayal of "living hearts," those seeking perfection and fulfillment in mortal life. It is self-consciousness that betrays both the poet and his audience when both confront the ineluctable truth that words cannot change or create things. Tragedy is that moment of discovery when words and things oppose each other instead of harmonically forming new perceptions. The poet must create because he is blind, and because he is blind his creation is necessarily an error. But tragedy is also heroic, a persistence in the face of certain failure. The shift from Helen's betrayal to "O may the moon and sunlight seem / One inextricable beam, / For if I triumph I must make men mad" is a shift in itself from self-consciousness to a liberation from it, a heroic disregard for the limits and perils of imagination. He knows that betrayal is inevitable but still pleads for the power to betray, to make men mad. In a sense, that shift shows that he has made himself mad.[17]

To understand the ontology of the speaker's creations, we need to examine the ambivalence of "madness." It is simultaneously a splitting off from communally held perceptions of the world, and therefore a kind of deprivation, as well as a Unity of Being, the subject's apparent possession of his object of desire. It is dream's union with reality, a loss of self-consciousness. Yet madness is also tragic, ending in the loss of both sun and moonlight; what the speaker creates exists only in madness and disappears with death or the dreary pressure of reality.

Where, then, does the speaker stand in relation to the dark and bright sides of the imagination? The desperate vigor of his apostrophe and the union of triumph with compelled madness suggests that he is flinging himself over to the side of the imagination, but key conditions of his utterance restrain him, sparing him from the charge of bombast. First, because the speaker's success is made uncertain with the conditional "if," he is not overtly claiming Homeric status. Furthermore, that uncertainty intercepts his commitment to the imagination, maintaining his detachment. Finally, the "triumph" is countered by the evil of its consequences, even though the speaker seems to plead for the beams' inseparability precisely because he must make men mad, as a measure, presumably, of his own authority, which he requires to know that he can exist on his own terms. But in spite of the ambivalence of this apostrophe, the lines still present a model of how the mind pursues ego-centered authority, a model that the speaker can authorize but not yet occupy.

His ability to occupy this poetic archetype is immediately made more certain as he points out that he has made a man, Red Hanrahan, mad:

> And I myself created Hanrahan
> And drove him drunk or sober through the dawn
> From somewhere in the neighboring cottages.
> Caught by an old man's juggleries
> He stumbled, tumbled, fumbled to and fro
> And had but broken knees for hire
> And horrible splendor of desire;
> I thought it all out twenty years ago:

Though he has created his own terms for poetic authority and then, with this stanza, fulfilled them, the meditation up to now has always brought discovery rather than support for a preconceived argument. Since he does not claim to authorize this archetypal model but only to fit into a prior pattern, his apparent passivity in the face of inevitable circumstances makes acceptable his merely implicit claim to poetic authority.

Simultaneous to and inseparable from the implicit claim in this stanza is a virtual coronation of ego-centered authority. Hanrahan is the vortex pulling fact into fabulation. Having already made us see empirical reality in terms of the fabulous, making "the moon and sunlight seem / One inextricable beam," the speaker has now reached into the objective world to pull it inside out, into subjective forms. Put another way, with this stanza objective reality is crowded out of consciousness to accept the tumescent presence of the ego's world. Though Hanrahan is purely fictional, he is made as much a part of the landscape as the great bog of Cloone and so is equally authentic.

The consequences of the ego's triumph are considerable and complex. Nonetheless, at this point the speaker does not know for

certain what he should do with "this absurdity." He has only shown
how to dispose of it: by casting suspicion on its relevance, sealing
it in the tomb of its actuality and crowding it out of his consciousness. Thus, it would not be accurate to say he has discovered a way
to reintegrate his divided identity, but rather that he is shrugging off
the chaff of objective circumstance to reveal the kernel of his self-
authorizing imagination.

But the ego's triumph depends on the speaker's transpersonality,
his movement away from the source of claims that are partisan
and self-serving. He must discover, not originate such claims so
that they emerge as inviolable truths rather than mere desires.
Hanrahan is the speaker's means to transpersonality here, for
through him the speaker can play two roles at once: poet/victim
and poet/victimizer. In the first role, he avoids bombast and self-
aggrandizement, and in the second he justifies his claims to poetic
authority.[18] As poet/victim, Hanrahan stands in for the embittered
speaker of the poem's opening, allowing the speaker to detach and
dramatize his rage. With a stand-in, he can appear less self-
involved, less finite, more authoritative. And while this poet/victim
role gives him greater freedom and distance in transpersonality,
the poet/victimizer role gives him greater authority, greater sway
over the mental obstacles to his re-creation. Specifically, it is a
clear sign of the speaker's triumph over the actual, over the pressures of self-consciousness, that he can call on Hanrahan as if he
were not a product of the speaker's own mind but a person existing
independently: "Old lecher with a love on every wind, / Bring up
out of that deep considering mind / All that you have discovered
in the grave . . ." And even as the speaker confesses that "I myself
created Hanrahan," even though he recounts his manipulations,
Hanrahan's suffering and circumstances are his, arising from his
independent nature rather than an author's contrivances:

> And drove him drunk or sober through the dawn
> From somewhere in the neighbouring cottages.
> Caught by an old man's juggleries
> He stumbled, tumbled, fumbled to and fro
> And had but broken knees for hire
> And horrible splendour of desire;
> I though it all out twenty years ago:

Our first thought might be that Hanrahan's independence reduces
the speaker's authority, but the opposite is true, for if the speaker
can create a character with the same ontological status as any
historical figure's, then—in the poetic field the speaker and reader

occupy—his work is scarcely to be distinguished from God's. In the same way, as his command that Hanrahan bring up truths from his "deep considering mind" reinforces the character's authenticity, it enhances the speaker's authority.

Yet if the speaker wields so much authority at this point in the poem, then "what is else not to be overcome?" It is death that the speaker must overcome in his pursuit of absolute authority even while it is toward death that his every transpersonal gesture leads him. What should clarify the speaker's dilemma here is the question of which Hanrahan story the speaker is referring to. Albright presumes that the poem refers to "Red Hanrahan" (26–28), in which Hanrahan is brought into the land of Sidhe, where he is offered immortal union with Echtge, Queen of the Fairies, but is too paralyzed to respond (*Mythologies,* 221). But David Lynch points to a much earlier, lesser-known tale, one presenting Hanrahan with what appears to be the opposite problem (17–21). Galatea-like, the woman of Hanrahan's dreams is incarnated as a mortal woman in love with him, but he is repelled by her and drives her away. However, the point here is that the unions in both stories threaten Hanrahan with satisfaction—the opposing ones of self and soul—and so they threaten him with the end of desire, which he needs to sustain his voice and his identity as a poet. The speaker faces just such a threat as he considers that

> Hanrahan rose in frenzy there
> And followed up those baying creatures towards—
>
> O towards I have forgotten what—enough!

It is the threat of the unnameable, the absolute authority of ideal beauty, which it is his part as a poet to recover and mediate for the reader. Beauty is the absolute authority for the speaker because it structures his thinking and values; it is the author of his purpose. And it is absolute because it can be approached only by the poetic act of transpersonal mediation. Unlike the speaker in *The Prelude,* the Yeatsian speaker mediates this beauty by poetic creation of a supreme selfhood rather than by a natural evolution within the individual ego. But for any poet of ego-centered authority, who must look to his own mind rather than to a prior principle, a Logos, for his epistemological structures and terms of value, there must be "a little space for the rose-breath to fill" even as he begs the Rose to come near (*Variorum,* 101.) Because the speaker must remain distinct from the divine and the permanent, he has to remain separate, but not detached, from his most essential nature.

Threatened by Unity of Being and thus forced back into separateness, the speaker must dismiss both Hanrahan and the man's wild desires and disappointments. The reason he gives for this dismissal, that he has "forgotten what," is peculiar, but this memory lapse is clearly necessary: to maintain his voice, he must remain unconscious of what the dogs bayed towards. Yet at the same time, by bringing to mind Hanrahan and the baying creatures, the speaker is pointing to the lost or refused union without having to refer to it. His gesture, of course, reminds us of Hanrahan's—and the speaker's—failure to recover ideal beauty and mediate it for the reader, and such a failure challenges the speaker's poetic authority. But the speaker does not retire, baffled. Instead he forgets, which means both that he once knew and that his dismissal of Hanrahan is a failure of will, not vision, thus justifying his opening complaint: failure must be blamed on his body, not his imagination.

The eighth stanza provides a necessary diversion from Hanrahan's and the speaker's willed loss so that the speaker can dwell on an archetype of loss:

> I must recall a man that neither love
> Nor music nor an enemy's clipped ear
> Could, he was so harried, cheer;
> A figure that has grown so fabulous
> There's not a neighbour left to say
> When he finished his dog's day:
> An ancient bankrupt master of this house.

Resurrecting his predecessor gives him a celebrated precedent for his perceived failure as a poet. The ancient bankrupt master was a victim of circumstances, so only the barrenness of reality can be blamed for his failure. Furthermore, the degree of his predecessor's suffering is also important to the speaker; that the man was so "harried" that no examples of passionate imagination could cheer him suggests a remoteness and dignity essential to a mind that must shrug off the consequences of the actual.

Yet what is especially interesting here is not the fact of the speaker's calling on his predecessor but his means of doing so. Where another modern poet might have relied on an imagistically direct representation or a narrative description of the ancient bankrupt master, thus compelling the reader to bridge the juxtaposition, this speaker in effect instructs the reader to watch him draw on the man's latent power to signify. He doesn't simply recall the man, but tells us he "must recall" him. The result of this self-consciousness is a presence that, as Eliot struggles to articulate, inverts modern "impersonality" yet remains impersonal through an archetypal intensification of personality (*OPP*, 299). Instead of the speaker's particular emotion of loss dissolving into the general image, achieving impersonal authority through surrender of personality, the general image of the ancient bankrupt master is annexed by the particular. The speaker takes on the properties of his predecessor and then moves on, still intact, still himself, to annex the energies of "Rough men-at-arms" who climbed the narrow stairs and of those

> Whose images, in the Great Memory stored,
> Come with loud cry and panting breast
> To break upon a sleeper's rest
> While their great wooden dice beat on the board.

In picking up these figures and examining them before the reader, the speaker arranges them in a tableau, in a world suited to the tragic-heroic personality he must create for himself. He annexes them so that they may exist on his terms, bearing his meanings. The more he annexes, the broader the sway of his authority; for creative survival he must aestheticize a selfhood before which his voice can fade and yet through which it can persist.[19]

But annexation is neither a smooth nor an inexorable process: we see an implicit competition between Hanrahan and the ancient bankrupt master, a tension between the speaker's inward and outward movements. As he approaches the goal of those baying creatures, the speaker is moving inward, expelling from consciousness the outer world in favor of the pure products of the imagination. Absolute inwardness brings absolute authority, but as the scent of the Rose breath tells us, absolute authority brings silence. Moreover, subjective and objective worlds can exist only in relation to each other, for they can be known only in relation. With no outer world, the inner world's primary quality, innerness, would vanish. The collapse of these worlds collapses the speaker's authority, so to maintain their relation and their separateness—or at least the appearance of separateness—the speaker must set at a distance the inner world expressed through Hanrahan and move out again into a recognizable empirical reality.

And it is in this move, from Hanrahan to the bankrupt master, where we see ego-centered authority clearly exerted over the reader. The speaker's predecessor in the tower, like the other his-

torical figures, exists in the mind only as a fabulation, his shape
and significance dependent upon imaginative re-creations. Thus,
appearing to have relaxed his claims to authority by returning to
empirical reality embedded in history, the speaker has in fact tight-
ened it. Making concessions only to a reality of his own construction, the speaker appropriates the actual to fuel the imaginative.
The speaker's mastery over perceived reality settles in the decep-
tively simple question:

> Did all old men and women, rich and poor,
> Who trod upon these rocks or passed this door,
> Whether in public or in secret rage
> As I do now against old age?

Seemingly a private question of no consequence beyond the
speaker's finite concerns, it extends his core strategy of remaking
the empirical world in order to sit at its center. The "old men and
women" he summons to the reader's mind exist only as ragers
against old age. Making a covert statement that his rage is justified
within his overt question solves the continual problem of ego-
centered mediation: how to displace from the finite speaking voice
the self-advertising quality of the self's attempt at vatic pronounce-
ments, in essence, how to achieve transpersonality. Asking the
question displays his power to summon past continuous spirits,
externalizing into perceived reality the purely mental act of sum-
moning, yet grants him a humility to counter the grandeur of these
verbal gestures.

He himself provides the answer to his question, thus sealing his
mastery of perceived reality—his own reality, that is, which the
reader shares in and he controls—and his independence from the
objective world:

> But I have found an answer in those eyes
> That are impatient to be gone;
> Go therefore; but leave Hanrahan,
> For I need all his mighty memories.

He identifies himself with those "impatient spirits" rather than with
the reader, staging their departure in such a way that only he, not
the reader, has access to what they have learned beyond the grave.
Of course, such a staging, by privileging the speaker at the reader's
expense, does not actually block the reader's access, because the
reader must know the answer for the question to have any relevance, for the poem to grant archetypal authority to the speaker.

The answer must be yes, they all did rage, thus justifying the speaker's own rage and further releasing the speaker from the finitude of idiosyncratic suffering.

This staged combination of innocent questions and curt commands carries the speaker surefootedly through to the end of the section so that he can end with sufficient hieratic presence to deliver a will. We see this combination again in the blend of contempt and deference in his return to Hanrahan: "Old lecher with a love on every wind, / Bring up out of that deep considering mind / All that you have discovered in the grave." Because the speaker is pulling Hanrahan out with him into the empirical world, not following him into pure imagination, Hanrahan hangs on to the same authenticity the old men and women have. Yet Hanrahan is also an intersection of the inner and outer worlds and so allows the speaker to address the reader from both perspectives. Like the dual roles of victim and victimizer, the perspectives of inner and outer are transpersonal shifts from personal finitude: private loss, expressed through Hanrahan, is given objective and thus unfixed identity, and as the questioner, the speaker can assume the dispassionate posture of the observer toward his own pain, instructing and even chastising. Not only is the speaker thus liberated from his private griefs, but he is enlarged by his liberation. Since Hanrahan partakes of empirical reality, the speaker's access to his soul is equivalent to another's access to, say, the soul of W. B. Yeats; the speaker can presume here the mediating powers of an oracle, of a transtemporal as well as a transpersonal authority. The fact that the speaker is unabashedly inquiring of one of his own creations means that his own imagination, besides being able to people the landscape, can transcend the reaches of mortal knowledge. His utterance claims that the imagination can extend life into death and probe the labyrinth of another's being.

The perspectives of outer and inner reality are both simultaneous and interdependent, holding in the suspension of the poetic field the tendencies toward self-pity and its opposite, bombast. Situating himself outside the reach of these oppositions, the speaker can draw on their more positive masks, personal immediacy and public relevance, as the address shifts from Hanrahan to himself:

> Does the imagination dwell the most
> Upon a woman won or woman lost?
> If on the lost, admit you turned aside
> From a great labyrinth out of pride,
> Cowardice, some silly over-subtle thought
> Or anything called conscience once;

What would be a hollowness in the speaker's lecturing posture is instead filled with the personal remorse in self-incrimination, and the softness of self-pity is hardened into public distaste for the cowardice of having turned aside.

Two related questions loom as central at the end of the poem's second section. First, we wonder not whether the imagination dwells on the woman won or woman lost, but why the speaker presents a question with such an obvious answer. Second, in these last lines, we must wonder at the juxtaposition of rebuke and approval for having turned aside.

The first question is simpler than the second. The speaker must ask it because he must stage himself as a vulnerable brooding questioner—he cannot seem to create but only to mediate a creation he seems to discover. What he discovers in turn points to his qualities as archetypal poet. The issue of the imagination, furthermore, must be raised as a set of alternatives: the heroic antithetical mind dwelling on the woman lost as opposed to the complacent primary mind dwelling on the woman won and thus experiencing no desire, no growth. Given these alternatives, the mind's proper path is clear, but the alternatives must be proposed for the path to emerge.

It is the consequence of the choice that reveals the contradictory response to turning aside. Discovering which the imagination dwells on, the speaker can chastise Hanrahan—and himself—for what is paradoxically a heroic and cowardly act at the same time. To have turned aside from the labyrinth's dangers and treasures exposes the speaker's fear of vanishing into the superior intensity of "another's being," but it also provides the opportunity to live in heroic consciousness of failure. In other words, he endures the benefits of a fortunate fall. In mastering loss, one becomes greater by that loss than if the possession had not been denied.

Now we can see the unity in the contradiction between rebuke and approval, an approval—or sense of relief—displayed in the warning "And that if memory recur, the sun's / Under eclipse and the day blotted out."[20] This absence of light is quite different from the "inextricable beam," for the blotting out of day not only thwarts the poet's power to illuminate but denies the possibility of any illumination at all. It is precisely this blotting out that the speaker wishes to avoid when he conveniently, impatiently, forgets what "those baying creatures" were heading towards. If memory of the infinitely desirable threat to his life and force of desire recur—if, in other words, he actually can imaginatively recreate this threat, it would annihilate him. We approve of this "turning aside" in our response to a certain brand of heroism in his declaration of failure. Thus, it is the speaker's observation—the text—that evokes this approval, not any assertion on his own behalf, for such claims would display a private need for an authority that this very need makes unavailable.

Avoiding self-congratulation, the speaker pulls further approval toward himself by creating in Hanrahan a character who can endure what he as speaker cannot, those thoughts and images from the past that "come again like a rope's end to smite us upon the face" (*Mythologies*, 354). And because the speaker is the source of this drama between Hanrahan and his torments, he can master his own anguish without facing it directly. He displaces it from its source within him, granting himself transpersonal freedom and the ability to exert aesthetic control, and thus authority, over its shape and meaning. His identity as creator preserves him from the reductiveness of a paralyzing self-conscious combat with his passions. He has created the arena and the combatants, an archetypal dramatic structure to shape and authorize cultural discord.

And so the end of the second part has shaped a speaker sufficiently detached from his trauma to master it, to move to a transpersonal position from which he claims title to an entire culture. The tension in this third part is between a self-conscious recognition of his inevitable crumbling to age and a defiant creation of a permanent tradition he can make over into an expression of his archetypified personality:

> It is time that I wrote my will;
> I choose upstanding men
> That climb the streams until
> The fountain leap, and at dawn
> Drop their cast at the side
> Of dripping stone; I declare
> They shall inherit my pride,
> The pride of people that were
> Bound neither to Cause nor to State,
> Neither to slaves that were spat on,
> Nor to the tyrants that spat,
> The people of Burke and Grattan
> That gave, though free to refuse—
> Pride, like that of the morn,
> When the headlong light is loose,
> Or that of the fabulous horn,
> Or that of the sudden shower
> When all the streams are dry,
> Or that of the hour

> When the swan must fix his eye
> Upon a fading gleam,
> Float out upon a long
> Last reach of glittering stream
> And there sing his last song.

The shift from meditation in the second part to declaration in the third is striking. The change in rhythm and line length gives the speaker not only a new voice but a new context and a new relationship with the reader, for even vehemence alone carries a degree of authority. Instead of sitting reverently across the table from him, as the second section prompted us to do, we now sit at his feet, looking down the mountain with him at the squalid world below. But ironically, it is in this third section that his authority begins to fray: the more he lays claim to, the more we see the tension between authority and Said's notion of "molestation" (84).

The first line, "It is time that I wrote my will," is, in valediction, a majestic admission of defeat. The will is an astonishing presumption, for it "implies you possess what you bequeath," and so stands as a "final exertion of personality" (Brooks, 14). The speaker's declaration, then, underscores the simultaneous extension and limitation of his selfhood. And contrasted with the poem's opening, it establishes a presence that is composed, detached, controlled. This personal control over personal events, prepared for at the meditation's end and solidified in the will statement, suddenly takes an apparently small step but one that lifts him in a giant leap of cultural authority as he moves from the first line to "I choose upstanding men." A similar leap from personal to cultural occurs from "They shall inherit my pride," to "The pride of people that were / Bound neither to Cause nor to State." Since a will distributes personal goods to a household of principally blood ties, it is quite a leap to have those goods become attitudes and the heirs a cultural category of the populace. The speaker now presumes himself to be the household head of a cultural elite, its father rather than just a member, possessing qualities that sustain and nourish a culture while elevating to a knight or priesthood those who share in them.

The speaker further extends himself in a strong web of images that express both pride and his own bond with the upstanding young men. Specifically, through imagery of dawn and twilight he maintains a continuity between himself and future generations: the light is waxing and waning simultaneously, each dying into the other's life and living into the other's death in Yeats's intersecting cones. The speaker thus draws strength from the young men as they in turn seem to draw dignity from him. Importantly, for here is the speaker's ground, this reciprocal relationship is necessary to a coherent reading, which in turn depends on our accepting as a premise that the speaker possesses such dignity. Moreover, these images of Fisherman, fountain, and dawn evoke "natural richness and vitality" as well as that grim archetype from the earlier poem "The Fisherman," the figure on whose behalf that speaker wished to write a poem as "cold and passionate as the dawn."

But the speaker of "The Tower" does not successfully demonstrate "the beneficent pride of Anglo-Ireland" and "the pride of a natural largesse that works through individuals" (Whittaker, 199). The speaker's authority begins to leak out under pressure of three interlocking difficulties in these lines:

> The pride of people that were
> Bound neither to Cause nor to State,
> Neither to slaves that were spat on,
> Nor to the tyrants that spat,
> The people of Burke and Grattan
> That gave, though free to refuse—

Briefly, because the speaker does not successfully identify the source and nature of the pride he exalts, he falls short of successful association with it and slips into the very sort of partisanship he claims cripples the independent mind. We cannot learn from this third section whether the pride is prior and external to the mind or intrinsic to certain minds, and therefore we do not know whether pride is collectively or individually held, what pride sustains, or what its bestowal on others can mean. Pride is the core of the poetic archetype that is to preserve the speaker's voice, so this uncertainty threatens to undo the poem.

To see more closely why the speaker seems unable to seize and master pride, in spite of his declamations to the contrary, we must first look at the problem of identifying its source. The images of pride present a self-generating magnanimity of self, an increase of vitality and growth for their own sakes. Pride must be, then, the Divine distributing its excess in the world. If pride is divine, and thus prior to the individual mind, neither the speaker nor any other can be its author or its sole possessor and distributor. Yet the speaker "declares" that "upstanding men . . . shall inherit my pride." To a certain extent, the speaker can evade the need to declare himself the origin of pride—one could argue that he is making a prediction about the inevitable rather than presuming that his desire creates inevitable circumstances, that their inheritance is predestined, not willed by him—but if the metaphor of will-writing is to have any meaning, then pride must be the speaker's to give, and its possession by upstanding men must be dependent upon the speaker's willing it to them. But as we have just seen, the degree of pride's divinity bears an inverse relation to its vulnerability to possession. If pride is eternal and continuous, as the references to Burke and Grattan suggest, then temporal figures like the Yeatsian speaker are only mortal vessels whose sole purpose, one that determines their identities, is to be the corporeal bearers of pride. Such a purpose makes the speaker at the most a caretaker rather than a squire.

The problem of the speaker's dubious status is compounded as we study his beneficiaries. I point out above that the speaker's expressed relationship to the upstanding young men is a rhetorical attempt to borrow dignity from and to ally himself with the virility of the coming generation. He is, therefore, dependent on them to display the value of his legacy. This dependence in itself weakens his authority, but the prestige of his legatees further debilitates him because it diminishes his role as possessor and distributor of pride. As "young upstanding men" they possess such virile independence of mind and imagination that the legacy of pride is superfluous. What makes them worthy to receive this Yeatsian pride makes the gift irrelevant. Consequently, we are left with two choices, neither of which strengthen the speaker's rhetorical position: either pride begins with the speaker, is defined and determined by him, thereby existing only by his account and necessarily perishing with him, or pride is automatically invested in new generations as individuals display their merit, leaving the Yeatsian speaker a phantom intermediary to fade into irrelevance with the dawn.

His declamatory assertion of a culturally regenerative pride is what threatens to annihilate him. His second interlocking difficulty leads from the first; in fact, he seems to be guilty of what by implication he is accusing others. Harold Brooks refers to the Protestant Irish and their tradition of the "whole man," a freedom from association with abstract or partisan ("partial") causes (199). Yet by his trumpeting of Anglo-Irish pride, the speaker himself seems bound to a partial cause. The need to speak on behalf of Protestant Irish pride thrusts him into the public world of partisan clusters, reducing him to one among many, not separate from but part of the masses. Placing himself on the level of other partisan causes in this way removes whatever distinction or claim to special ascendancy claimed by his rhetoric. Worse, such partisanship prevents him even from possessing, much less passing on, this pride. If in the vividness of shower, fountain, and fabulous horn he brings his idea of pride to our consciousness, it must exist independently of his agency and authority.

The speaker's third difficulty with pride comes in the conflict between collective and individual possession, between a sense of community and an intense consciousness of solitude. The pride he must appeal to and appear to pass on must seem collectively held; the proud acknowledge each other in unspoken maleness as a brotherhood set above and apart from the rest of the world. Pride is collectively held, shared, and reinforced, the identity of this brotherhood of the proud determined collectively. But the speaker's pride is solitary,

> that of the hour
> When the swan must fix his eye
> Upon a fading gleam,
> Float out upon a long
> Last reach of glittering stream
> And there sing his last song.

There is in the swan's passing no sense of a collective pride or tradition of noble departures, but the opposite, a death with no audience but the dying self. If there were a brotherhood of the proud existing prior to the speaker's attempt to link himself to it, then the significant feature of his identity would be held collectively, not individually; what transcended his passing would bear no evidence that he had existed. Furthermore, participation in this collective identity removes the need for the entire poem's meditation: no problem of dissociated identity could exist to generate the poem. And if the speaker's pride is then only a soaking in self-regard, a swan listening to itself sing, then the pride is neither generative nor divine but merely the desire for a pride to preserve personal essence in one's descendants. The very presence of the poem expresses desire for pride rather than pride itself, for pride is silent, making itself felt in its actions, not in self-congratulatory accounts of such actions. The most the speaker can do here is mediate pride, presenting it to us without being able to touch it himself: he must either block its divinity or vanish before it. Its necessary impersonality lifts it beyond his reach, so that his attempt to synthesize the dusk of his passage with the dawn of young upstanding men is blocked by the persistent contradiction between solitary self-regard and the cultural authority of an acknowledged collective pride.[21]

He fares better in his declaration of faith, for this second legacy can begin and end in the ego:

> And I declare my faith;
> I mock Plotinus' thought
> And cry in Plato's teeth,
> Death and life were not
> Till man made up the whole,
> Made lock, stock and barrel
> Out of his bitter soul,
> Aye, sun and moon and star, all,
> And further add to that
> That, being dead, we rise,
> Dream and so create
> Translunar Paradise.

Faith is more accessible to the speaker because it is belief that implies opposition to itself, generally one that is empirically based, and so Faith carries a recognition that its claims lack universally felt authority.[22] Further, his declaration of faith is a way of sanctifying the solitary self-regard he is left with; it becomes all he needs to overcome what makes relevant his deterioration in the empirical world. For if I read Yeats's misreading of Plato and Plotinus correctly, the two, for Yeats, represent any body of thought insisting that the empirical world exists according to the blueprint of a prior Idea, or Logos.[23] The speaker is mocking and crying in the teeth of Logos-centered authority, declaring faith in the imagination, in the mind's power to shape perceptions of the empirical world, saying that what the mind perceives, is.

Yet the very boldness of this declaration, its defiant colloquial blare, begins an undercutting of faith that ends with the idea of "bitter soul." The soul, which we may suppose houses the imagination, is limited in its authority by the same bitterness that demands exercise. Being bitter at the inevitable limits of empirical existence, the soul is compelled to reshape what it perceives, to make one inextricable beam, but it is unable to blind itself, to escape self-conscious realizations that all creation begins and ends in the mind. The poet cannot forget that he is not the Wizard at all but only the little fat man behind the screen.[24] Yet although the mind cannot make actual its imaginative perceptions, it can make that failure irrelevant by seeking a condition of mind that accepts failure with the same equanimity as triumph. The world thus loses its power to imprison the mind in circumstance. Moreover, physical reality loses its authority over such a mind.

But unfortunately for the speaker, the declaration of faith, like the assertion of pride, is not quite the same as its display and possession, for the need to declare it demonstrates the absence of equanimity. He is at most in a state of self-conscious desire for such faith, for if he possessed it he would have no need to defy a Logos-centered authority that could exert no pressure on him. The need to speak, however, does not leave him powerless. Even though he is thrust back into the role of desiring mediator, unable to possess the authority of faith and pride, he can act ex officio, wielding the authority of one who has possessed them and now wishes to pass them on. We have a model for this mediating relationship in *A Vision*. Silence and perfection characterize phase 15, where no human life can exist—it is the complete integration of desire and its object. Phases prior to 15 carry a sense of anticipation, and those following carry a sense of loss. It is thus from these latter phases only that the poet can speak, needing to speak precisely because he does not possess either faith or pride.

Daniel Albright rightly calls the "Translunar Paradise" passage the climax of the poem, but there are more important reasons for doing so than the ones he provides (41).[25] It is at "Translunar Paradise" that the poem shifts from expressing desire to anticipating desire's absence. It is only by absenting himself from desire that the speaker can move toward the dispassionate autonomy of ego-centered authority, though of course he cannot fully destroy his desire without destroying himself. His valedictory lines once more presume authority without having to assert it; rather than long for a remade self, the speaker soaks it with praise:

> I leave both faith and pride
> To young upstanding men
> Climbing the mountainside,
> That under bursting dawn
> They may drop a fly;

How different these lines are from those opening the will. Gone are the antagonism, defiance, and struggle. Emphasis on the past-ness of things detaches the speaker from the finitude inevitable to desire, which by definition limits authority. The more desire can be muted, the greater the transpersonal distance from the finite self.

Emphasis on the pastness of conflict begins in the turning from Translunar Paradise:

> I have prepared my peace
> With learned Italian things
> And the proud stones of Greece,
> Poets' imaginings
> And memories of love,
> Memories of the words of women,
> All those things whereof
> Man makes a superhuman
> Mirror-resembling dream.

This odd combination of airy disregard and reverence for these traditions requires scrutiny, but we must first confront the uncertainty in "I have prepared my peace / With . . . ." Does this statement mean that the learned Italian things were the means to the peace preparation (Brooks, 14)? Or was peace prepared with these other artistic traditions in the sense of peacefully ending a conflict, burying the hatchet? Interestingly, the presence of this uncertainty is what in a sense removes it and detaches the speaker from cripplingly dependent relationships to prior artists. Or, as Whittaker puts it, with great accuracy but little desire to resolve the uncertainty, "penury of [imagination] and magnificence now meet and are reconciled in serene ambiguity" (201). Such ambiguity removes the speaker from the field of conflict; by meditating on them he has used learned Italian things to prepare his peace, measuring himself against them to discover and define himself. This self-definition, however, must and does take place in a way that liberates him from his predecessors or at least that reduces his dependence on them. That release or reduction comes, first, in his ambivalent tone, and second, in the way he changes their status from fathers to material for art.

The ambivalent tone is also heard in the edge of contempt in "learned Italian things," that tradition withering as what composes it is reduced to "things." Furthermore, "things" makes "learned" facetious, as if the speaker is merely using the term in parodic imitation of the naive. In the same way, the synecdoche "proud stones" treats the Greek tradition as a set of ruins, reducing its cause for pride. Yet the speaker remains dependent on these traditions. By supposing a competition with them, he shares their status even as he tries to reduce it. Therein lies the ambivalence: for his contempt to have ground, he must revere them.

The speaker tampers even more drastically with the status of these traditions, doing so, however, without an overt competition that would otherwise display his anxiety and reduce his authority. The prepositional phrase describing how the speaker has prepared his peace strings together a number of objects unrelated to specific artistic traditions:

> Poets' imaginings
> And memories of love,
> Memories of the words of women,
> All those things whereof
> Man makes a superhuman
> Mirror-resembling dream.

The category being assembled is not a set of competing artistic traditions but all that generates passionate expression and reflection, whether these things be art or personal suffering. Such a category subordinates the imaginative efforts of other traditions to the level of private experience, which has use and value only as raw matter for the speaker's own art. The speaker's consciousness—the reader's poetic world—is constituted solely by the imagination; any possible competitor can exist in this field of perception only as fuel for art. But finally, the speaker does not rest even with this reduction of all that is not himself, going on to abandon this posture of lofty solitude by having made his peace with all that had previously stirred him, in his previous bitterness, to artistic exertion. Stressing the pastness of conflict is a means of leaving the field both undefeated and unchallenged; the speaker transpersonalizes himself toward the vanishing point of detachment and silence.

Yet because the speaker cannot both maintain a voice and achieve absolute authority over the world he perceives and mediates for the reader, he can only announce his departure. In the speaker's self-staging we have an analogy to Richard's abdication speech in *Richard II* (IV i 201–21). While the enthroned but uncrowned Bolingbroke remains silent—absent—to avoid moral competition with and direct challenge by the legitimate king, Richard displays his right to the throne by his self-generated ritual of abdication, a ritual bringing to the foreground all that makes him king. Richard's catalog of royal trappings is at once an abdication and an assertion of his legitimacy.

Two key gestures in the speaker's own abdication passage raise shields of ambiguity, allowing him to retire farther from the field. "Poets' imaginings," being both singular and without either definite or indefinite article, characterizes his poetic identity as simultaneously personal and archetypal, both subjectively felt and objectively perceived as a standard. Thus, he alone becomes the source of an archetypal form that, of course, he cannot occupy as he speaks, but instead can point to as a laureateship he has previously occupied. His status here is authoritative precisely because it is unfixed; he cannot be located and circumscribed because he is espousing no particular cause. Contrapuntal to this gesture of aggressive withdrawal is the notion of a "superhuman / Mirror-resembling dream," lines that suspend assertion and withdrawal. "Dream" tends to undercut the authority of the imaginative world, implying that this world is challenged by a more substantial alternative, the objective realm of the actual. Yet that dream is "superhuman," beyond the lesser nature of the empirically verifiable. Because the speaker in this way maintains equal tension between both positions, he absents himself from partisan claim and therefore from any partisan gain in status as a finite being, removing the imaginative realm from the jurisdiction of the actual world to that of his own progressively more elusive ego.

The next stanza, rather indifferently inserted, proposes with the impersonal authority of the imagist poetic that this making of superhuman dreams is elemental and inevitable, a natural function of the universe rather than a process of self-advertisement thrust forward by an individual mind:

> As at the loophole there
> The daws chatter and scream,
> And drop twigs layer upon layer.
> When they have mounted up,
> The mother bird will rest
> On their hollow top,
> And so warm her wild nest.

The speaker's simile interprets in natural terms the continuous energies of the imagination, likening them to the principles conducting natural growth so that the imagination might share in their authority.[26] Leaving faith and pride to young upstanding fishermen works to the same rhetorical effect:

> I leave both faith and pride
> To young upstanding men
> Climbing the mountain side,
> That under bursting dawn
> They may drop a fly;
> Being of that metal made
> Till it was broken by
> This sedentary trade.

The speaker appropriates the empirical authority of nature to re-lease imaginative processes from an origin in finite being, showing that they exist within nature, on the same terms as natural proc-esses. The speaker does not claim that the imagination is somehow identical to nature, but that they both are equally "real" and equally perpetual. Finally, though, the speaker reaches for a status greater than nature's, reducing nature to mere symbol. Specifically, as many critics have pointed out, the references to fishing are sym-bolic rather than mimetic: it is any image of single-minded and passionate commitment to solitary pursuits of mind, pursuits that somehow integrate self and circumstance. The speaker does not wish to participate in nature but to make natural images, and the structures of thought that "nature" brings to mind participate in his intellectual system.

Finding a hole in Yeats's rhetoric, Marjorie Perloff reminds us that in his youth Yeats never was "of that metal made" (572). He never could count himself among the vigorous, unself-conscious heroes who rode horses, fished, and got shot. We might counter, of course, by charging Perloff with the biographical fallacy, but because specific features of the poem demand that we associate the speaker with a public conception of the W. B. Yeats who lived at Thoor Ballylee and invented Hanrahan, we cannot ignore the pressure to locate the speaker in our shared, public world. Though the poem is an act of self-staging, even self-making, the self cannot re-create what publicly exists prior to the poem. The poem can alter perceptions, but it cannot place the empirically verifiable under the jurisdiction of the imagination. And to evade the prob-lem, saying that the speaker refers to a world of the imagination in which he had been of that metal made, trivializes and makes irrelevant both the speaker's assertion and, by association, the whole poem.

A good way to make sense of the passage and to resolve the problem is to examine what is meant here by "climbing the moun-tain side, / That under bursting dawn / They may drop a fly." The solitary yet participatory action of fishing at dawn forms Yeats's opposite, his mask, which he has wrought and reached by the same process that has broken him: the sedentary life of reflection upon and re-creation of experience. Reflection brings the remorse of failure and of missed opportunities, which are both generically equivalent to the aging and death of the body. Thus the speaker—the dramatized version of W. B. Yeats we perceive here—can quite legitimately presume that he was of that metal made, that he can pass on a kind of faith and pride. They are his not because he can speak with and from them but because he has created them. Moreover, that sedentary trade has indeed broken him from his creative product. Who would not be bitter and broken as a result? That is why the "it" rather than an "I" of "Till it was broken" emphasizes the thingness of the self, just as the body is a "battered kettle at the heel." This thingness of the self reminds us that self-staging is a kind of self-creation. The speaker is a thing created by the speaker, who is self-authorizing to the extent that he is self-objectifying in self-conscious poetic reflection. Making himself the object rather than the subject of these meditations secures a temporary release from finite being. The creator, at least, is freed.

The final verse paragraph of "The Tower" is a valediction to end all valedictions. The speaker achieves the greatest transpersonal distance from his circumstances, dismissing himself with a cold, impartial eye and liberating himself in the union of chance and choice:

> Now shall I make my soul
> Compelling it to study
> In a learned school
> Till the wreck of body,
> Slow decay of blood,
> Testy delirium
> Or dull decrepitude,
> Or what worse evil come—
> The death of friends, or death
> Of every brilliant eye
> That made a catch in the breath—
> Seem but the clouds of the sky
> When the horizon fades;
> Or a bird's sleepy cry
> Among the deepening shades.

The "Now" thrusts all the previous lines into the past as a finished event, saying that whatever lies behind the speaker is now composed, in both senses of the word, in an aesthetic pattern. As he has made his self, now shall he make his soul, that transtemporal and essential identity remaining after the body's death.

David Lynch dismisses this posture of soul-making as a "merely rhetorical triumph," claiming that it is unearned "self-invented integrity" (13). My objection to Lynch's position is to the word "merely." The speaker's triumph is indeed rhetorical, one for which I have tried to demonstrate the basis, but it is pointless to diminish it as somehow a show, as if there were some alternative "actual" triumph that the speaker ought to have achieved but did not. There is no useful difference here between rhetorical and actual triumphs; rather, the distinction should be between assertions from a finite, partisan source and those from a transpersonal, impartial one. The speaker slips into bombast in his claims for Anglo-Irish pride, claims based solely on partisan need, a fragmentary perspective. But on the other hand, where poetic images imply, unprodded by exposition from a finite source, that the imagination reshapes the speaker into an archetypal presence, one therefore invested with cultural authority, the speaker triumphs because he is not the author of the statement of that triumph.

The principal reason for the speaker's success is his apparent surrender in the end to deterioration and death. However, this surrender is at the same time a measure of reasserted control over the meaning of his circumstances, a jujitsu in which the act of yielding to perceived circumstances slackens them into malleability. By denying the significance, not the fact, of death, even requiring death in order to frame his dignity, the speaker pulls his circumstances under his control. It is he who is to compel his soul to study in a learned school, not those circumstances that have beaten his body. It is his own mind, not scythe-swinging Time, that has surrounded him with visions of decay, delirium, decrepitude, and death. He triumphs because he has absorbed all conflict. Gone is the defiant swan song, superseded now with the bird's sleepy cry. Nor is the sun blotted out. It sets with inevitable naturalness. Without defiance, the speaker is no longer measuring himself against his circumstances and thus no longer being dwarfed by them. Choosing his fate, besides enlarging him, identifies him with principles of generation and degeneration, entwining all enemies into the fabric of his own being.[27]

Choosing one's fate, which is inevitably death, is also a sinking into silence. His valediction must point to his mastery over fate; it must be propositional, yet not doubtful. Like Tennyson's Ulysses, the speaker tries "to project the achievements of the past into the present and on to an open future" (Whittaker, 198). However, Yeats's speaker is sufficiently self-aware to see the limits of such projections, as Ulysses does not. The speaker in "The Tower" admits and embraces his death wish, in this way orchestrating the kind of death and funeral it should be. Whether the speaker finally can compel his soul to study and to watch worse evils blend into the shadows is really not an issue. He succeeds by projecting a character who has passed through defiance and who therefore can credibly meld ego and circumstance together. Such a staging shows how chance and choice meet, leaving us to presume the speaker capable of reaching the point toward which he can now only show the way. He establishes himself as an archetype.

There is much critical debate about what sort of note the poem ends on, but it is clear that it brings us to silence.[28] The speaker can triumph, can become his own author, only by allowing his finite form to vanish and be defeated; the poem ends with "the deepening shades," not with a fisherman rising to drop a fly. The most the speaker can do is to show the reader how to die, achieving immortality by archetypifying himself into the indifferent dying, in archetypal form standing as a model, a way of perceiving and responding to the modern world. Were the ending different, were he to live on, reappearing transformed among his descendants, he would be trying to escape his fate rather than choosing it. Ego-centered authority depends on leaving behind in the reader's mind a model of resistance to decay that points to the inevitability of that decay. The ego and its imagination can only then become the lords of reality, though not of a terribly glorious one. And therein lies the heart of Yeats's modernism: he admits the intractability of the circumstances and the futility of quarreling with them, but he still creates an ego, a private source of desire, that can adjust its perceptions of reality to grant the ego both vitality and meaning.

4

Speech without Self: Logos-centered Authority in *Four Quartets*

"I don't know what it is, if I have not defined it, about Eliot that is so slimy. It is the affectation of authority, an offensive leaking from above so that the water is polluted wherever he appears in print."
—William Carlos Williams (*Selected Letters* 225)

When the mind is conscious of having itself created the interpretive structures by which it knows the world, it submits to ego-centered authority. When the source of that structure is outside and prior to the individual mind, the mind submits to a Logos-centered authority. Logos-centered and ego-centered authority are perfect and complete forms that can only be mediated, never achieved or fully internalized. Given these necessary conditions, a poetic speaker must mediate, and when mediating the authority of the Logos, the speaker's position between the Logos and the reader must be uncertain and elusive, simultaneously of both worlds and neither world.

But how do we distinguish between a poem of Logos-centered authority and its opposite, particularly considering that no poetic speaker can be fully committed to either one? In poetry of ego-centered authority, the only universe is the universe of the mind contemplating its relationship with earlier and other manifestations of itself. Using the term "Greater Romantic Lyric," M. H. Abrams describes this structuring as "a self-educative journey," both of the lyric speaker and the human race, moving from a natural and happy unity, through progressive division, estrangement, and conflict, to a crisis that eventuates in "a new and complex integrity" (454). *Four Quartets* is certainly an educative journey, but not of the "self"; the very notion of independent selfhood dissolves in Eliot's verse. Also, though *Four Quartets* projects "a new and complex integrity" at the end, it is not the integrity of the self but of the cosmos to which the self is subordinate.

In David Ward's reading of *Four Quartets,* Eliot positions the speaker "to direct the reader's experience more and more, to marshal his ghosts into a formal pattern, to persuade the imagination into a special way of seeing" (234). This description accords well with two points of my argument: that by directing the reader's thinking, the speaker exerts authority over him; and that this authority can be sustained only by drawing the reader in so that he subordinates himself to the Logos, the formal pattern revealed by the speaker's discourse and example.[1] The speaker's presence must be undeniable yet invisible, directing the reader's understanding of the Logos yet restraining the charge that he authorizes it. For while a Romantic might have a "ready-made carapace" of external authority in religion, Eliot has only his own "propositions" (Weatherhead, 33). To justify these propositions, the speaker must be disembodied, emerging from no particular time or place or set of circumstances, representing not a typical human identity but a point of view or set of lenses through which to see the world. To assume this point of view, and so to make present the Logos, an "ideal construction" integrated with past and future (Ellis, 101–2), the speaker must also be abstracted from time. Moreover, like the speaker in the invocation passages in *Paradise Lost,* he must remain distant enough from the reader's level to assert oracular authority, yet close enough to gain access to the reader's mind. And the Logos that the speaker mediates must draw on the resources of the generic ego, one describing the species rather than the individual. Such an authority is presented as a continuous and uniform tradition, one that is sustained by individuals and sustains them in turn by finding recurrent and unchanging roles for individuals to occupy. These roles give an otherwise anonymous reader an identity and a consequence, as well as preserving the authority of the Logos. The reader is thereby incorporated in the Logos, occupying its structure.

In a sense, Eliot inverts the Romantic tendency to internalize the divine, the Logos, in the ego's private energies, engaging in a "reverse romantic displacement of religious terminology to secular experience" (Bornstein, 129). This inversion locates the divine outside the ego, which in its turn is pressured to immerse itself in the Logos. Eliot's purpose in integrating the modern ego with its presumed origin, the Logos, is to overcome the ego's "partial view" of reality, wherein the mind knows itself as distinct from what it observes (Ellis, 104).[2] Such a mind is inadequate to full apprehension of reality, which does not tolerate the distortions of analysis—the only means available to the partial view (Ellis, 94). Thus, because a voice requires a consciousness distinct from its surroundings, the speaker of *Four Quartets* is limited to the inadequacies of the partial view. The border of mediating speaker and Logos is the scene of a constant struggle. To overcome the limitations of the partial view, the ego desires to submit to Logos-centered authority. But because submission brings silence, the ego must at the same time resist the Logos. Ironically, though *Four Quartets* is a poetic attempt to subordinate the ego, to compel an acknowledgment of its source of meaning and being, this attempt relies, finally, on the efforts of an individuated ego.[3]

How Eliot overcomes the presence of this ego forms the subject of the chapter: his poetic speaker manipulates our reading by manipulating the identity of the projected reader. This manipulation arises from the pattern of mediation; our access to both the Logos and the projected reader is dependent upon the speaker's presentation of them. To keep from appearing to color what he mediates, the speaker of *Four Quartets* "effaces" himself (Kenner, 170–72). He is not absent but merely removed from the locus of thought and feeling, projecting a set of circumstances that the projected reader must inhabit. The speaker slips in and out of the scenery he describes, merging himself alternately with the projected reader and with what this reader is made to see. These are feats of transpersonality, transformations of identity a poetic speaker must perform in order to avoid being circumscribed and thus limited by qualities equating his status with the reader's. This transpersonality by effacement makes the speaker's relationship with the reader infinitely plastic and the speaker himself generally impossible to locate in the sense that we can locate and list the qualities of the speaker in "The Tower." And because of this elusiveness and plasticity, the projected reader is made infinitely malleable, taking on a set of attitudes and apprehensions originating in the speaker but located in the projected reader's mind. With his creating hand thus made invisible, the speaker cannot be subject to reader-inflicted irony. He can legitimately mediate the authority of the Logos.

Still, complete effacement is impossible as well as undesirable. At a number of key points in *Four Quartets* the speaker emerges as a circumscribed persona, as what I call the "speaking ego." He surrenders his hieratic position and lapses into an attitude that circumscribes him with wryness or irritability or despair: "The moments of happiness—not the sense of well-being, / Fruition, fulfillment, security or affection, / Or even a very good dinner." Such resurgences—or descents—into the projected reader's more cramped reality foreground the gap between the ego and Logos, between the narrowness of our perspective and the breadth and depth of the authority the speaker mediates. Moreover, these appearances of the speaking ego dramatize the difficulty of reorienting the self toward the Logos. And because the speaking ego is discredited, Logos-centered authority is enhanced rather than undermined. Ultimately, these emergences reinforce the speaker's textual voice because of the distance from ego-centered gestures the text must maintain. The speaking ego, emerging at the end of each quartet but "Little Gidding," models the limits and failure of the ego-centered position.

This question of the speaker's shifting status and identity illuminates the difficulties with Eliot critics who read his poetry in general and *Four Quartets* in particular as Romantic, that is, as the product of a conflict between the intuitive, visionary subconscious and the rational shaper of consciousness (Spurr, xii).[4] These critics must, consequently, label Eliot a failed Romantic because he apparently shrinks from the fertility of his own creative energies (Bornstein, 104–12). Such a reading of Eliot, though provocative, is both inadequate and unfair, suffering from the either/or fallacy that poems are either Romantic or failed Romantic.

Although these critics do provide a useful structure for describing the tension between ego and Logos in *Four Quartets,* their bias in favor of ego-centered authority begs the question of its superiority. Also, to claim that the visionary faculties are overwhelmed by the rational, that the ego is pressed into a mold and forced to submit to a rationalistic set of *a priori p*rinciples, is to miss Eliot's premises: that the poem's projected reader occupies the concepts, rather than the reverse, and that the reader serves as their instrument. These concepts authorize the mind of the projected reader, giving it shape and meaning. In a poem of ego-centered authority, as most Romantic poetry tends to be, the opposite is true: it is the imaginative mind that gives birth to ways of interpreting experience. As I shall argue, the point of origin for all mediating structures in *Four Quartets* is the Logos; efforts on the ego's part to create such structures are discredited from the start. Eliot is not a failed Romantic but anti-Romantic.

Thus, the issue is not whether Eliot cringes before his own creative forces, but whether or not he convincingly constitutes the projected mind with Logos-centered structures that can sustain and assure value. The success of the poem depends on how successfully he shows that the mind cannot achieve form without prior shaping principles to identify it. Because of his manipulations of mediating authority, he does succeed, as I will argue in close readings. Yet Eliot must and does return to the ego ultimately, doing so not because the ego is expansive and the Logos constrictive but because the mind can know itself and maintain consciousness only when it can locate its boundaries. In *Four Quartets* it is only by acknowledging the authority of the Logos that the ego can learn these boundaries and live.

In a poem of Logos-centered authority, such as *Four Quartets,* the speaker exists as a lens through which we are to see not the speaker or his acts of mind, but the reader's placement in the structure of reality. To counter this view by claiming that there is a strong speaker presence in *Four Quartets,* a presence as clearly felt as the speaker of *The Prelude,* is to miss the point. What distinguishes these two positions is not the comparative vigor of the speakers but their point of focus and relationship to their origins. To authorize the reader's interpretations of experience, the speaker positions himself at the periphery of the reader's world, between the reader and the Logos.[5]

The speaker's location—his position in relation to the projected reader and the Logos—is the key to the speaker's authority, for this position either justifies or undermines the way he projects and characterizes the reader. He assumes the role of guide through each section, the author not of the presented experience but of its interpretation, its meaning. He is not visible or present to us as Virgil is for Dante, or even as the speaker of *The Prelude* takes on an imaginable shape for us. Rather, he exists as a set of instructions and precepts pushed into circulation in the projected reader's mind. Yet because the movements of each quartet are mutually responsive, there is no central authoritative presence, only a pointing toward that presence by the forward movement of each poem. By "forward movement" I mean less a particular direction and more an accumulation to achieve a particular shape, as a rolling snowball accumulates snow. Even though the strong, stern, occasionally caustic tone of the speaker makes him a strongly felt presence, he does not and cannot serve as the authorizing center because he must not tamper with his status as mediator.

Integral to the speaker's situation and identity is the interdependence of time, ego, mediating authority, and the musical form of the poem. The form speaks clearly to Eliot's purpose: the repetition, reexamination, and elaboration of particular themes is antichronic, evoking a centrifugal continuity that generates possibilities from itself while still remaining constant. This generative constancy works to reorient the mind of the projected reader, turning it back to face and acknowledge its source.[6] The form of *Four Quartets* imitates the Logos: our encounter with the poem is analogous to the speaker's encounter with the still point.[7] Like the Logos, the poem can be known only within a temporal and thus fragmented consciousness. In Bradleyan terms, knowledge means consciousness of "the relations between parts;" true apprehension is thus impossible (Ellis, 104). The conflict between mediated knowledge and immediate apprehension, between ego and Logos, is expressed in the tension between linear and circular movement, time and timelessness, change and stasis, becoming and incarnation. This primary struggle is resolved less by a commitment to one side or the other than by a statement of the kind and degree of subordination the ego is required—or privileged—to acknowledge. By "Little Gidding," notions of subordination and submission evaporate, for these terms express an exertion of power, not authority. Authority prevails when those under its sway—in this case, the speaker and the projected reader—identify themselves with it.

This chapter focuses on representative passages in each quartet that demonstrate the speaker's three principal gestures: establishing the authority to mediate, overcoming threats to that authority, and reorienting the projected reader toward an acceptance of a Logos-centered authority. Aside from some necessary eddying from the true direction because of the projected reader's and speaker's failures, *Four Quartets* moves forward in the convergence of speaker and projected reader. This convergence occurs as the speaker leads the projected reader through three levels of apprehension: the concrete, the abstract, and the figurative or symbolic. At the first level, principally in "Burnt Norton" and "East Coker," the projected reader is an ego detached from his surroundings, made discontinuous from them and from himself in an awareness of loss, of the irretrievability of the past and the inaccessibility of the future. His world is purely concrete, filled with images of things without apparent context, purpose, or meaning. The ego flounders at this level, paralyzed and ungrounded, self-aware only by negation. The speaker seizes control of this ego by implanting his own perceptions and interpretations in the projected reader's. In this way, the speaker creates a sense of elusiveness and mystery, transpersonally creating the reader while seeming to be identified with him.

The second, or abstract, level, is marked by second-person address and a shift to abstract language. This pair of conditions carves away the ego of the projected reader, stripping it of its autonomy and its powers to sense and judge, to mediate its own experience. This abstract level of apprehension follows inevitably from the concrete: after the speaker has appropriated and interpreted the projected reader's perceptions, and then removed even those, he leaves him with no qualities or attributes but a general sense of longing and vacancy. The speaker even supplies the object of longing—not the Logos, but the stance and state of mind appropriate to accepting the Logos as prior and absolute authority. At this stage, the projected reader does not even desire his earlier dream of autonomy.

At the third, or figurative, level, consciousness is a recomposed ego acknowledging that the mind derives its structure and powers from a prior pattern. To survive, the mind must receive the generative powers of the Logos, not try to replicate them from within. The lyric second movements of each quartet and most of "Little Gidding" are utterances from this third level, where consciousness is marked by iconic, symbolic language: words having vertical as well as horizontal referents, linking the temporal and the timeless, the ego and the Logos.[8]

Before examining in detail the levels the projected reader ascends through, we need to see how the speaker first secures authority over the projected reader. At the opening of "Burnt Norton" and "East Coker," there is an ante-stage in the reader's progress that does not so much shape or direct the reader as try to establish sufficient authority in a speaker presence that is sufficiently diffuse to blend with the mind of the projected reader. As "Burnt Norton" begins, the speaker is disembodied and unfixed, yet still an ego wrestling with a purely conceptual world, suspended between the certain and the propositional: "Time present and time past / Are both perhaps present in time future, / And time future contained in time past." A rhythmic litany on cosmic issues is interrupted, briefly, with a "perhaps." But the force of that qualifying, uncertain "perhaps" is almost dissipated in what follows:

> If all time is eternally present
> All time is unredeemable.
> What might have been is an abstraction
> Remaining a perpetual possibility
> Only in a world of speculation.

This if/then clause has the impersonal force of syllogistic reasoning, yet at the same time it permits doubt just as "perhaps" does;

the unredeemability of time remains only a proposition, however compelling. Because of the tentativeness of the speaker's conditional clauses, David Ward argues that "Eliot chooses not to speak with authority" (228). I think, though, that Ward is misled by referring to Eliot rather than the speaker, therefore missing the point that the speaker does speak with authority, doing so because he allows the force of syllogism rather than assertion to make his claim. For the speaker's is not the circumscribed voice of a self-regarding persona, but what I have called a textual rather than personal voice, one that examines experience with the keenest disinterest. The effect of this abstract, impersonal, logical, but propositional voice is to transpersonalize the speaker, situating him between the Logos and the private, limited world of the projected reader. And because the speaker can only mediate, not serve as the source of those principles, that situation is vital to his poetic authority. Paradoxically, if he located himself at the source of those principles rather than at their periphery as a nonentity witnessing their effect, he could not claim any sort of oracular access to them. Conversely, if he were not propositional but unyieldingly certain, the speaker would still be just as far from the Logos, just as trapped in finitude as his reader. Because the Logos does not speak, speech must come from the ego, yet authoritative speech does not come from a clearly delimited ego. By being impersonal—devoid of references to personal circumstance, feeling, or identity—and yet propositional, the speaker emerges from the text here only ectoplasmically, a presence from a world not our world, yet without pretensions to an infinite grasp of all things and principles. This ante-stage occurs at the opening of "East Coker" as well, where the speaker is less diffused into a priori principles but still transpersonalized far beyond the mortal scope, distributed among the conditions he describes:

> In my beginning is my end. In succession
> Houses rise and fall, crumble, are extended,
> Are removed, destroyed, restored, or in their place
> Is an open field, or a factory, or a by-pass.
> Old stone to new building, old timber to new fires,
> Old fires to ashes, and ashes to the earth
> Which is already flesh, fur and faeces,
> Bone of man and beast, cornstalk and leaf.
> Houses live and die: there is a time for building
> And a time for living and for generation
> And a time for the wind to break the loosened pane
> And to shake the wainscot where the field-mouse trots

> And to shake the tattered arras woven with a silent motto.
> In my beginning is my end.

The implied "I" here takes on the features not of a person but of a process, and one not abstractly conceived but physically apparent, as if we had empirical evidence for the speaker's transpersonality. Contrasted with the "Burnt Norton" opening, the language projects a more sharply defined speaker, establishing a clearer if less mysterious authority. This greater clarity is the beginning of the speaker and reader's convergence: the speaker's sphere of authority retreats as the reader's consciousness is extended and reoriented.

Each of the quartets furthers the convergence of speaker and reader, weaving together in a spiral the concrete and the abstract, the ego and the Logos. In "Burnt Norton," the spiral is at its widest. The speaker has unlimited mobility, entering the mind of a reader he has himself projected. Thus, the projected reader must interpret the speculative experience in the rose garden according to the terms the speaker has set up:

> Footfalls echo in the memory
> Down the passage which we did not take
> Towards the door we never opened
> Into the rose garden. My words echo
> Thus, in your mind.
> > But to what purpose
> Disturbing the dust on a bowl of rose-leaves
> I do not know.

Instead of telling the reader what he, the speaker, has experienced, as would be the case in a poem of ego-centered authority, the speaker tells the reader what he, the reader, has experienced. The "passage" is one neither he nor the reader took, so he presumes a shared experience. The explicit statement of control in "My words echo / Thus, in your mind" echoes as the footfalls do, both referring to and constituting his memory at the same time. In effect, the speaker annexes the projected reader's memory, where images of unexamined experience wait to be interpreted and categorized. This annexation requires that the speaker assume a double part, directing the poem's progress and experiencing its events alongside and through the reader, as if Virgil had slipped inside Dante instead of walking ahead of him.

Yet, as he does throughout *Four Quartets,* the speaker pauses just as he implicitly asserts authority, backing away from further explanation and thus from further assertion with "I do not know." But because the speaker has remained invisible thus far, his disclaimer masks more than it reveals: since we do not know any more than he does about the purpose of the dust being disturbed, his ignorance does not distinguish him from us and so does not go very far toward limiting him to a specific identity. Furthermore, we have been directed to look not at the speaker but at the speculative experience. Because his ignorance is ours, at this point he is practically indistinguishable from us. Put another way, both the ignorance and the deferred presence of oracular understanding exist on his authority, as does, in fact, the projected reader. The speaker's challenge is to displace himself from any apparent or accessible origin, to efface himself yet direct the projected reader's consciousness at the same time. Eliot makes an analogous claim when he said he wanted to write poetry "that in reading it we are intent on what the poem points at, and not on the poetry" (Matthiessen, 90).

In "East Coker," the latter part of the first movement places the projected reader at the first stage again and embeds him in a stasis, immobilizing him, while the speaker remains elusive, providing the means and the terms by which the reader experiences the vision to come:

> Now the light falls
> Across the open field, leaving the deep lane
> Shuttered with branches, dark in the afternoon,
> Where you lean against a bank while a van passes,
> And the deep lane insists on the direction
> Into the village, in the electric heat
> Hypnotised. In a warm haze the sultry light
> Is absorbed, not refracted, by grey stone.
> The dahlias sleep in the empty silence.
> Wait for the early owl.

Telling the reader not what to do but what he sees, the speaker neither witnesses nor participates, expressing no attitude toward the scene lest he solidify his identity. And because the account of the experience is equivalent to the experience itself, the speaker effaces himself. That is, he displaces himself from the locus of poetic creation almost completely, emerging in the shadow of second-person address. To the extent that the speaker is invisible, the ego of the projected reader is alone with his consciousness. At the first level, the concrete world, speaker and reader appear to be one, the speaker articulating the reader's thoughts but without explicitly asserting the authority to mediate. This is a stage of ego-centered authority in a poem of Logos-centered authority, so the ego must of necessity appear passive, paralyzed, and directionless, as he does here.

Yet the projected reader has progressed from his condition in "Burnt Norton," where the concrete level of language displays the ego at a loss, detached from inner or outer sustenance and conscious of itself as little more than a set of narrow limits. Ego-centered consciousness is consciousness of absence. In the "East Coker" version of the concrete level, the ego has in one sense come forward, having passed into the second level in "Burnt Norton," and in another, back. Diminished, it nonetheless is being prepared for vision, filled with a sense of mild but focused anticipation:

> In that open field
> If you do not come too close, if you do not come
> too close
> On a summer midnight, you can hear the music
> Of the weak pipe and the little drum
> And see them dancing around the bonfire
> The association of man and woman
> In daunsinge, signifying matrimonie—
> . . .
> Keeping time,
> Keeping the rhythm in their dancing
> As in their living in the living seasons
> The time of the seasons and the constellations
> The time of milking and the time of harvest
> The time of the coupling of man and woman
> And that of beasts. Feet rising and falling.
> Eating and drinking. Dung and death.

As Derek Traversi observes, this vision parallels the vision in the garden of "Burnt Norton" (130). But a sign that the projected reader has grown since then, grown at least according to the terms of Logos-centered authority, is that he directs his attention outward rather than inward. But the reader is not yet prepared to disperse or reorient his ego, for he has not yet come upon something of sufficient value to replace it. The "romantic possibilities of human love," held up as a redemptive possibility in "Burnt Norton," are discredited here in "East Coker" as a "mere human order" (Weatherhead, 40). But on what basis? Perhaps this vision of earthy harmony is not painful enough to suit Eliot; perhaps he is demanding more consciousness, a more painful awareness of the ego's severance from the Logos. The vision's failing is clearly not its evanescence. It vanishes because of its content and consequences: "Dung and death." George Bornstein argues vigorously that this passage is an "imaginative eruption" that, overtaking Eliot with its power and vitality, he must then stifle unnaturally to preserve the forces of rationality, to avoid collapsing the divine nature worship or humanism (157). But presupposing that Eliot's anti-Romanticism results from failed Romanticism, Bornstein does not read *Four Quartets* on its own terms. Given that, for Eliot, modern consciousness is incapable of self-restoration, unlike its Romantic predecessor, it requires generative forces that must come from somewhere other than primal history.

However, "dung and death," appearing suddenly at the end of this passage celebrating a pattern of seeming fecundity, does betray the struggle of the ego—in this case, the speaker's ego within the projected reader's—against absorption into a prior pattern. The speaker is only faintly disguised behind this comment authorized only by the speaking ego, deliberative, not descriptive: "death" is perhaps a logical consequence, but "dung" expresses personal revulsion. As Bornstein argues, there is nothing inherently repulsive about the clumsy shoes or country mirth (158). But the reason this vision must repel the presiding ego is not, as Bornstein supposes, because of Eliot's neurotic fear of romantic vitality. Rather, it is a fear of the ego's death, as die it surely would if absorbed into the earthy harmony of the dancers. And without a distinction between individual selfhood and collectivized Other, harmony cannot be mediated and thus cannot be known. This fear illuminates the walls of the speaker's ego, shaking, for the moment, his authority to mediate. The speaker must apprehend harmony rather than be apprehended by it, and so must not "come too close."

And just as the speaker must shrink from the threat of harmony, he must evade the walls of his ego and resume his transpersonality:

> Dawn points, and another day
> Prepares for heat and silence. Out at sea the dawn wind
> Wrinkles and slides. I am here
> Or there, or elsewhere. In my beginning.

The description of a warm, damp dawn is all we have to summon an image of the speaker, who makes his transpersonality explicit as his specificity dissolves into "here, / Or there, or elsewhere." The speaker exists only in our sense of this scene, and the projected reader is left on the concrete level in a halcyonic inertia.

The projected reader reaches the second, or abstract level in the second movement of "Burnt Norton." The speaker does not assume a more fleshly presence, but he does display the sense of an audience, the sense that an idea must be explained, rendered in words. And as that idea is explained, the concrete world of things and events evaporates:

> At the still point of the turning world. Neither flesh nor
> fleshless;
> Neither from nor towards; at the still point, there the dance is,
> But neither arrest nor movement. And do not call it fixity,
> Where past and future are gathered. Neither movement
> from nor towards,
> Neither ascent nor decline. Except for the point, the still
> point,
> There would be no dance, and there is only the dance. . . .
> Yet the enchainment of past and future
> Woven in the weakness of the changing body,
> Protects mankind from heaven and damnation
> Which flesh cannot endure.

The oppositions, "flesh" and "fleshless," "from" and "towards," "arrest" and "movement," "ascent" and "decline," are presented as the reader's unspoken conclusions, which the speaker automatically dismisses as inadequate to comprehend the Logos.

Having done so, the speaker has placed himself in a rhetorical position between knowledge and ignorance, the Logos and the reader's ego. In that space between, he can elude the immobility of the former and the responsibility of the latter. Also, though the Logos exists solely on his terms, he does not stage himself as its creator. That is, having banished the empirical world from the reader, the speaker can derive a purely conceptual one that is apparently not subject to any prior authority. Also, the litanic rhythm and diction—principally the relentless "neither"—tend even more to nick at the projected reader's ability to grasp the Logos independently of the speaker's mediation. As a result, the projected reader is stripped of his language and his power to form ideas. Thus, when he is told that "Here is a place of disaffection," the projected reader has not merely had this place pointed out to him, but he has been put there by the speaker. In this way, the poetic authority of a transpersonalized speaker creates what seems merely referred to. As an invisible mediator asserting no individual will, the speaker can presume to instruct us not to "call it fixity." His authority is such that we cannot even choose to think of "it" as fixity. Certainly we have not been presented with an array of alternatives. The speaker's authority is assured here, carried by an arrogant evasiveness and the sheer mystery of transpersonal effacement. When he reaches "I can only say, here we have been: but I cannot say where. / And I cannot say how long, for that is to place it in time," given reality is such that the lack is not in him but in the language available to him, which is the language limiting the reader. The less information, empirical or conceptual, there is available to the projected reader, the more dependent he must become upon the speaker's mediation. As I shall argue in more detail, this dependency is a necessary second step in the projected reader's progress toward reorientation, his acquiescence into prayer.

But throughout *Four Quartets,* the speaker recoils, gently, from complete acquiescence to the Logos because consciousness demands separation of self and Other. No reorientation or acquiescence is possible unless or until a boundary can be defined by a relentless and concentrated effort, in a passage through doubt that winds at times back around the ego. The first such recoiling occurs at the end of the second movement of "Burnt Norton," as the speaker returns to construct a hypothetical ego:

> Time past and time future
> Allow but a little consciousness.
> To be conscious is not to be in time
> But only in time can the moment in the rose-garden,
> The moment in the arbour where the rain beat,
> The moment in the draughty church at smokefall
> Be remembered; involved with past and future.
> Only through time time is conquered.

Moments of timelessness are possible only in time, in those moments constructed and preserved in memory that can have meaning only when framed by a context of flux, surrounded by time. In other words, consciousness of the timeless—in memory—occurs only when the mind has accepted time's continuity. Thus, there is an underside to the claim that "only through time time is conquered." Timelessness must be felt in time for there to be consciousness of it; time is not conquered at all, because the timeless moment is ultimately dependent upon it.

At this point in "Burnt Norton," the speaker has returned us to the concrete level, to the world of the solitary ego, but this world has been reoriented. The mind, through memory, has been set once more in relation to things of the empirical world, however temporarily. The moments described in this passage are unacknowledged failures as transcendent moments, but they are harbingers of the consciousness to be pursued in "Little Gidding," directing contemplation toward the permanent and essential. But the projected reader is still lodged in an ego-centered perspective: he can conceive of the permanent in personal terms alone. Because memory dies with the individual, the "timeless," lodged in the ego, is time-ridden after all. Not until the mind can see itself as an extension and repetition of other minds, as it does in "Little Gidding," can it seize permanence and consequence.

To clarify this necessary connection between time and mind, and to assess the state of the projected reader's ego at this point in *Four Quartets,* we need to go beyond the conventional wisdom that "Burnt Norton" is about finding either redemption or escape from time in timeless moments recovered by memory. Memory in "Burnt Norton" is personal memory, the ego's solitary efforts to maintain itself in the face of time's continual pulling away of choices, consequences, and possibilities. The ego recoils from the Logos because at this point in *Four Quartets* the Logos is too much a mystery, too much a featureless abstraction to be acknowledged as an originating authority. The projected reader of "Burnt Norton" is not yet equipped to read the world from a Logos-centered perspective. His reorientation is inadequate: he does not yet have access to the mysteries of the figurative level, where Logos and ego can intersect in symbol. The projected reader retreats to the isolation of the ego, to the consolations of personal memory, to the only place where ego-centered consciousness can accommodate the timeless. The speaker pulls him back from retreat, thrusting him ahead to the second level. The personal—and thus stunted—version of timelessness in memory is inadequate because it is inert.

On the return to the second level, the speaker does not merely describe to the projected reader a world cut off from sensory investigation. Instead, his deictic language places him there:

> Here is a place of disaffection
> Time before and time after
> In a dim light: neither daylight
> Investing form with lucid stillness
> Turning shadow into transient beauty
> With slow rotation suggesting permanence
> Nor darkness to purify the soul
> Emptying the sensual with deprivation

> Cleansing affection from the temporal.
> Neither plenitude nor vacancy.

The paired negations form a perfectly symmetrical structure—a blank center with felt absences on either side. This language of the second level is necessarily abstract, for while the concrete would summon images to mind, the abstract removes them, leaving blanks where mental pictures might have been. Since the mind's ego-centered authority constructs ideas and patterns from its apprehension of the material world, removing images removes the ego's ability to form ideas. Moreover, the less the speaker summons or has contact with the empirical world, the less he shares with the projected reader, and the less he is subject to the empirical circumstances containing the projected reader. As a consequence, at the second level the speaker seems all the more oracular and elusive.

"Here" is a place where the mind cannot arrive deliberately; it matches no prior expectations because the mind cannot conceive of such complete absence. Defined by circumstances, the ego loses identity when separated from them. When placed "Here," the projected reader must peel back layers of negation to arrive at the still point, yet bound as he is to ideas authorized by the ego, he is left with only the negations themselves, not with what they point to. And only when he is fully stripped of his pretenses to independent reasoning, when he no longer reaches inside for an explanation of his experience, is he properly oriented to acknowledge Logos-centered authority.

But as we see in the next lines, even the speaker is not fully reoriented; the text simultaneously authorizes the projected reader's view of modern experience and undercuts the speaker's own ego-centered voice—and by extension, any ego-centered authority. The projected reader, rendered passive and paralyzed "Here" on the abstract level, has modern experience properly mediated for him:

> Only a flicker
> Over the strained time-ridden faces
> Distracted from distraction by distraction
> Filled with fancies and empty of meaning
> Tumid apathy with no concentration
> Men and bits of paper, whirled by the cold wind
> That blows before and after time,
> Wind in and out of unwholesome lungs
> Time before and time after.

Eructation of unhealthy souls
Into the faded air, the torpid
Driven on the wind that sweeps the gloomy hills of London,
Hampstead and Clerkenwell, Campden and Putney,
Highgate, Primrose and Ludgate. Not here
Not here the darkness, in this twittering world.

The speaker quite deliberately provides the categories through which modern experience is to be understood. The place of disaffection is not mediated through concrete description but through an editorial. Abandoning the second-person address, the speaker slips again from the second level into the concrete world, his ego reemerging in distaste. The ego drawn in this passage, what I have called the "speaking ego," is isolated from both the physical world and a redemptive position oriented toward the Logos. Individuals are reduced in consequence, but there is nothing to replace them. First we see a flash of "time-ridden faces." Then men shrink to the status and size and indistinguishability of bits of paper, and then the landscape falls away and the people blur into the horizon, fading as we rise above "the gloomy hills of London" and its environs. We are never let in close; the figures are thrust from us by their supposed insignificance. They live only as an intellectual category.

The nauseated mind revealed in these lines is another version of those behind the "time-ridden faces." The text provides here the other view of a return to the ego: rather than the inevitable refuge of enduring consciousness, as it was for "the moment in the draughty church at smokefall," the isolated ego is inert, sealed off by self-created boundaries of feeling.

There are two direct and seemingly opposed consequences to this pulling back from the physical world into the self. The ego as an isolated, nauseated entity is further discredited: its passivity is reinforced along with its inability to shelter transpersonal consciousness—mind extended beyond sensations of personal limits. Yet even though the speaker emerges for a moment as a circumscribed consciousness, his failure strengthens the text's authority by dramatizing rather than asserting the need for the Logos' restoration. Through his own failure he wins the day, "insisting" in the direction of the quartets to come.

But within the next verse paragraph, the speaker reemerges with a command to:

Descend lower, descend only
Into the world of perpetual solitude,

> World not world, but that which is not world,
> Internal darkness, deprivation
> And destitution of all property,
> Desiccation of the world of sense,
> Evacuation of the world of fancy,
> Inoperancy of the world of spirit;
> This is the one way, and the other
> Is the same, not in movement
> But abstention from movement; while the world moves
> In appetency, on its metalled ways
> Of time past and time future.

The speaker exerts authority here both directly and indirectly: his imperative mode separates the scene of utterance into commander and commanded. Rather than continue describing the descent, the speaker insists on it, for his purpose is different at this point. As we have seen, on the first, concrete level, the speaker attributes to the reader, without insisting, a set of intellectual and emotional responses to the world. And on the second, abstract level, the reader has no choice but to "descend," based on his disgust with the world, a disgust engineered and authorized by the speaker's mediating authority. Importantly, this descent must be compelled; the speaker must be clearly detached from the projected reader to demonstrate that the urge to descend "into the world of perpetual solitude" is not authorized by the ego. Not much is generated by the ego in *Four Quartets* except longings and attitudes and despairing interpretations of everyday experience. Any progress or significant action toward reorienting the ego is imposed, urged by speaker command.

Examining the second, or abstract, level of ego reorientation points to the speaker's source of mediating authority and the Logos's source of absolute authority. In the universe of *Four Quartets,* things originate from words; ideas about the thing give it form and meaning by giving it a name and a category. Existence is determined by Logos-centered mediation.[9] The Logos is the source of necessary coherence and communication among egos struggling to sort, order, and comprehend. Thus, the farther we go out into the world of things-in-themselves, and the farther we move from the mediating, ordering influence of the Logos, the less we are buttressed by authority. Thrown back on itself, the ego is ill-equipped to forge meaning in the world. Without authority, the raw ego is as ungrounded, undirected, and inchoate as the world it seeks to press into form:

> And so each venture
> Is a new beginning, a raid on the inarticulate
> With shabby equipment always deteriorating
> In the general mess of imprecision of feeling,
> Undisciplined squads of emotion. And what there is to
>   conquer
> By strength and submission, has already been discovered
> Once or twice, or several times, by men whom one cannot
>   hope
> To emulate—but there is no competition—
> There is only the fight to recover what has been lost
> And found again and again: and now, under
>   conditions
> That seem unpropitious.

Disintegrated from a sustaining culture, acting in solitude, the ego can at most repeat, never regenerate.

The speaking ego displayed in the above passage ("So here I am"), modeling the projected reader, has not progressed far toward acknowledging the Logos, particularly considering the distance needed to achieve the posture of prayer in "Little Gidding," where the ego can intersect the Logos. But the second level does mark a kind of progress for the projected reader: what the ego author-izes—sensations—can be annihilated with a few words. For if words are removed, or replaced, their referents are likewise re-moved from consciousness and thus from perceived reality. The reader is therefore the captive of the word, and once the periphery of private sensation is stripped away by abstract language, what remains of the ego must acknowledge that consciousness depends on and is generated by a set of prior categories. After the second level, the projected reader must face the fact that he is without authority, and so without anything.

The third, figurative level of ego reorientation, the level from which the speaker addresses the reader in the lyric passages, is accessible to the projected reader only intermittently, and only in the latter quartets, "Dry Salvages" and "Little Gidding." By "accessible" I mean the projected reader's presence on the level, the degree to which the speaker has him partake of the eternal patterns of the Logos, placing him inside—with the speaker—rather than outside, alone in the ego. The language of this level evolves in *Four Quartets* from the inaccessible and forbidding to the intimate and inviting. This transition matches the movement of the projected reader's reorientation; where in "Burnt Norton" and "East Coker" he is sealed off from the Logos, made to focus on the inadequacy of the solitary ego, in "The Dry Salvages" and "Little Gidding," though still commanded by the speaker, he is treated as an initiate, almost an equal.

We must clarify now how "figurative" is to be used here, and in what sense it is a "level." For my purposes, "figurative" language is symbolic, referring to spiritual concepts or responses as they intersect things and ideas, incarnating within the outlines of empirical objects. For instance, let us look at the notorious opening to the second movement of "Burnt Norton": "Garlic and sapphires in the mud / Clot the bedded axletree." For these lines to have meaning to the fallen projected reader, they must have some kind of vertical reference. That is, when the search for meaning breaks the confines of concrete reference, that reference must extend "vertically," toward the Logos, to signify a spiritual conception extended from its conventional empirical context. The syntactic attachment of these words compels the reader to fashion an idea that will accommodate their clashing or incongruous associations. The pairing of "garlic and sapphires" taunts the reader with its mystery, exposing the relationship between speaker and projected reader and reinforcing the speaker's authority: the gap between the words' conventional meaning and the speaker's Logos-centered purposes is a model of the gap between Logos and disoriented ego. "Taunting" perhaps overstates my case, but because there is no immediate ground in "Burnt Norton" for interpreting these lines, the intention to obscure is clear. The tools of interpretation come to hand only from continued reading and study of the entire poem. *Four Quartets* performs in effect the same tasks the speaker explicitly urges upon the projected reader.[10]

But what does the presence or absence of the figurative level signify for the authority of the speaker and the status of the projected reader? At the figurative level, nature and spirit, the concrete and the abstract, the empirical and the conceptual, ego and Logos, are united. In "Burnt Norton" and "East Coker," the lyric passages are oracular, uttered from the figurative level to comment on cosmological events in natural terms:

> Time and the bell have buried the day,
> The black cloud carries the sun away.
> Will the sunflower turn to us, will the clematis
> Stray down, bend to us; tendril and spray
> Clutch and cling?
>   Chill
> Fingers of yew be curled

Down on us?

. . . .
What is the late November doing
With the disturbance of the spring
And creatures of the summer heat,
And snowdrops writhing under feet
And hollyhocks that aim too high
Red into grey and tumble down
Late roses filled with early snow?

Because the mind demands meaning from language, language used in a conventionally meaningful context begs explication. And if the meaning is not apparent according the mind's own conceptual authority, such as it is, the obscurity must result from the speaker's superior understanding, on which the reader depends to render the language meaningful. Because only figurative language requires mediation—though this language itself is a medium—meaning can emerge only on the mediating authority of the speaker.

Thus, the figurative language of the third level performs a number of functions at once. First, it enacts the Logos for the projected reader. In other words, it does not merely propose the ideas of the originating pattern of experience and consciousness, but it promises the interpenetration of the idea and the ego's solitary consciousness. Second, by a progressive lightening of the Logos's mystery, as I shall examine in the next section, the projected reader moves progressively, if intermittently, toward the figurative level. This level, where figurative or symbolic language is uttered and understood, is presented as a goal, the end to a beginning, the *paradiso* of *Four Quartets*.

The struggles between ego and Logos and the interpenetration of thing and idea coalesce in the idea of timelessness in time, which also can be enacted only on the figurative level. The figurative implies a concrete and temporal reference to a continuous and atemporal form or concept, just as the ego is a concrete and temporal version of the originating form authorizing it. When the ego apprehends itself symbolically, it sees itself in its proper relation to its author, identifying itself according to terms of Logos-centered authority. The act of symbol-making is an act of union. When a symbol's terms are fully apprehended, and the ego fully acknowledges his own presence in the symbol, it fully unites temporal and atemporal, ego and Logos, in an epiphanic moment.

Both a more intimate tone and a more sustained use of symbolic or figurative language combine in "The Dry Salvages," where the river and sea as empirically felt things merge with ideas of a continuous self and ungraspable eternity. And with this merging comes a diminishing of the speaker's oracular powers, a shift in the nature of his authority from the hieratic to the avuncular, continuing the demystification begun in "Burnt Norton." As the third quartet begins, the speaker casts off the oracle's robes: "I do not know much about gods. . . . " But this dismissal and the modest "I think" that follows is swallowed by the elaborate claims for the river's enduring force:

> I do not know much about gods; but I think that the river
> Is a strong brown god—sullen, untamed and intractable,
> Patient to some degree, at first recognised as a frontier;
> Useful, untrustworthy, as a conveyor of commerce;
> Then only a problem confronting the builder of bridges.
> The problem once solved, the brown god is almost forgotten
> By the dwellers in cities—ever, however, implacable,
> Keeping his seasons and rages, destroyer, reminder
> Of what men choose to forget. Unhonoured, unpropitiated
> By worshippers of the machine, but waiting, watching and
>   waiting.
>   . . . .
> The river is within us, the sea is all about us;
> The sea is the land's edge also, the granite
> Into which it reaches, the beaches where it tosses
> Its hints of earlier and other creation. . . .

Holding the speaker's modesty in the face of the monumental river nullifies the speaker's presence, or rather, his self-characterization. He is transpersonalized by an inversion of ego. This idea of riverness takes on an authority quite apart from its apparent source. As David Ward explains, the river is "a measure against which the brevity of man's personal hopes and achievements can be measured" (254).[11] This distance between mere ego and the river's awesome eternity, paradoxically, enhances the speaker's authority to mediate. The more the speaking ego as a detached consciousness is diminished, the more the Logos—as it is mediated in the poem—can emerge as the originating authority.

In some sense, Eliot is reworking Wordsworth's deified man of *The Prelude.* "The soul when smitten thus by a sublime idea" is an ego conceived as a collective and supreme essence who "takes her rest with God" (VII 672–73). The Wordsworthian version of this continuous ego is the pinnacle of being, imitating the Logos rather than flowing into it, existing according to its own purposes, self-directed, adjunct to the Logos rather than subordinate to it.

But the Eliot version, enacted in the river symbol, is farther from our conscious reach and subordinate to its Logos, the sea. For Ronald Bush, the river is "that 'untamed and intractable' portion of the self that makes itself available to the passions of God and the devil" (217). Traversi describes the river as "a symbol of the history of the human race which each individual accumulation of experience in time in some measure recreates" (153). Ward echoes Traversi, but takes it further: "an individual's life . . . is a distillation of the life of many generations into one experience." In Ward's view, the individual is dissolved into both past and future, each addition one of quantity rather than kind. The human community yearned for in "The Dry Salvages," then, is united in a shared experience that is not the raw material of experience, but the experience, as it were, "when developed by a process which universalizes it" (260). This "development" is cultural mediation: for experience to be shared, for there to be contact between individual minds, it must be mediated by images from the Logos. Consequently, we need the river symbol as a way to mediate our understanding of our places in the continuous ego, which, subordinated to the sea/Logos, is our avenue to it.

Yet it is not wholly accurate to say that the ego is diminished by its subordination to the river. Rather, the ego is transpersonalized, merging on the figurative level with the river, an aspect of the Logos's originating authority. Here the ego, as river, merges not with the Logos, still unapproachable and unfathomable as Logos, but with the ego, the accumulation of limited selves continuing

> in the nursery bedroom,
> In the rank ailanthus of the April dooryard,
> In the smell of grapes on the autumn table,
> And the evening circle in the winter gaslight.

The intimacy implied in the modesty of "I do not know much about gods" is furthered: "The river is within us, the sea is all about us." Because the speaker has buried himself in the river's deification, the projected reader is less likely to dismiss this broad claim, which furthermore would be meaningless were it not uttered on the figurative level. This is not the first place in *Four Quartets* where "we" is used, but it is the first place where this construction is used to amplify—transpersonalize—the contents of the individual consciousness. But this primary form of the ego expressed by the river image neither justifies the projected reader's separation nor allows him the honor of being distinguished from his circumstances. On the contrary, the ripples of symbolic riverness and the more intimate address transindividualize the ego, implying two paired models: the individual and the historically continuous ego, as well as the historically continuous ego and the Logos. Our relationship to the river expresses our relationship to the combined energies of the continuous ego, and in turn, the river's surrender to the sea expresses the ego's proper orientation toward the Logos. The continuity of selfhood carried by the river is what the speaker urges the projected reader to accept in "Little Gidding." Just as "Time is a 'felt whole' in which there is a moment of knowledge" (Ellis, 98), historicized selves compose a total self.

The Logos presented in "The Dry Salvages" is mysterious and unfathomable, but as this quartet progresses and the ego's reorientation proceeds, the speaker addresses the projected reader in a new tone of intimacy; ego and Logos are expressed in analogous terms. At the same time, a continuity between them is emphasized: the river both composes the sea and vanishes into it. The succeeding movements of "The Dry Salvages" present and defend the response appropriate to the revelation of this new ego's relationship to the river (primal, continuous ego) and the Logos. This response—a willed acceptance of subjugation, diminished prospects, small rewards—is displayed in the laborious questioning of the second movement. The response is dramatized by the speaker's litanic effacement. In the first stanza, the speaker refashions himself to become another projected reader, but one who articulates his own condition. By doing so he effaces his presence as directing mediator in order to authorize, quite invisibly, the model of a reader who is beginning to grasp the true insignificance of the solitary ego:

> Where is there an end of it, the soundless wailing,
> The silent withering of autumn flowers
> Dropping their petals and remaining motionless;
> Where is there an end to the drifting wreckage,
> The prayer of the bone on the beach, the unprayable
> Prayer at the calamitous annunciation?

This effacement into the reader is similar to what occurs when the speaking ego emerges only to be shown its error in doing so. Because the speaker has remained elusive, chameleonic, he can create characters as a playwright does, investing them with a variety of points of view to let the text order and reform them rather than arrogating the authority to do so in a monophonic narrative voice.

The less distinct the speaker is and the more polyphonic, the more authority is left to the ordering principles we ascribe to the text, and the more secure that authority is.

Let us look at the results of this particular episode of effacement. The above stanza is apostrophic, yet without apparent audience other than the projected reader.[12] But at the same time, we can hardly suppose that the speaker would turn to the reader for information, particularly when an answer to the question follows immediately:

> There is no end, but addition: the trailing
> Consequence of further days and hours,
> While emotion takes to itself the emotionless
> Years of living among the breakage
> Of what was believed in as the most reliable—
> And therefore the fittest for renunciation.

These apostrophic questions create a model of a new relationship between speaker and projected reader, a more equal, companionable one. But what makes this exchange a model of a relationship rather than an actual one? First, because the catechismal form requires a set of answers as well as a set of questions, the projected reader is introduced as a second generator of poetic text. Yet at the same time, of course, there is still an actual projected reader listening to both question and answer. In this way the projected reader is given the questions appropriate for him to ask at his particular level of understanding. Providing these questions, then, allows the speaker to control the significance of and the terms by which any question can be put together. Also, the very utterance of the question reinforces the speaker's authority—that is, the authority of the mediating voice—as well as the speaker's appraisal of human consciousness, purpose, and experience.

Essential to this new relationship between speaker and projected reader is the movement to the third, figurative level. By presenting the series of questions in seafaring terms, the speaker brings the projected reader from the abstract to the figurative level. That is, the speaker locates the projected reader on a plane of understanding created by figurative language, dramatizing the way to achieve this new, higher level of reorientation: by perceiving figuratively— seeing the empirical in terms of the eternal, and vice versa. The projected reader is to know himself by what he sees in the mirror of this new projection. It tells him, first, that he and the speaker are on the same "drifting boat," that they share essentially the same plane of understanding and the same fate. Consequently, the projected reader must see that his status has been elevated, that to accept the speaker's projection of reality is in some way to restore both a purpose and a relationship to the Logos.

The prosaic looseness as well as the comparatively intimate tone in "The Dry Salvages" are also functions of the speaker's transpersonal effacement. The closer the projected reader moves to the correct attitude, the less iconic and the more prosaic the language becomes, as in this passage uttered from the abstract level:

> I have said before
> That the past experience revived in the meaning
> Is not the experience of one life only
> But of many generations—not forgetting
> Something that is probably quite ineffable:
> The backward look behind the assurance
> Of recorded history . . .
> For our own past is covered by the currents of action,
> But the torment of others remains an experience
> Unqualified, unworn by subsequent attrition.
> People change, and smile: but the agony abides.

Though such passages in "The Dry Salvages" are commonly charged with being sentimental and flabby (Traversi, 152), I am arguing that the shape of the projected reader has changed by this point in *Four Quartets*. The speaker does not instruct so much as clarify an established view. The projected reader is being reoriented to accept immersion in the Logos—taking a kind of pleasure in achieving ploddingness—as the only available redemption from the pointlessness of perceived isolation:

> There is no end to it, the voiceless wailing,
> No end to the withering of withered flowers,
> To the movement of pain that is painless and motionless,
> To the drift of the sea and the drifting wreckage,
> The bone's prayer to Death its God. Only the hardly, barely
>   prayable
> Prayer of the one annunciation.

The litanic questioning in the second movement of "The Dry Salvages" stresses the ego's inability to embody truth and know it, to experience events and mediate them simultaneously, and to serve as its own authority in defining itself. In the third movement, which attempts to dignify and construct from the ego's failure the correct attitude toward it, the speaker draws on the spiritual authority of Krishna:

> Fare Forward, you who think that you are voyaging;
> You are not those who saw the harbour
> Receding, or those who will disembark. . . .
> At the moment which is not of action or inaction
> You can receive this: "on whatever sphere of being
> The mind of man may be intent
> At the time of death"—that is the one action
> (And the time of death is every moment)
> Which shall fructify in the lives of others:
> And do not think of the fruit of action.
> Fare forward.

Just as he does in the opening to this quartet, the speaker effaces himself to disappear into a more substantial authority. And because he never asserts that authority as his own, he can speak through it without much anxiety.

The speaker's repeated gestures of self-effacing transpersonality into Logos-centered authority coalesces in his use of Krishna. As we shall see, Krishna's sententiae are inserted in the text in a way fully consistent with the exigencies of Logos-centered authority. They emerge not in Romantic declarations for the autonomous self but in a voice heard from within, audible only when integral to the thinking of the projected reader, who has by now been stripped of ego-centered illusions because of his passage through the second, abstract level in "Burnt Norton" and "East Coker."

Considering the authority he eventually vests himself with, the speaker begins the third movement with a modesty that is almost excessive: "I sometimes wonder if that is what Krishna meant— / Among other things—or one way of putting the same thing." The series of enigmatic metaphors that follow serve the same rhetorical function as the river description—to dwarf the display of modesty:

> That the future is a faded song, a Royal Rose or a lavender
> spray
> Of wistful regret for those who are not yet here to regret,
> Pressed between the yellow leaves of a book that has never been
> opened.

Following this passage on the figurative level, the speaker anticipates Krishna's admonition, putting it in his own terms at the concrete level:

> When the train starts, and the passengers are settled
> To fruit, periodicals and business letters
> (And those who saw them off have left the platform)
> Their faces relax from grief into relief,
> To the sleepy rhythm of a hundred hours.
> Fare forward, travellers! not escaping from the past
> Into different lives, or into any future;
> You are not the same people who left that station
> Or who will arrive at any terminus . . .
> At nightfall, in the rigging and the aerial,
> Is a voice descanting (though not to the ear,
> The murmuring shell of time, and not in any language)
> 'Fare forward . . .

Here continues a pattern in *Four Quartets* that emphasizes its modernism: symbolic meanings are not derived from "medieval analogues," but from the text itself (Bornstein, 156). The analogues, having perished in excesses of orthodoxy, lose cultural authority. In such a vacuum of authority, the speaker of *Four Quartets* co-opts Krishna's authority by anticipating it. By addressing the projected reader at the concrete level, the speaker prepares the ground so that the projected reader's inductive grasp of Krishna's abstractions depends on the speaker's terms. Krishna's words are mediated by the speaker's concrete references to travel: meaning is funneled from the concrete to the abstract. This funneling unites concrete and abstract, fashioning travel into a metaphor for the correct orientation toward the Logos, authorizing a structure of thinking that perhaps is not what Krishna meant at all. But the legitimacy of the speaker's reading of Krishna is finally irrelevant. The way to read the world, the basis of the ego's reorientation, is not Krishna's but the speaker's, even though it is done in Krishna's name. Following the ironic but inviolable principle of Logos-centered mediation, the speaker ascends to prophetic authority by denying his own access to it, turning plagiarism and the sin of pride inside out.

We need to examine more closely this principle of mediation, so prevalent in *Four Quartets* because it is philosophically inseparable from the poem's claims about the mind's nature and purpose. Because the speaker mediates Krishna's voice by anticipating it, when he does call upon its oracular authority, it cannot be readily distinguished from the speaker's own. Though he seems to have obliterated himself by transpersonality, vanishing into the ethos of Krishna, this Logos-centered authority has, in fact, been reinterpreted in the speaker's terms. I place "reinterpreted" in the passive voice for good reason: the speaker's agency is not felt. Because the speaker's vocal boundaries are difficult to define, drawing the line between mediation and fabrication becomes problematic to the point of pointlessness. And because the only textual presence from which the speaker can be distinguished is the projected reader, to say that we hear not from Krishna but from a mediated or recreated version of Krishna is ultimately not useful. Because a poetic speaker's selfhood is determined—or left undetermined— by his verbal gestures, the more they refer beyond his own self- hood, the less distinct he becomes and the wider the scope of his authority. As we have seen, a speaker's indistinctness—or degree of transpersonality—is, within limits drawn in "Little Gidding," directly proportional to his authority to mediate.

But what about the projected reader's response to Krishna's words? By this point he is stripped of ego-centered illusions, purged in a willed passivity. A sign of this condition is that the speaker's tones are gentler, less scolding; he has moved closer to the reader than in the previous quartets. Two other features suggest intimacy: the speaker's conversational musing—"I sometimes wonder"—and the fact that he invokes Krishna rather than trying to thrust home his message on the strength of sheer obscurity, as he does in "Burnt Norton." He needs to draw on Krishna's author- ity both to stay ahead of the reader and to have an authority to mediate. But more important, as we shall see more clearly in "Lit- tle Gidding," the projected reader is moving closer to the speaker. First, the reader has progressed, having reoriented his ego to ac- knowledge Logos-centered authority. Second, the speaker, to as- sert full control over the shape the projected reader takes, must make that reader over in his, the speaker's, image. And to do this he must reduce and delimit himself, emerging as a speaking ego to serve as a place for him and the projected reader to intersect.

To suggest movement toward this intersection, the language of the figurative level is more discursive and prosaic than formal and oracular. The lyrical fourth movement, for instance, though im- paled with vertical reference, is still grounded in common experience:

> Lady, whose shrine stands on the promontory,
> Pray for all those who are in ships, those
> Whose business has to do with fish, and
> Those concerned with every lawful traffic
> And those who conduct them.

> Repeat a prayer also on behalf of
> Women who have seen their sons or husbands
> Setting forth, and not returning:
> Figlia del tuo figlio,
> Queen of Heaven.
>
> Also pray for those who were in ships, and
> Ended their voyage on the sand, in the sea's lips
> Or in the dark throat which will not reject them
> Or wherever cannot reach them the sound of the sea bell's
> Perpetual angelus.

This is clearly a voice conscious of being caught in the rhythms of work and loss, subject to indifferent forces of overwhelming magnitude, modeling the correct attitude for the projected reader. As with the speaker of its closest counterpart, the fourth movement of "Burnt Norton," the speaker here prays for both himself and the reader. But the prayer here is far less enigmatic and does not presume to an authority or an understanding greater than the reader's: the speaker in this latter passage does not answer his implied question as he does in the "clematis" passage. The figurative language, though religious, is not arcane and hieratic, and the syntactic rhythms, though formal, are far more conversational than in previous lyric passages. The worlds of speaker and reader intersect, the reader's elevated to the symbolic and the speaker's lowered to the empirical. They merge in sympathy and in a sense of community.

This intimacy between speaker and reader, and their tendency to converge, demonstrate the stability—not fixity—characterizing the relationship between solitary egos reoriented toward a community that acknowledges a Logos-centered authority. That is, "Dry Salvages" works to reorient the ego at least partially by drawing it into a sense of tragic community, a shared understanding of the world as Lilliput. But my emphasis here is on a presumed commonality of understanding reached on the figurative level of language, an understanding in which both of them—and by extension, all those similarly enlightened souls—partake in a cycle of loss, uncertainty, and heroic paralysis that together form a tradition and thus define a culture:

> Where is then end of them, the fishermen sailing
> Into the wind's tail, where the fog cowers?
> We cannot think of a time that is oceanless
> Or of an ocean not littered with wastage

> Or of a future that is not liable
> Like the past, to have no destination.
>
>   We have to think of them as forever bailing,
> Setting and hauling, while the North East lowers
> Over shallow banks unchanging and erosionless
> Or drawing their money, drying sails at dockage;
> Not as making a trip that will be unpayable
> For a haul that will not bear examination.

And in figurative language that presumes a shared understanding of the reoriented ego, the speaker announces:

> For most of us, there is only the unattended
> Moment, the moment in and out of time,
> The distraction fit, lost in a shaft of sunlight,
> The wild thyme unseen, or the winter lightning
> Or the waterfall, or music heard so deeply
> That it is not heard at all, but you are the music
> While the music lasts. These are only hints and guesses
> Hints followed by guesses;

The "most of us" and what follows create a sense of intimacy within a special, elevated sphere where speaker and projected reader are equals, each knowing the same experience and knowing it equally.

But what is the link between the convergence of speaker and projected reader and its situation on the figurative level? In the context of poetic utterance, references to the empirically known— winter lightning, wild thyme, the waterfall, the shaft of sunlight— at once compress the spiritual and the physical into one figure and extend the empirical vertically. Given the speaker's habit of oracular clothing, we can think of the speaker as providing the vertical referent and the projected reader the empirical. Together they form a symbol expressing the incarnation as well as the means and direction of the reader's progress. And the speaker's continued presence as a prophetic voice, however restricted it is to hints and guesses, depends on his service as emblem or evidence of the Logos.

This service, though, is threatened by the necessary convergence of speaker and projected reader. Emerging at the end of the fifth movement as a speaking ego once more, the speaker sets forth the reasons for a sense of dignity in the solitary ego:

> And right action is freedom
> From past and future also.
> For most of us, this is the aim
> Never here to be realised;
> Who are only undefeated
> Because we have gone on trying;
> We, content at the last
> If our temporal reversion nourish
> (Not too far from the yew-tree)
> The life of significant soil.

The speaking ego here is trying to preserve the value of individual effort, but expresses its dignity in terms dependent for their meaning on communal acceptance. In other words, because the value of individual effort is contingent upon its contribution to other individuals, the speaker cannot ground his claims on any inherent value. The only authority for these claims lies with the audience. As a result, he is identifying himself with the projected reader to gain the sustenance of communal authority rather than compelling the reader to identify himself with the Logos-centered authority he mediates. In such a position, the speaker is distinct and circumscribed and vulnerable, in a way beneath and dependent upon the projected reader.

This passage shows a reversion to egocentrism, a muted attempt to celebrate the efforts of private ego, however collectivized and culturally entrenched. This celebration has been much attacked critically; Ronald Bush's assessment is one of the gentler ones as he describes Eliot's shift from "private guilt" to "collective guilt . . . through Krishna and then as an anonymous prophet. . . . [Eliot] adopts the rhetoric of public wisdom [and] has slipped into journalistic cliche" (223). But such views miss the point that the poem is not yet at rest. If this longing to find purpose in the fundamental nobility of human striving reduces us to cultural fertilizer—mere dung and death—then the ego is looking in the wrong place for sustenance. Quite apparently, his reorientation is not yet complete.

In "Little Gidding," the speaking ego does not reemerge. That is, the speaker does not impersonate a self-willed, self-directed mind. The convergence of speaker and projected reader is essentially completed: both occupy the figurative level of understanding. Mystery returns to descriptions of the Logos, but it is a mystery presumed accessible to the reader in that he is instructed in postures of prayer rather than subjected to descents, as in "Burnt Norton," or denied the sustenance of vision, as in "East Coker," or saddled with world-weary stoicism, as in "The Dry Salvages." The speaker remains oracular by strewing about symbolic references, but they reverberate in an air of spiritual prosperity missing from the other quartets, a prosperity available to both speaker and projected reader equally. The "otherworldly" quality of "Burnt Norton" is united with the "earth of 'East Coker'" (Weatherhead, 46).

In the first movement, mingled with the empirical description of "Midwinter spring" is a figurative language investing the scene with a significance beyond what the accurate recitation of the weather provides: the fire is "pentecostal," and the "soul's sap quivers." As in "The Dry Salvages," the figurative level here is not expressed as oracular dicta intended to cow and baffle the reader, but as a scene empirically witnessed yet spiritually apprehended, equally accessible to both speaker and projected reader:

> Midwinter spring is its own season
> Sempiternal though sodden towards sundown,
> Suspended in time, between pole and tropic.
> When the short day is brightest, with frost and fire,
> The brief sun flames the ice, on pond and ditches,
> In windless cold that is the heart's heat,
> Reflecting in a watery mirror
> A glare that is blindness in the early afternoon.
> And glow more intense than blaze of branch, or brazier,
> Stirs the dumb spirit; no wind, but pentecostal fire
> In the dark time of the year. Between melting and freezing
> The soul's sap quivers. There is no earth smell
> Or smell of living thing. This is the spring time
> But not in time's covenant.

The speaker's mediation provides the reader with language for grasping the experience, but proof of their participation in this experience is that the speaker does not distinguish between them: the "glare" does not "blind you" but "is blindness." The speaker maintains his edge of authority, his prior knowledge, but he does so with a sense of wonder that still situates him with the reader: "Where is the summer, the unimaginable / Zero summer?" Yet at the same time, wonder is not in itself sufficient achievement; to end the poem with this passage would celebrate the ego's apprehension of epiphany. The ego must deny itself the pleasure of pure wonder, pure apprehension, to avoid ego-centered rationalist constructs:

> You are not here to verify,
> Instruct yourself, or inform curiosity
> Or carry report. You are here to kneel
> Where prayer has been valid.

It is surely a sign of the reader's progress that he has arrived "here" at the "intersection of the timeless moment" rather than having still to "fare forward." But though his faculties are now more fully engaged, able to hear "the communication of the dead," he must continually deflate the ego, replacing consciousness of self with "indifference," a consciousness of his situation on the outer rim of the turning world. In this state, the mind is emptied of such irrelevant particularities as self, things, and person—that is, of the principal constituents of the individual mind. The ego ceases to matter to itself, directed instead, almost by default, toward the permanent and ideal revealed through "communication with the dead." The speaker's urgent refusal to particularize or locate himself dramatizes this same indifference; the mind is defined by what it desires:

> There are three conditions which often look alike
> Yet differ completely, flourish in the same hedgerow:
> Attachment to self and to things and to persons, detach-
>   ment
> From self and from things and from persons; and, growing
>   between them, indifference
> Which resembles the others as death resembles life,
> Being between two lives—unflowering, between
> The live and the dead nettle.

The effect of this apparent indifference is impersonality—more specifically, an impersonation, the ability to flit between the dead "touched by a common genius" and the living deceived by a thrush, between the voice of the Logos and the mind of the projected reader, thinking both sets of thoughts yet the source of neither. This pattern of elusion and impersonation is most baldly performed after the lyrical section in the second movement, where the speaker divides himself into speaker and reader:

> Over the asphalt where no other sound was
>   Between three districts whence the smoke arose
>   I met one walking, loitering and hurried
> As if blown towards me like the metal leaves
>   Before the urban dawn wind unresisting.

> And as I fixed upon the down-turned face
> That pointed scrutiny with which we challenge
> The first-met stranger in the waning dusk
> I caught the sudden look of some dead master
> Whom I had known, forgotten, half recalled
> Both one and many; in the brown baked features
> The eyes of a familiar compound ghost
> Both intimate and unidentifiable.
> So I assumed a double part, and cried
> And heard another's voice cry: 'What! are you here?'
> Although we were not. I was still the same,
> Knowing myself but being someone other—
> And he a face still forming; yet the words sufficed
> To compel the recognition they preceded.
> And so, compliant to the common wind,
> Too strange to each other for misunderstanding,
> In concord at this intersection time
> Of meeting nowhere, no before and after,
> We trod the pavement in a dead patrol.

While insisting on an urban setting, the speaker at the same time blocks us from locating it in any specific urban setting, overturning expectation with paradox: "the recurrent end of the unending," "loitering and hurried," "intimate and unidentifiable." The landscape of the scene is internal but actual, or rather, external but imaginary, recognizable but inaccessible.[13]

The difficulty in locating the scene inside or outside the imagination testifies to its purpose. As in the descent passages of "Burnt Norton," the speaker is displacing conventional categories of thought and sensation from the projected reader, thus overriding the mind's authority to mediate reality. The scene at the uncertain hour occurs in a place we can recognize but not naturalize or know fully. It remains the speaker's world, and we remain dependent on him for an understanding of the event. Yet in contrast to the earlier, abstract passage in "Burnt Norton," here the speaker relates his own experience, not the projected reader's. While the incantatory abstractions of "Burnt Norton" strip the projected reader of selfhood ("Desiccation of the world of sense, / Evacuation of the world of fancy, / Inoperancy of the world of spirit"), this latter passage from "Little Gidding," vibrating in a multiplicity of symbolic references, introduces a new kind of self, the composite identity.[14] And because these selves span the centuries, their intersection—"the sudden awareness that one is not an isolated being, but a focus for a collective simultaneity"—pulls together time and the timeless

(Ward, 275). In place of Dante and Virgil are the recurring roles of speaker and listener, master and disciple, roles in which the individual loses his irrelevant singularity by occupying them.[15]

The speaker enacts the composite self by doubling and even trebling his identity, dramatizing the arbitrariness of our distinctions between individuals. While the speaker claims to be assuming a "double part," he is actually assuming a triple one, staging the scene even as he performs in it, thus obscuring, partially, at least, his role as stage manager. Without abdicating the authority of that role, he situates the "dead master" as the speaker. Yet by "communicating with the dead," he stabilizes the need for mediation, providing the source of the dead master's dicta while at the same time displacing himself from that source: "Let me disclose the gifts reserved for age / To set a crown upon your lifetime's effort. . . . "

His dual impersonation creates a structure of roles that models the mind's proper stance toward time and circumstance. According to this structure, we are all versions of the same pattern. And to understand this pattern we need a sense of history: without a knowledge of one's place, of the fact that each mind is at best an echo of earlier minds, the ego can do nothing but imagine itself unique and thus ultimately without context or meaning, paralyzed in "futility and anarchy."

At the close of *Four Quartets,* the discursive and the oracular are united, crystallizing the reader's experience in symbol. The rhythm of the language is no longer meditative, but sharp, urgent, and direct:

> Why should we celebrate
> These men more than the dying?
> It is not to ring the bell backward
> Nor is it an incantation
> To summon the spectre of a Rose.
> We cannot revive old factions
> We cannot restore old policies
> Or follow an antique drum.

The reader is being lectured to, as usual, but the speaker and the projected reader are clearly of one party, of one large community that has voluntarily joined in the new understanding of the ego's place and purpose in history and of his kinship with the dead. How far the projected reader may have come by this point is suggested in one of Eliot's general claims for art's purpose:

For it is ultimately the function of art, in imposing a credible order upon ordinary reality, and thereby eliciting some perception of an order in reality, to bring us to a condition of serenity, stillness, and reconciliation; and then to leave us, as Virgil left Dante, to proceed toward a region where that guide can avail us no farther. (*On Poetry and Poets,* 94)

This quotation is especially interesting in that it unites the social and the spiritual so that "serenity" follows naturally from "order." And since "order" must have a public, cultural context to have any meaning, and "serenity" must follow from order, that pre-beatified state must require a cultural unity as well. The problem of the whole poem is underlined here: how to bring the "intense initial experience" of "Burnt Norton" into a broad cultural context to give private experience a cultural authority, extending it beyond the self to incorporate a community (Weatherhead, 36).

A close reading bears out the speaking ego's transpersonality. Who constitutes "we" is uncertain; the projected reader at this point is not a person but a culture, a community by an ethic of perpetuity for its own sake:

> These men, and those who opposed them
> And those whom they opposed
> Accept the constitution of silence
> And are folded in a single party.
> Whatever we inherit from the fortunate
> We have taken from the defeated
> What they had to leave us—a symbol:
> A symbol perfected in death.
> And all shall be well and
> All manner of thing shall be well
> By the purification of the motive
> In the ground of our beseeching.

Were the projected reader not of cultural scope here, the passage would be meaningless; the actions of the individual are irrelevant. The ego exists as defined by his culture, and so to reorient one is to reorient the other. The poem culminates in the advent of this new projected reader, for it has been the speaker's project throughout to subvert the ego, to reintegrate it in a communal identity.

Here at the end of "Little Gidding" the speaker's exhortations are more acceptable, too, because the distinctions between "I" and "you" are gone. According to the terms the speaker has established, he can speak as the projected culture for the projected culture because he is never clearly circumscribed as an individual. An even stronger basis for his vatic position is that he has brought with him the projected reader, who is disoriented in "Burnt Norton" and "East Coker," and then reoriented in "The Dry Salvages" and "Little Gidding," elevated to the speaker's level of understanding though not to his oracular stature. Our implied unity with the speaker therefore demands that we either accept the shared, coherent reality as he has outlined it or do without one entirely. The speaker controls the terms of discourse, so no alternatives beyond "daunsinge at twilight" emerge.

The lines quoted above provide an illuminating inversion of the inheritance passage in "The Tower." Unlike the Yeatsian speaker, in *Four Quartets* the archetypal poet does not take tradition into himself. Rather, tradition takes poets into tradition: "the past experience revived in the meaning / Is not the experience of one life only / But of many generations." For Eliot, it is not poets who sustain tradition, but tradition that sustains poets. Inevitably, art and the creative faculty that generates it are relevant only to the extent that they can shift the mind away from itself and toward the vortical, originating harmony of the Logos. Poetry and poets are to be synchronic, barren of idiosyncracies that might fix a word in time or place. Words cannot be seen to originate in an individual mind:

> And every phrase
> And sentence that is right (where every word is at home,
> Taking its place to support the others,
> The word neither diffident nor ostentatious,
> An easy commerce of the old and new,
> The common word exact without vulgarity,
> The formal word precise but not pedantic,
> The complete consort dancing together)
> Every phrase and every sentence is an end and a
> beginning,
> Every poem an epitaph.

For Eliot, the aesthetically and spiritually correct use of language is one displaying the relationship between the mind and its context, the world generated by the Logos in its own image. That world is euphonious, harmonious, and synchronic, every word expressing the Word, every ego revealing the Logos. David Ward's analysis of the stated purpose, "To purify the dialect of the tribe," is very telling here. To "purify" is to refresh the language of humans continually, as poets must do; but to do it in such a way that language is brought more closely into contact with these resilient assumptions . . . which control our behaviour in ways so subtle that we cannot always determine them. (280)

We cannot control our behavior, our thinking, because it is language that mediates our basic assumptions about purpose and identity. If we exist only in terms of the Logos, our highest goal can only be to know those terms, not seek to challenge them.

At the end of *Four Quartets,* where is the reader left and in what shape? Assured that "we shall not cease from exploration," the speaker and projected reader are brought to a condition of static continuity: "And the end of all our exploring / Will be to arrive where we started / And know the place for the first time." But this is a peculiar place to occupy. Knowing what lies ahead, linearity having been exposed as falsehood, "we" have already arrived at what lies ahead.[16] Yet at the same time, on the authority of Julian of Norwich, we cannot be well until some future point:

> And all shall be well and
> All manner of thing shall be well
> When the tongues of flame are in-folded
> Into the crowned knot of fire
> And the fire and the rose are one.

The fire and the rose are not one at the moment of utterance and audience.

In his work on this particular problem, William Spanos finds two mutually exclusive tendencies at work: "re-collection" and "repetition." For Spanos, to re-collect is to create a spatialized fictional account of experience, a series of events made synchronic and therefore accessible:

> . . . temporality, as difference, is ontologically prior to Being as Identity and thus a re-collective understanding, in wilfully attempting to reify or spatialize time from the backward perspective of the privileged 'wisdom' of tradition inevitably falsifies being.

The poem as a whole, Spanos says, defies the coercion of re-collection with the more liberating "repetition," which is "retrieving or repeating beginnings in the sense of remembering in and for the present . . . the open ended or historicity of being. . . ." (549).

Though I think Spanos sees very clearly the end problem of Being versus Becoming, he ignores the fact of the reader's growth and change—the poem does not circle, but spirals—and he dismisses the very possibility of Logos-centered authority. That is, he does not acknowledge the poem's premise, that by definition the Logos is generative. Not seeing the premise, he cannot see where the poem is trying to take him. Clearly, the ego's efforts at re-collection, at fashioning a fixed pattern as a way to read experience, are failures. But they fail not because re-collection is a misreading of reality but because the ego is inadequate to the task; the ego is not creative. The repetitive tendency Spanos identifies is therefore not a preferable, more authentic gesture but simply the best the mind can do. And even repetition, insufficient as it as, comes only after discipline, submission, and prayer. At the end of *Four Quartets,* Being, though not achieved, is not withheld, either. Immediacy and deferral, anticipation and vision, are made into simultaneous possibilities to preserve the speaker's voice and the reader's presence. The speaker suffers the same necessary failure Yeats does: as long as the speaker can speak, there can be no union. The projected reader's apparent movement is partly accounted for by the purgatorial image, the spiral of circularity and ascent, but his progress is more a reorientation, a change in kind, away from linear and thus ego-centered movement. This change loosens the ego's grip on the mind so that the Logos is "Not known, because not looked for / But heard, half heard, in the stillness / Between two waves of the sea." In this pattern, all is always now, but the "condition of complete simplicity" has still not been attained except in spasms because it costs "not less than everything," not less than consciousness itself. Consciousness knows only parts, not wholes (Ellis, 104). The projected reader can see only the route to the union of fire and rose. That union, still deferred, is actual but unavailable, more than proposition and less than reality.

In spite of this limitation, the projected reader is transpersonalized along with the speaker, redistributed beyond personal and historical boundaries, passing "Through the unknown, unremembered gate / When the last of earth left to discover / Is that which was the beginning." But the more the reader's individuality is dissolved and distributed as the speaker incorporates him into the Logos, the more inclusive the time reference and thus the less relevant the distinction between immediacy and deferral. Given the constraints of language that prevent this distinction from being completely blurred, the foregrounded display of the fire and rose symbol in the immediacy of the present tense is as far as any speaker could go toward uniting the consciousness of the projected reader, which is necessarily divided between witnessing the vision and bearing witness to the act of witnessing. Because poetry is inherently testimonial, the ego cannot dissolve into the Logos and at the same time report that dissolution.

Ronald Bush describes the resolute irresolution of the poem's end in this way: "At the most, art can create an iridescent structure of indeterminacy, whose disciplined openness, the analogue of spiritual humility, makes it available to moments of grace" (205). But there is more iridescence than humility in the fire and the rose. The moment of the ego's surrender to the Logos is actual, but not present. The speaker projects the immediacy that the fact of his mediation defers.[17]

5

Williams's Unmade World: Co-extensive Authority in *Paterson*

3

I gave away the money that you had been saving to live on for the next ten years.
The man who asked for it was shabby
and the firm March wind on the porch was so juicy and cold.

4

Last evening we went dancing and I broke your leg.
Forgive me. I was clumsy, and
I wanted you here in the wards, where I am the doctor.
—Kenneth Koch
"Variations on a Theme by William Carlos Williams"

The poetic speaker of *Paterson* escapes the pressures of both ego-centered and Logos-centered authority, the pressure on the one hand of mediating a self-generated and supreme creative ego, and on the other, of mediating the Word. He advocates and derives his voice from co-extensive authority, which is grounded on the position that neither ego nor Logos can create authentic forms that reality can inhabit. Instead, those forms must emerge from the "interpenetration" of subject and object, resulting from an act of perception by a nonspecific consciousness, an act that animates both subject and object. Thus, the poetic focus is not on one or the other but on this effort and the consequences of mutual animation.[1]

Four interrelated terms are key to my study of *Paterson:* "contact," "local," "co-extension," and "marriage." The first, "contact," refers to the mind's direct and intimate relationship with reality rather than with terms about it, defeating the ego's efforts to mediate.[2] Contact, for Williams, is the only basis for poetic authority—not only because it is the sole path toward authenticity, but because it is the only way to bring reality to a moment or an

144

object or a mind.[3] Williams is concerned not with unity but with "continuity," wanting "a renewal of 'the close tie between the poet and the upsurging (or down-surging) forms of his immediate world'" (Mazzaro, 70).[4] Contact with the "local" is what permits thing and idea to intersect, thus granting cultural authority to the art generated from it:

> 'Look at your feet and you will know what is actual and at the same time universal, that you exist, the universal in the particular. . . . It is in the universal diversity of place that the actual gets its definition and vigor and that love itself is generated. . . . [W]hen we experience an actuality, when we experience a vivid moment of passion . . . then a literature is born.' (Quoted in Mazzaro, 112)

Williams's language seems troubling at first: is it not redundant to say that we "experience an actuality"? Indeed, what else is there to experience? The premise is that the inactual, the illusory, the inauthentic, are primarily what we experience instead of the thing itself. In this way, Williams's poetry authorizes the reader's experience of the actual, as mediated by that poetry. That authority is founded on contact with the local, the intersection of the actual and the abstract, the thing and the idea. At this intersection, the mind can apprehend reality and at the same time apprehend other minds apprehending reality. Contact is thus inherently generative, and thus authoritative.

But to see how contact with the local grants poetic authority, we must examine the idea of "co-extension," which describes the poet's necessary transformation to cope with his material:

> The inevitable flux of the seeing eye toward measuring itself by the world it inhabits can only result in himself crushing humiliation unless the individual raise to some approximate co-extension with the universe. This is possible by aid of the imagination. Only through the agency of this force can a man feel himself moved largely with sympathetic pulses at work—.(*Imaginations*, 105)

Co-extension is the result of transpersonality, expressed not as a distribution but as a heightening of the ego. This passage, like most in *Imaginations,* is difficult. On first reading it seems as though Williams is pushing forward an egotistical sublime, making the mind its own measure and measuring the world according to the terms of ego-centered authority. Rather, the imagination is guided by sympathetic pulses, urgings to seek likenesses between self and object. Indeed, with what Bernard Duffey calls a "denial of transcendence," Williams is not in the least exalting the ego. Ultimately, the speaker's relationship to his material "is not only a cutting off of alternatives to presence; it is a limit upon presence itself, confining it to the poet's own presence within it" (Duffey, 215). His purpose is not imperial, but a negotiated impersonation, deriving knowledge and understanding by examining the areas of contact. Nor is it a union with or immersion in the object. Coextension, the result of transpersonality, is a nonhypothetical act of the imagination, true according to the premise that

> In the composition, the artist does exactly what every eye must do with life, fix the particular with the universality of his own personality—Taught by the largeness of his imagination to feel every form which he sees moving within himself, he must prove the truth of this by expression. (*Imaginations*, 105)

This passage points to key constructions of subject and object. First, if the objective world is composed of particulars, there is no overriding *a priori* idea giving it shape and purpose. Yet at the same time, "Williams's gathering of local detail [in *Paterson*] does not reveal the priority of things to ideas but, on the contrary, unveils the true ground of ideas as the undetermined relation of things" (Riddel, 14). But for the mind to live in such a world, the mind must determine those relations at all costs. Moreover, in this vacuum of authority, the self does not necessarily thrive or rise to greatness. The mind's "universality" brings it no closer to godhead, but depersonalizes it, detaching it from particularity and distinct selfhood. The universal mind is nonspecific. Just as "Anywhere is everywhere" (*Paterson*, 235), anyone is everyone. Nor does the subject provide the original pattern by which things are known and understood. The universal mind "fixes" the particular, holds it in place so that it can be seen and known; it does not create the object, but by articulating its contact with the mind it gives life to the object.[5]

Like all exercises of transpersonality, the specific mind becomes nonspecific in the poetic act. The difference with co-extensive authority is in the disposition of the subject, the poetic speaker, who claims priority for neither the ego nor the Logos in structuring perceptions of the objective world. Williams's speculations about the "life" of Shakespeare in *The Embodiment of Knowledge* and *Imaginations* directly address Williams's notion of the ideal poetic speaker and its source of energy, truth, and art. He makes an implicit distinction between writing that is "pure," unmediated, unself-conscious, and writing that is about something else—about Shakespeare, for instance:

> "Realism" has one inevitable catch in it: it is not susceptible to writing, to being written as a transcription of events or even facts. . . . To transcribe the real creates, by the same act, an unreality, something besides the real which is its transcription, since the writing is one thing, what it transcribes another, the writing a fiction, necessarily and always so. (*Embodiment of Knowledge,* 13)

An assembly of details about Shakespeare's life would be irrelevant, "unreal," because they would not enact the life itself. But on the other hand we have an unself-conscious purity of writing, exemplified by Shakespeare's investment of selfhood in his dramatic characters: "But to have written a hundred characters is *himself* [emphasis his], true, actual. He could not distinguish between the thinker and the doer. He could not himself, a sham, appear" (*Embodiment of Knowledge,* 14). Instead, Shakespeare "melted himself into that grossness, and colored it with his powers" (*Imaginations,* 258). For Shakespeare, Williams argues, writing is Being: "It is pure writing that can't get away from itself to be thought. Thought is not writing, to write betrays both writing and itself. So Shakespeare is disclosed fixed in a world, as actual as a tree." Williams then links the idea of pure writing with action and contact:

> Shakespeare's weakness in thought is his peculiar strength: he is not divorced by thought from a persistent actuality. . . . He stands outside the thought which encloses his work not in "thoughts" their trouble. He is not a dealer in abstractions using a play as a subterfuge, words, writing as a means. But the writing is the all and only. (*Embodiment of Knowledge,* 14)

Though there is much to unpack here, it will suffice to point out that writing not circumscribed by self-consciousness and self-regard demonstrates by definition that the poetic mind is in contact with its material. It thus has the authority and authenticity to present that reality freed of the baggage of prior and abstract discourse. Williams, a few lines before the above quotation, makes a startling remark: "—the futility of deeds, and that man is real only as imaginative speech." This remark, which he does not elaborate on, suggests that deeds in themselves are divorced from speech, and thus ironically do not act in the world. It is only through imaginative speech—contact between mind and world in a mutual infusion of being—that the inertia of divorce is broken and the mind is brought into the world: "Poetry is the one purely articulate form, more so than action which involves the mind so scantily, or to know" (*Embodiment of Knowledge,* 66). There is no life, no utterance, without contact between subject and object. Neither exist without contact. Thus, for Williams, far more than for Eliot, "each new venture / Is a new beginning, a raid on the inarticulate," except that it is not a raid at all, but a cooperative act of making. Williams has no fear of the inarticulate; he would, in fact, dismiss the term along with its negative connotations. The choice of "inarticulate" over, say, "inchoate," points to Eliot's distaste for what is un-formed—not made in acknowledgement of the Logos. What "the inarticulate" is to Eliot, "divorce" is to Williams: "a green bud fallen upon the pavement its / sweet breath suppressed" (*Paterson,* 22).

For Williams, it is not the poet's job to make, but to marry; the co-extensive speaker is not the vortex of poetic creation. In the composition process, the act of "raising" the self stirs an interplay of sympathetic energies between subject and object, transforming the self into its objective equivalent. The result neither glorifies nor annihilates the self, but regenerates it by establishing relations with its circumstances. The marriage metaphor is not accidental—marriage is life-giving, generative, providing the inaugural pattern of being: "the two partners do not become one, as in some ideal union, but they join in their separateness and therefore incorporate a third" (Riddel, 26). The mind, raised by co-extensive imagination, feels itself "moved largely with sympathetic impulses at work." The adverbial positioning makes it unclear whether the mind is moved extensively or whether it is predominantly with sympa-thetic impulses that it is moved. But in either event, the result of this contact is sympathy, as if the mind were replaying a subjective representation of the object. The poetic mind is sympathetic rather than creative, yet does not in its sympathy subordinate itself to the object. As in the typical marriage, neither has priority or author-izes the other. What does authorize, what does create, is the action of co-extensive imagination. Marriage in co-extension is an author-ity devoid of coercion or annexation of the inchoate on behalf of ego or Logos. Thus, marriage is also a rescue: the poetic speaker married by co-extensive imagination to the objective world res-cues, "redeems" both the self and object. But the key here is that for Williams, neither the imagination nor the objective world in itself provides the form of the poetic speaker's utterance.

Thus, the speaker makes no grandiose claims for himself: he is more observer than participant. This separation from the narrative action gives him a greater authority to mediate our perceptions, crafting a version of vox populae rather than vox cathedra. Carl Rapp's vigorous if unconvincing argument for Williams's Romanticism proposes that for Williams, as for Keats, the "true poet" seeks:

> the achievement of a standpoint outside the normal course of experience. Only from such a standpoint—outside of, or independent of, ordinary experience—can experience itself be contemplated as a whole. Naturally, this involves a certain renunciation of self, but the self renounced is merely the finite self. . . . In recompense for the renunciation of this ordinary self, the poet gains access to many selves, in fact to the whole range of human experience. (Rapp, 16)

Rapp's use of "ordinary experience" here is unnecessarily confusing. As both poet and doctor, Williams immersed himself in "ordinary experience," if by ordinary we mean common, unstartling. If on the other hand he means ordinary in the sense of conventional and unexamined, rote event, his statement becomes useful. The speaker has "many selves" because of his co-extensive impersonations, though those "selves" do not contain sufficient integrity to warrant the term. A more important problem is that Rapp misreads the speaker's persona when he refers to "renunciation" of self. There is no renunciation of self because the self does not compete with or subordinate itself to the objective world; instead, it seeks only to ignite the imagination by revealing that world.

My method in this chapter is to track the speaker's transpersonal movement through each book of *Paterson,* from Williams's premises to his tentative conclusions. I will thereby show what generates the speaker's co-extensive authority and how the poem supports it. The movement of *Paterson* is not so much in a pattern of linear logic but an accumulation of recurrent, related images that Williams calls "homologues." This organization is crucial both to the speaker's authority to mediate and to the core of his claim, which are interpenetrating. Because the speaker does not seem to be weighing and selecting images, but merely to observe them whirling in the mind, he is neither their source nor even their mediator. Mediation does occur, of course. The prose passages, staged as if the mind, following an association of thoughts, chanced upon them, are indeed mediated by the speaker to provide a ground for the mind's contact with Paterson's history and landscape. And where the speaker does not distinguish himself from the reader or locate himself in the poem's action, the speaker's experience is equivalent to the reader's. The speaker is dislocated, generally not the center of the events he displays. Nor, as is the case in *Four Quartets,* is the reader the center of those events. Rather, it is the events themselves that are the focus, so that the issue of the speaker's authority to mediate is not really raised, and the validity of the speaker's self-characterization is not threatened by the acceptance or rejection of his authority. For it is the growth of neither the speaker nor the reader that *Paterson* dramatizes, but the growth and progress of the representative man-city—and the modern ethos in general—toward a redemption through the imagination's contact with reality.[6] Thus, the agent of redemption is the nonspecific imagination, which purges the mind of false, preconceived forms.

However, there is yet another vocal layer above the speaker's, what I am calling the textual voice projected from the reader's interpretive act.[7] This voice is by definition not from an individual speaker. It is a voice only in the sense that it is a point of view, or the intersection of many points of view. Thus, it is the interpretive act demanded of the reader that demonstrates how language redeems: it demands the reader participate—it demands contact, a marriage of word and mind that projects a marriage of world and mind, with the poem as minister, the mediating authority that structures thought with a measure of authenticity. Art allows a

> fixation by the imagination of the external as well [as] internal means of expression the essential nature of technique or transcription. Only when this position is reached can life proper be said to begin since only then can a value be affixed to the forms and activities of which it consists. (*Imaginations,* 105–6)

It is Williams's task in *Paterson* to show that authentic values do not exist without the mediation of his art, that everyday experience is a divorce of self and object, and that the poetic imagination is equipped to marry them.

Implicit in the poem's movement are certain premises and lines of argument. Briefly, the preface's premises are that beauty "is locked in the mind past all remonstrance," that is, that everything of worth is inert, not expressed and brought into being. The second premise is that there is no *a priori* pattern, no Logos, to provide meaning to experience. As a result, we must operate inductively, beginning in the concrete world:

> To make a start,
> out of particulars
> and make them general, rolling
> up the sum, by defective means
>
> —(*Paterson,* 3)

A corollary to the second premise is that "we know nothing, pure / and simple, beyond / our own complexities." To make his next leap of logic—that meaning can be created by approximate co-extension with the universe—he presumes an essential identity between man and city, supporting this claim with images of particulars "rolling up" into a whole:

> Rolling
> up! obverse, reverse;
> the drunk the sober; the illustrious
> the gross; one. . . .
> Rolling up, rolling up heavy with
> numbers. . . .
> Rolling in, top up,
> under, thrust and recoil, a great clatter:
> lifted as air, boated multicolored, a
> wash of seas—
> from mathematics to particulars—
> divided as the dew,
> floating mists, to be rained down and
> regathered into a river that flows
> and encircles:
> shells and animalcules
> generally and so to man,
> to Paterson.
>
> (3–5)

These images of unified multiplicity, birth, and natural rhythms counteract the images of the inert and sealed in. In this argument by panorama, expressed in participial phrases and subjectless verbs, events are without apparent agency. This argument, by concluding with an account of the coming of rain, displays the overcoming of divorce as a natural and inevitable pulling together of particulars. Apparently none but the forces of nature are at work here.

Book 1 authorizes the perception of both the problem and solution: the poet as city, Paterson. As part of this identity, the poet

Paterson possesses an equivalent, non-specific anonymity that grants the poem's disclosures a broader authority:

> Paterson lies in the valley under the Passaic Falls
> its spent waters forming the outline of his back. He
> lies on his right side, head near the thunder
> of the waters filling his dreams! Eternally asleep,
> his dreams walk about the city where he persists
> incognito. Butterflies settle on his stone ear.
> Immortal he neither moves nor rouses and is seldom
> seen, though he breathes and the subtleties of his
> > machinations
> drawing their substance from the noise of the pouring
> > river
> animate a thousand automatons. Who because they
> neither know their sources nor the sills of their disappointments
> > walk outside their
> bodies aimlessly
> > for the most part,
> locked and forgot in their desires—unroused.

(6)

This opening passage presents Paterson as a sleeping giant whose mind is numbed because it has no contact with an environment to which it is integral. As a sleeping immortal—immortal because archetypal—he both contains and withdraws from the people forming the elements of his being, the extensions of his mind into the world. Paterson's inhabitants are the equivalent of the mind's co-extensive responses to the inhabitants of its own world; the mind is populated with figures extracted from experience. Thus, to be asleep, out of touch with the world around the mind, is to be out of touch with even the contents of one's own mind. Only the possibility of arousal keeps the mind from death.

To be aroused, Paterson must listen to the "spent waters" of the Falls, which currently fall on his "stone ear." The Falls form the primary symbol of Book 1, describing at different times the rush of immediate experience, language, and the confused flow of thought:

>   He
> lies on his right side, head near the thunder
> of the waters filling his dreams!
> . . .
> (What common language to unravel?
> . . combed into straight lines

from that rafter of a rock's
lip.)

. . .

Jostled as are the waters approaching
the brink, his thoughts
interlace, repel and cut under,
rise rock-thwarted and turn aside
but forever strain forward—or strike
an eddy and whirl, marked by a
leaf or curdy spume, seeming
to forget.

(6–7)

This spread of references is not evidence of confusion or inconsistency. Rather, it suggests an identity among the three, or what should be an identity; if the mind were fully engaged with its circumstances, then experience, reflection, and expression would indeed be inseparable. This kind of figural integration is the poem's principal means of overcoming divorce, the split between mind and world, idea and thing. By locating his argument in such an irrefutable presence as the Passaic Falls, the speaker establishes the fundamental authority of his approach and displaces his agency and responsibility.

But before the speaker can present any sort of apotheosis, the images forming the ground of his argument must accumulate to complicate the scene. The apparent randomness in the way the speaker presents the lyric and prose sections serves this accumulation by removing the sense of an authorial hand, thereby sparing the speaker an ironic challenge and reinforcing the view that the poem presents things as they are. But more important, this method demands a way of reading that enacts the co-extensive mind, the only mind that can marry experience. That mind works associatively, seeing and expressing the shared patterns in divergent phenomena. Those patterns emerge in the act of reading to show the means of redemption, of bringing order to experience. When seen in each other's terms, the apparently disparate take on both life and meaning by generating further understanding, further patterns that echo or map onto yet other disparate things.

In the first section of Book 1, a multitude of recurrent images creates a pattern of isolation, waste, and violence. We are given "evidence" of the divorced minds and feelings in the first letter from "Cress":

In regard to the poems I left with you; will you be so kind as to return them to me at my new address? And without bothering to comment upon them if you should find that embarrassing—for it was the human situation and not the literary one that motivated my visit. (7)

Cress's letter, in fact, exists only because there is no contact—emotional or intellectual—between her and Paterson. Likewise, the "low mountain" is not loved but suffers ignorance and rape; with "Pearls at her ankles, her monstrous hair / spangled with apple-blossoms is scattered about into the back country" (8). David Hower, the "poor shoemaker," at first saw the Notch Brook pearls as "hard substances" to be thrown away. When these "substances" are revealed to be pearls, the mussels bearing them are "gathered by the millions and destroyed often with little or no result," and an exquisite pearl "was ruined by boiling open the shell" (8–9).

Williams summarizes these events with a characterization of the Paterson persona and his role in the poem. Paterson is simultaneously hero and villain, the redeemer and the one in need of redemption. As man and city, Paterson is both the poet and the people:

> Who are these people (how complex
> the mathematic) among whom I see myself
> in the regularly ordered plateglass of
> His thoughts, glimmering before shoes and bicycles?
> They walk incommunicado, the
> equation is beyond solution, yet
> its sense is clear—that they may live
> his thought is listed in the Telephone
> Directory
>
>   —(9)

Here we see the essence of the poet's subjective animation, or "approximate co-extension with the universe": the speaker creates an identity between object and its subjective animation. The problem co-extensively displayed here is that there is no contact between objects—the people—and consequently none between analogous or related thoughts within the poetic mind. Disconnection from one's surroundings implies the mind's equivalent disconnection from its own contents. Means of connection, then, are interdependent; growth and interplay within the mind require contact with the objective world, a contact forged by approximate co-extension. And what rescues Williams and *Paterson* from the poles of Logos-centered or ego-centered authority is that neither the mind nor the objective world creates a prior structure. Rather, it is their interdependence that Williams insists upon. He presents both the problem and the solution at the same time, the speaker all the while disclaiming authorship. By making prose and poetic descriptions rub up against each other, the speaker ensures that they inform each other without exerting the pressure of a mediating voice.

Language charged with forging a relationship between idea and thing fails when the mind seeks a predetermined effect rather than an actual relation or understanding. That is, when the mind imposes a construct unauthorized by the thing itself, there is no mutual informing of mind and thing. Language fails the event, which remains unarticulated and therefore undisclosed, while the mind receives no new seed to regenerate itself with new patterns and definitions. This failure of language is first enacted in the description of the "wild and cultured life" in the Ramapos. This passage is rich with a multitude of ironies in the contrast between a nurturing beauty of place and an ugliness of circumstance. George Washington rests in the Ramapos after "the traitors' hangings." What amazes the narrator of the story of Jackson's Whites is not the brutality inflicted upon innocents but the peculiarity of the resulting mixture: "natives of Barbadoes speak with an Irish brogue." The slaves never rise above thingness, never achieving self-determined actuality, because the prose narrator makes no co-extensive effort to understand the events he describes. He makes no visceral contact with the events but mediates with prior—and thus inauthentic—sentiments, concluding with the trivializing structure of ironic contrasts. The blur of languages and deracinated cultures referred to echo the narrator's own separation from the reality his words do not express.

In contrast with Jackson's Whites, the nine African women perched on the log display a marriage of self and world, a marriage generating both a temporal and a cultural continuity. But the more important contrast for Williams's rhetorical purposes is that it is the lyric speaker rather than a prose narrator who presents the scene. Consequently, it is the lyric voice and text, representing the co-extensive imagination, that emerges as the authoritative point of view. The speaker's authority is reinforced even further by the contrast between the poetry of the African wives and the prose of Sarah Cummings. The prose narrator fails by his surrender to pietistic sentimentality, another prior form imposed on the event. His account robs the Cummings marriage of particularity; husband and wife each fills preestablished roles, without contact:

> She had been married about two months, and was blessed with a flattering prospect of no common share of Temporal felicity and usefulness

in the sphere which Providence had assigned her; but oh, how uncertain is the continuance of every earthly joy. . . . When they had enjoyed the luxury of the scene for a considerable length of time, Mr. Cummings said, "My dear, I believe it is time for us to set our face homeward"; and at the same moment, turned round in order to lead the way. He instantly heard the voice of distress, looked back and his wife was gone! (14–15)

The language without marriage to the event describes another absence of marriage, without enough proximity to the event for us even to know whether the fall was an accident or a suicide. But whether willed or unwilled, Sarah Cummings's fall was uncontrolled, a surrender rather than a willed participation.

The leaps of Sam Patch (15–17) serve as the climax of the first section because they embody a solution to the problem of divorce and the poet's role in that solution. The rush of water, which expresses the daunting ideal of unity between thought, experience, and articulating language, offers the alternatives of participation or surrender. The poet can either match the falls, rising in approximate co-extension with it, or despair, "crushed in humiliation." When "speech" does not "fail" Sam Patch, he leaps and lives, in effect enacting the falls in approximate co-extension. The effect is a "wonder," bringing a new life to Sam Patch and a new relationship with the falls. In his successful leaps, Patch neither appropriates nor is subordinated to the falls; he participates in it, sharing its force and immediacy to redefine both himself and the falls in the new, authentic relationship he creates. The falls are seen in terms of the man, and the man in terms of the falls. Sam Patch's leaps model Williams's definition of the poetic act: a Shakespearean purity of purpose uniting thought, language, and experience.

The second part of Book I meditates on the falls and attempts to reinforce the homologue that will redeem the mind from divorce. As the speaker puts forward his homologous images, he must also cope with the paradox of the unmediated voice, of making "I" simply an "eye." The speaking subject must not pull the focus onto itself as a mediating identity:

> There is no direction. Whither? I
> cannot say. I cannot say
> more than how. . . .
> Why even speak of "I," he dreams, which
> interests me almost not at all?

(18)

Williams sidesteps the problem of the idiosyncratic I by stripping it of authority, showing how it flounders when divorced from the world of particulars. The I, as the above lines suggest, is a null point, the center of only a void. And the first person singular is submerged in Paterson's dream, the speaker can remain retired from narrative presence. Consequently, when the "I" surfaces again, we cannot clearly delimit or identify it unless we read it as a dramatization of Paterson's thoughts. Bernard Duffey identifies the subject's movement as the "three acts" of *Paterson:*

> (1) uncertain awareness of the external world; (2) uncertain awareness of internal turmoil; (3) occasional resolution formed by the interaction of the two. Or, poet meets Paterson, poet recoils into self, poet enacts a discovered oneness with the city. (Duffey 74)

For Duffey, the drama of *Paterson* is the movement in and out of the self, which becomes a useful construct if we can link it to Williams's purpose: to make contact with the world and thereby overcome divorce and death.

What the speaker does move in and out of is an impersonation of the character Paterson. Where he slips out reveals the gap between effort and achievement:

> But never, in despair and anxiety,
> forget to drive wit in, in till it discover
> his thoughts, decorous and simple,
> and never forget that though his thoughts
> are decorous and simple, the despair
> and anxiety: the grace and detail of
> a dynamo—
>
> (27)

The poet's impediments, despair and anxiety, are to be overcome, not ignored, with wit as a "wedge" to penetrate the thoughts of Paterson, the poetic subject. And wit—an insight dispassionately passionate—is a condition of mind that turns outward to construct a way of seeing the world where the speaker has no role. Its authority is founded on the fact that comments on the world, not on the speaker. And armed with the interpenetrating wedge of wit, the poet can find his "despair and anxiety" have taken on—through the eyes of wit—the "grace and detail of a dynamo," the beauty, symmetry, and impersonality of a machine. The speaker's emergence from his subject does not comment on him or solidify his identity in any way. Rather, the emergence illustrates that the poet's proper move toward his subject is neither absorption by an ego nor annexation by the Logos, but penetration by the co-extensive mind.

With the issue of the speaking "I" thus shouldered aside, the speaker can concentrate on reinforcing his dual claims that mind and world are divorced and that poetry is the only redemptive means available. He is faced with "a mass of detail / to interrelate on a new ground, difficultly," from which he must form "an assonance, a homologue / triple piled / pulling the disparate together to clarify / and compress" (20). Such images of vital unripeness as the "bud forever green, / tight-curled, upon the pavement" and the "Two halfgrown girls hailing hallowed Easter" bring forth not only a series of divorce homologues but the tragedy of thwarted possibilities, the "unfledged desire, irresponsible, green, / colder to the hand than stone." Presenting the problem of divorce in these homologous images enacts the solution but does not reveal how the solution can come about. To do so, the speaker collects homologous images of contact between mind and world:

> The theme
> is as it may prove: asleep, unrecognized—
> all of a piece, alone
> in a wind that does not move the others—
> in that way: a way to spend
> a Sunday afternoon while the green bush shakes. . . .
> On the embankment a short,
> compact cone (juniper)
> that trembles frantically
> in the indifferent gale: male—stands
> rooted there.
>
> (20)

But the action of the imagination on the mind is continuously problematic: "Stale as a whale's breath: breath!" Breath and gale (inspiration) are also homologues, suggesting that language can be caught too easily in recycled wind, the gross stale breath of one's own received notions or preconceptions never generated from contact with particulars. Such a wind cannot shake the mind's green bush but merely fouls the attempts. The wind must make contact, circulate, a movement central to the third part of the book.

But let us dwell for a moment on the image of the shaking bush, which perfectly expresses the necessity for contact between imagination and reality, and the untenability of life without it. With no bush to shake, there is no evidence of the wind's existence, and without the wind, the bush cannot display the fullness of its nature, its flexibility, and ability to change shape, to be altered by the imagination. In the context of this emblem, the speaker's absence—even as a mediator—is clear; the interplay between wind and bush is a natural one, with no prior cause beyond the forces of nature. Mind and world interact according to an agenda that neither one originates or determines.

Like its predecessor, the third part of Book 1 begins with the speaker confessing his undoing. But now he is distributed evenly into three persons: the second, the first, and the third:

> How strange you are, you idiot!
> So you think because the rose
> is red that you shall have the mastery?
>
> . . . .
> But, creature of the weather, I
> don't want to go any faster than
> I have to go to win.
> > Music it for yourself.
> He picked a hairpin from the floor
> and stuck it in his ear, probing
> around inside.
>
> > > > (30)

Divided this way, the speaker has no essential selfhood. He assaults his own enterprise, responds to that assault, and then sinks once more into the person of Paterson to probe inwardly, searching for a "heroic dawn of desire" that "is denied to his thoughts." The problem is self-consciousness, the self divided against itself, divorced from itself and thus from the world, with no object for his thoughts and thus no thoughts. This same inertia, another sign of divorce, is felt throughout the third part in the numerous examples of the withheld, the undispersed, the packed seed. The doctor absent-mindedly withholds his medical attentions while scraping the label off of a mayonnaise jar. The cornucopian mansion is sealed up "in time of general privation" (33). The "non-purveyors" of knowledge in universities create "an impossible moat between the high / and the low where / the life once flourished" (34). Eels are plundered and horded by the "black crowd," and the ones "who prepared the nets were not the ones who got the most fish" (35). With this plunder, waste, and hoarding of riches comes ruin. On the one side is the unredeemed world of "Tenement windows," and on the other, its "complement exact," the untouched mind in abstract removal: "a mathematic calm, controlled," with "the same blank and staring eyes" (38).

Book 1 ends with a modest moment of equilibrium between the still unmarried mind and reality:

> Plaster saints, glass jewels
> and those apt paper flowers, bafflingly
> complex—have here
> their forthright beauty, beside:
> Things, things unmentionable,
> the sink with the waste farina in it and
> lumps of rancid meat, milk-bottle-tops: have
> here a tranquility and loveliness
> Have here (in his thoughts)
> a complement tranquil and chaste.
>
> (38–39)

There is a certain measure of heroism in contriving a sustaining complement to the ubiquitously ugly, but that aesthetic heroism is ultimately impotent. That complement is "'locked in the mind past all remonstrance,'" never made manifest—unlike the too-visible waste farina—but merely referred to in his surrender to explicit mediation. This complement, however tranquil and chaste, cannot redeem the world but only provide a temporary retreat from it. Thought remains sealed up, living as mere potential,

> snail-like, upon the wet rocks
> hidden from sun and sight—
>   hedged in by the pouring torrent—
> and has its birth and death there
> in that moist chamber, shut from
> the world—and unknown to the world,
> cloaks itself in mystery—
>
> (39)

The only redemptive element here is in thought's possibilities, which are parodied; Paterson's shifting of change in his pocket is homologous to a loud but harmless earthquake, its harmlessness further emphasizing the mind's inertness and failure to marry. The speaker vanishes in the attempt to justify his complementive method by drawing on the authority of tradition, using the Symonds quotation that describes "the harmony which subsists between crabbed verses and the distorted subjects with which they dealt" (40). Still, the best that can be achieved is an imitative "harmony" between verse and world, imagination and reality. But imitation cannot heal divorce.

Book 1 describes Williams's view of the wasting spiritual disease of the times, divorce and its economic counterpart, nondistribution. Though focused in Paterson as a sense of place, the book ranges through history, its many voices expressing place and time rather than the contents of a particular consciousness. As a next step, Book 2 sets forth the poet's mission to bring coherence and purpose to a chaotic and disjointed world, and it measures his chances of success by dramatizing the poet's situation between the divorced realms of mind and object. This place is the intersection of multiple points of view in a non-specific consciousness, that is, in the "single" consciousness of the man/city/poet Paterson. Using the Klaus Ehrens passages and the images of music as an ordering principle, the speaker attempts a homological alliance between the forces of poetry and those of nature. As Book 2 begins, the giant Paterson gives a primitive but assured self-assessment:

> Outside
>   outside myself
>   there is a world,
>   he rumbled, subject to my incursions.
>
>   (43)

This is the voice of a god-poet venturing forth who "instructs his thoughts" on the park, the "female to the city." This mission, relentlessly phallic, proves ego-centered and a failure; reality submits to no single mind, whether it be Klaus Ehrens's or Alexander Hamilton's. The book ends with a descent into the pinched, paralyzed mind of Cress, the would-be poet so reduced by self-consciousness that even her anger is muted. In the shrinking from reality that Cress represents, the poet loses his place at the subjectless intersection of mind and world that his stroll through the park had briefly provided. At the end of Book 2, the lines of inner and outer experience are thrown back into parallel: the speaker is driven inward, descending to recover the sustenance of an internal unity and to reexamine the inventing powers of the self. In the first part of Book 2, the speaker's presence is exquisitely problematic. The continuous "Walking" gives the speaker a subjectless presence and expresses the poet's shadowy relationship to the empirical world.[8] It draws a thin line of mediation around the events in the park, inserting the man/city/poet Paterson in the poem as a character, a tentative center, yet still providing the appearance of immediacy. Positioned this way, the subjectless presence of the speaker is situated as a reader. In turn, the reader is placed in such proximity that the act of reading enacts the speaker's experience. In the context of reading, then, Williams's dicta about divorce are dislocated from any idiosyncratic source and become part of the reader's own inner landscape. Williams thereby avoids what his speaker and poet figures do not—the lapse into ego-centered vision—and justifies his poetics of co-extension. His method of identifying the problem of divorce enacts the solution.

Still, the very need for transpersonal investigation, for the supposed redemption by phallic incursions, suggests an inner uncertainty about how much the poet should unself himself in transpersonality and how much of the ego must remain in order to sustain imaginative activity. Three areas reveal this tension most clearly: the characterization of the poet as phallus, the passage on "invention," and the power of music (poetry) to focus and centralize activity—to describe and thus to mediate human purpose.

The phallic images of the poet in the first part of Book 2 are ubiquitous: Paterson's "incursions," the observation tower, the man combing the "collie bitch" (53), Paterson's ascent with the "ground dry," roots "writhing upon the surface" (44). These images have the positive connotation of procreative power and reciprocity with the reality it invades, but they are gestures of an effort that fails because it insists on ego-centered authority. It thrusts the initiative upon the poet, so that the resulting contact between mind and world is on his terms, thus calling into question the authenticity and the authority of his expression.

The pressure to exert ego-centered authority is also apparent in non-phallic images, as shown in the following contrast between different episodes of contact. First, after "hard going" through "stubble and matted bramble," simply experiencing his reality without ordering it, the poet is rewarded with "a flight of empurpled wings," the intersection of reality with imaginative "ardor" (47)—contact.[9] The prose description of the midnight encounter with the mink (46) covers the same ground, but points to an entirely different response: instead of delighted curiosity, the two policemen try, most ineffectively, to trap and kill the mink as a way of making it accessible.

Phallic, ego-centered efforts are more subdued in Williams's core polemic:

> Without invention nothing is well spaced,
> unless the mind change, unless
> the stars are new measured, according
> to their relative positions, the
> line will not change, the necessity
> will not matriculate: unless there is
> a new mind there cannot be a new
> line, the old will go on
> repeating itself with recurring
> deadliness . . .

(50)

Because there is no explicit statement of agency here, this passage implies only that the poet is the primary source of measurement, the legislator of reality. The focus is on the desperate need for poetry, and the consequences of its success or failure. The issue of agency does not arise overtly because the passage discusses the result, not the process of contact. Though "invention" is the action of the mind on its surroundings, it acts under the authority of the new measure, a relationship between mind and thing based upon their "relative positions," on the circumstances of their contact rather than on either a fixed Logos or a self-promoting, self-creating ego.

With invention as the primary method, the speaker pursues a "measure" that will order the world of the park. This measure is expressed in his efforts to identify the various sounds and voices as a species of music. After much aimless walking ("Mount. Why not?"), the speaker hears

>   Voices!
>   multiple and inarticulate   .   voices
> clattering loudly to the sun, to
> the clouds. Voices!
> assaulting the air gaily from all sides.
>
> —among which the ear strains to catch
> the movement of one voice among the rest
> —a reed-like voice
>   of peculiar accent

(54)

Though the speaker, like the reader, is not a participant but an observer and interpreter, he searches for a center, a source of clarity. And true to the principles of invention, the ordering "reed-like voice" is intrinsic rather than extrinsic to the reality that must be re-composed. Any resulting order is therefore based upon the voice's position "relative" to the other voices. This democratic relativity is short-lived, however, as the pressure of the poetic mind makes itself felt. The voice, as manipulated by the speaker, is now more prophetic than Orphic, and begins to annex the other senses:

> Stand at the rampart (use a metronome
> if your ear is deficient, one made in Hungary
> if you prefer)
> and look away north by east . . .
> —and the imagination soars, as a voice
> beckons, a thundrous voice, endless
> —as sleep: the voice
> that has ineluctably called them—
> > > that unmoving roar!
>
> . . .
> —his voice, one among many (unheard)
> moving under all.
> > > The mountain quivers.
> Time! Count! Sever and mark time!
> > > > (55–56)

Much like the observation tower that "stands up prominently / from its pubic grove" (53), this voice, homologous to the Falls in Book 1, is explicitly declared the primary mediating authority, ordering perceptions and commanding an audience. The voice, or more properly, the music informing it, manifests itself more concretely in its effects on certain picnickers:

> > > but Mary
> is up!
> > > Come on! Wassa ma'? You got
> broken leg?
> . . .
> > —lifts one arm holding the cymbals
> of her thoughts, cocks her old head
> and dances! raising her skirts:
> > > La la la la!
> > > > (57)

The music, the aural presence in the landscape and the blood, is equated with generative sexual principles, and more important, sets the terms of condemnation or praise by which the other picnickers are to be judged. And because Williams is concretely generic in his descriptions of the picnickers, any individual's failure

to join the galvanic unity of musical and sexual energies condemns
the class or culture or ethos that produced him. The first part of
Book 2 ends with the homologous union of the Falls, the phallus,
the voice, and the music's call to unity, to enact, in essence, the
poetics that have brought these images together:

                                              There where
        the movement throbs openly
        and you can hear the Evangelist shouting!
                                       —moving nearer
        she—lean as a goat—leans
        her lean belly to the man's backside
        toying with the clips of his
        suspenders   .
        to which he adds his useless voice:
        until there moves in his sleep
        a music that is whole, unequivocal . . .
        Sees, alive (asleep)
                    —the fall's roar entering
        his sleep (to be fulfilled)

                                          reborn
        in his sleep—scattered over the mountain
        severally   .
                —by which he woos her, severally.

        And the amnesic crowd (the scattered),
        called about—strains
        to catch the movement of one voice
                                                    (59–60)

At a call to unity from a single voice, the picnickers are pulled
from their inertia and disorder into the unity of a curious crowd in
a "cramped arena . . . at the base of the observation tower" (63).
It is, indeed, through the very singularity of the voice that the
appeal to order is felt, promising a redemption, or at least "pleasure," to those "poor souls" with "nothing else in the world . . ."
(62). The singular voice—identified with the observation tower, the
point of both reference and vision—is homologous to a phallic
pressure that the ego exerts to situate itself in the place from which
the world is to be "measured." This place is not relative, but centralized: Ehrens's voice is not heard in the context of other ambient
voices but itself creates the context by which we are to know and
judge the other voices.
    Still, the speaker works both to justify and to mask the fact that
Ehrens's authority is ego-centered. The ground he has to penetrate

is rocky and hard, desperately in need of redemption: "roots, for the most part, writhing / upon the surface" (44). His age and apparent surrender to the larger, ambient will guiding him suggest that as a prophet, he is only the voice of Another greater than he. Also, the contrast with Hamilton's messianic economics makes Ehrens's efforts seem full of charity, centered not in personal vision but in the welfare of the people. However, though Ehrens's vision is on the surface the antithesis of Hamilton's, in that Ehrens wants to give money generally while Hamilton sought to collect it through general taxation, they present a single pair of Janus faces. Both espouse centralized authority and control—Hamilton through the Federal Reserve System and Ehrens by the imposition of his own personal vision upon the lives of his audience. Neither plan can be integrated with either the phenomenal world or their own selves as they exist "relative" to the world the two occupy. Hamilton's plan, according to Williams, was to use tax money to fund private enterprise, thus drawing off money from the many to put it in the hands of a few. This plan represents withdrawal rather than penetration. On the other hand, Ehrens's gestures are well intentioned, but futile, "as of scattering money to the winds" (72), rooting nowhere. If Hamilton's plan was deliberate and villainous, Ehrens drowns in a wholly personal vision of unity.

It is mildly heretical, admittedly, to claim that Williams has somehow criticized the phallic presence, since his poetics have always employed such metaphors. Nonetheless, given that the phallic principle is utterly at odds with the stated principle of invention, which insists on relative positions serving as the shape of continually changing order, and given that Ehrens is ultimately impotent, the failure of the ego-centered phallus is inevitable. In *The Visual Text of William Carlos Williams,* Henri Sayre takes a similar view, but sees the failure of what I am calling the ego-centered, phallic principle as a failure from Williams's imperfect design. In Sayre's conception, "the initial project of the poem is ameliorative and idealistic. It would end opposition through synthesis . . . [and] make a world which is essentially heterogeneous into one that is homogeneous" (93). But by "the end of his career," Sayre explains in his introduction, "Williams had realized the futility of trying to achieve any synthesis" of mind and world (5). Sayre is correct that the poetic speaker/artificer—for him, Williams—struggles to reform heterogeneous reality into homogeneous art. However, it is the deliberate structure of the poem itself that disrupts the move toward homogeneity, dispersing ego-centered authority into the textual voice and the authority of "co-extensive approximation." The poem's authority and necessary dynamism depend on Ehrens's failure. Without the resulting descent, without the acknowledgement that "the world stays" in the face of any contrivance of the imagination, *Paterson* cannot track the poetic adventure with the authenticity that poetic authority requires. The ego-centered push toward homogeneity is ultimately shown as the imagination's unnatural withdrawal from the phenomenal world:

> The bird, the eagle, made himself
> small—to creep into the hinged egg
> until therein he disappeared, all
> but one leg upon which a claw opened
> and closed wretchedly gripping
> the air, and would not—for all
> the effort of the struggle, remain
> inside

(73)

Yet as the second part ends, there is a reactive movement inward, from an external to an internal landscape. This movement is the self-conscious collapse of ego-centered authority into memory, the only place where images can be more or less under his control. In an apostrophe to the Beautiful Thing, the speaker narrows the arena of consciousness to the two of them, lover and beloved, to examine his relationship with the clarifying artistic impulse:

> Why should I move from this place
> where I was born? knowing
> how futile would be the search
> for you in the multiplicity
> of your debacle. The world spreads
> for me like a flower opening—and
> will close for me as might a rose—
>
> wither and fall to the ground
> and rot and be drawn up
> into a flower again. But you
> never wither—but blossom
> all about me. In that I forget
> myself perpetually—in your
> composition and decomposition
> I find my .   .
>
>   despair!

(75)

In this passage the speaker reveals the incompatibility between external reality and the internal apprehension of the Beautiful Thing, which as the moment of illuminating contact between reality and imagination, is immediately lost in the flood of phenomena. It is the irritation of this incompatibility that urges the mind to attempt exertions of ego-centered authority. The phenomenal world, whose rhythms of growth and decay are relentlessly constant and multitudinous, are evidence of a chaotic and perpetually ephemeral enormity whose ultimate form the mind cannot know and from which the mind therefore cannot draw authorizing self-knowledge. But the Beautiful Thing, which permits intermittent understandings of form in the external world, does provide the sustenance of authority because it instructs the mind in its own nature. However, the intermittence of the Beautiful Thing amplifies the failed promise of the phenomenal world; in the constant withholding of sustenance, the speaker finds "despair," which is both a fate and a prize. Despair, which drives the descent, is ultimately necessary and possibly restorative.

The center of Book 2's third section is the descent into "memory," a removal to a place where imaginative resources can be reassembled, and contact with the self re-established. To understand who or what "descends," and why descent is necessary to Williams's quest for co-extensive authority, we must first see how descent is effected. Because the speaker is a nonspecific presence, the descent is generic, expressed in homologous images and voices to ensure the reader's interpretive participation and thus to dislocate the descent from any singular ego:

>   Look for the null
>   defeats it all
>
> . . .
> The descent beckons
>   as the ascent beckoned
>   Memory is a kind
> of accomplishment
>   a sort of renewal
>
>   (77)
>
> . . .
>   Bow, wow! A
>   departing car scatters gravel as it
>   picks up speed
>
>   (79)
>
> . . .
> Her belly   .   her belly is like a white cloud   .   a
> white cloud at evening   .   before the shuddering night!
>
>   (85)

The sex/night/descent homologues bring into focus the tension in Williams's feelings about descent, suggesting an obscurity, excitement, and confusion that come close to overwhelming the promise of renewed generative power. This descent seems to bring no new vision but instead blurs the boundaries between self and Other. Descent offers no new vision, of course, because it is a shrinking from contact with the outside world to recover the self.

But descent in *Paterson* is a rhetorical act as well as an act of mind. The reader is made to descend, too, from the broad scope of multiple homologues into the individual mind of Cress, from mathematics to particulars. The result enacts the virtuous necessity of descent in the midst of its admitted neurosis. Cress's prose brings her in contact with the reader—giving her a life and a sense of reality she did not have before and would not have had without this "Shakespearean" portrayal. But more important, the descent enacted in her letter grants her a renewed contact with herself as well. Given context and meaning by Williams's terms of descent, that "Memory is a kind / of accomplishment / a sort of renewal," Cress's letter, derived as a literary entity, authorizes her new understanding of herself and her halting moves toward restoration. After much invective, when the "anger and the indignation" has helped "pierce through the rough ice" of blocked creative faculties so that she can begin "thinking and feeling in terms of poetry again" (89), we can see her letter—in its literary context as a passage in *Paterson*—as a purgative descent into a sealed, bilious consciousness. Her contact with her own submerged consciousness redeems her mind and spirit because it returns her voice, and with it the ability to shape perceptions of herself and her world. She is released momentarily from her inertia, with a reawakened desire to struggle and live.

The inclusion of her letter also demonstrates why descent into the self permits ascent into the world: it raises the mind from its reduction to the level of mere circumstance by reintroducing the self to its faculties of imagination and reflection. But neither position nor movement, ascent into circumstance nor descent into the self, is secure. Consciousness, and thus existence, depends on continuous movement between self and Other, remaining at neither pole very long, for continuous proximity to either one prevents contact. The poetic mind too immersed in its circumstances cannot distinguish itself from them and is thus denied the faculty of imagination and the reward of self-knowledge. Similarly, the poetic mind submerged in itself, sunken in continuous descent, can also know neither itself nor the world. In Williams's poetic, that circulating, alternating contact depends on a homologous relationship between mind and world, a relationship that must periodically snap under the weight of self-consciousness so that perception—and thus knowledge—can always be made new. Circulation demands that mental structures continually break up, that words "slip, slide, perish, / Decay with imprecision"; fixity is atrophy.

This poetic of descent places an enormous burden on the poet, who, to maintain authenticity and credibility, must enact the circulatory process without seeming its source. At the same time, he must ensure that this process is controlled, that it display the structure it enacts. Moreover, this movement of consciousness between mind and world must seem to be a primary fact of existence, based upon their relative interaction rather than on either a prior design or one springing from the imagination. It is this demand that distinguishes Williams's poetry from the poetry of Logos- or ego-centered verse. Williams accomplishes this relative interaction through what I have called the textual voice, whose authority is based on the composition of homologous particulars from which meaning is synthetically abstracted by the reader. Because our self-consciousness as readers makes us aware of our own role in authorizing the poem's view of the world, the question of meaning's authorship becomes too problematic for that role to be assigned to the speaker.

The action of the reader's mind on the textual voice becomes clearer from the situation of Cress's letter in Book 2. The descent from the world into the self is an act specifically hers but generically the poem's. Her descent is only perceived as such in its homologous context as the central emblem of descent in the midst of a number of descent images. Treated as a poetic figure, she can—almost—be abstracted into a set of desires and circumstances that lead to descent. Her intensely personal expression thus ironically becomes generic, and the homologous arrangement of descent imagery projects a textual voice that authorizes the descent interpretion. I say that she can "almost" be abstracted into the generic pattern of the textual voice because, as many critics have complained, Cress takes over Book 2.[10] However, the complaint's accuracy does not necessarily grant it relevance. Cress's presence, however overwhelming, is entirely in keeping with Williams's plan for *Paterson*. To see more fully how her letter works in the poem, we must first examine the challenge she poses to both Williams and *Paterson*. Her charge, like Edward Dahlberg's in Book 1, is that Williams sees literature "as something disconnected from life" (86). The letter's inclusion, of course, seems to substantiate this charge fully: Cress is transformed from a person into a motif. Yet if we both accept this charge as valid and simultaneously claim that her letter throws Book 2 and perhaps the entire poem off balance, we are in effect saying that Cress's life overwhelms Williams's art. He gives her Shakespearean presence (in Williams's sense of the word) apart from the apparent formal demands of the poem; her character seems then to exist for its own sake, not joining the swirl of particulars described in the poem's preface but "asserting itself as itself" (Sayre, 101). Williams's inclusion of the letter gives her a life that she did not have before, creating in the minds of the readers a vision essentially equivalent in fullness and clarity to the vision of Marcia Nardi created in the minds of those, like Williams, who actually knew her. This essential equivalence merges or blurs art and life, rendering both Cress's and the critics' accusations irrelevant.

More important than the deflection of criticism, however, is that the great weight of Cress's letter furthers rather than obstructs Williams's design. Her principal complaint, that she is too fettered by her circumstances to write, provides a set of particulars to serve as evidence of the blockage that drives the poet from the park. Cress's neurotic failures are thus identified both with the poet's efforts to have language redeem the world and with the cultural sins creating the need for the redemptive poet. Furthermore, having released such a powerful figure as Cress into the poem, Williams deflects the focus from the authorial presence of the poet in the park, consequently enhancing the authority of that presence by removing from it any elements of idiosyncrasy or neurosis. Williams makes Cress the embodiment of poetic error and failure while at the same time using her as evidence for his cultural posture. Paradoxically, to divide the focus between the shadowy authorial presence and the disordered Cress is ultimately to demand of the reader an interpretive effort that will synthesize the two. From that implicit demand for synthesis the textual voice emerges.[11] Yet there is no real synthesis, no resolution. The confusion and neurosis that prevails at the end of Cress's letter deny closure, showing that descent is never a place to stop but a preparation for reencountering the world.

Book 3 shows a reduced poet attempting to recover and maintain a textual authority for the poem by transpersonalizing his poetic struggle with tradition into a quarrel of destructive elemental forces—wind, fire, and flood—and by using historical episodes of the Indians' mistreatment by murderous Europeans as homologues for the damage the European literary tradition has done to American poetry. According to Williams's staging of this struggle, tradition's mediation of art and reality deadens the mind, preventing the emergence of the Beautiful Thing, the elusive, epiphanic moment of contact between the creative mind and chaotic reality.[12] After describing tradition's destruction, the speaker seeks to replace it by a merging of language and unmediated consciousness to create a coextensive moment that replicates apprehension of the Beautiful Thing.

We must first look closely at how the speaker characterizes the literary tradition that provokes his enmity. Using first the figure of the library, he immediately undermines that image's nurturing associations:

                                 A cool of books

will sometimes lead the mind to libraries
of a hot afternoon, if books can be found
cool to the sense to lead the mind away.

For there is a wind or ghost of a wind
in all books echoing the life
there, a high wind that fills the tubes
of the ear until we think we hear a wind,
actual .

                        to lead the mind away.
Drawn from the streets we break off
our minds' seclusion and are taken up by
the books' winds, seeking, seeking
down the wind
until we are unaware which is the wind and
which the wind's power over us
                    to lead the mind away.

                                    (95–96)

This passage sets up what ought to be a positive view of literary tradition; the library is initially a refuge from the pressures of reality, the pressures that were so debilitating in Book 2. Yet what the library actually offers is distraction, encouraging an anti-creative passivity, providing only echoes and ghosts of a vanished vitality. The library image is particularly disarming, however, because after the speaker rises from the descent of Book 2, entering the new world naked, ungrounded, and undefined, a refuge seems the logical place to go, and passivity in the face of unapprehensible experi-

ence the logical attitude to assume. But it is Williams's very point to insist that the ungrounded mind need not and should not look to tradition to shape an identity, cultural or personal, for those "few" who do "go / to the Coast without gain" (11). Also, tradition is not only no help to the bewildered consciousness; it is dangerous. Williams explicitly—and thus unconvincingly—assails the library as a place of "stagnation and death," but a more damaging attack comes from the image of traditional authors as moths:

> And as his mind fades, joining the others, he
> seeks to bring it back—but it
> eludes him, flutters again and flies off and
> again away

(101)

The implicit claim of this image is that the mind belongs to either the self or to tradition, but not to both. The mind's alternatives to the library, which seals it off from contact with the world, are stagnation on the one hand and rebellious conflagration on the other.[13] The great Paterson fire, used as a figure for the transmogrifying heat of poetic effort, begins in another closed-in space:

> It started in the car barns of the street railway company, in the paint shop. The men had been working all day refinishing old cars with the doors and windows kept closed because of the weather which was very cold. There was paint and especially varnish being used freely on all sides. Heaps of paint soaked rags had been thrown into the corners. One of the cars took fire in the night. (115)

Even more effectively than the library, this homologue for the poet's mind confined by tradition emphasizes the danger of being sealed off from the phenomenal world. Without an authentic context outside itself, the mind destroys its own objects.

When tradition lays claim to poets, they are made passive and impotent, unable to move to new moments of understanding, clarity, and grace. There is an inevitable, explosive clash between the mind's expectations, which are grounded in the received literary tradition, and the authentic presence of the object requiring an artistic response. In his initial encounter with the Beautiful Thing, the speaker cloaks her in the trappings of romance; the purpose of the encounter is to possess her, to make her over to suit his image of the ideal. He fails in this attempt, and the blame is laid at the feet of a literary tradition that prevented him from seeing her clearly from the beginning:

> Haunted by your beauty (I said),
> exalted and not easily to be attained, the
> whole scene is haunted:
> > Take off your clothes,
>
> (I said) . . .
> (Then, my anger rising) TAKE OFF YOUR
> CLOTHES! I didn't ask you
> to take off your skin . I said your
> clothes, your clothes. You smell
> like a whore. I ask you to bathe in my
> opinions, the astonishing virtue of your
> lost body (I said) .
> > —that you might
>
> send me hurtling to the moon
>
> > (104–5)

Williams is perhaps too explicit in his staging of this encounter—the baldness of his metaphors weakens their impact—but he manages to make the passage work by venting irony against the speaker and still finding tradition at fault for that failure. The poem's textual voice comments with implicit irony on his fury and disappointment. The speaker's stated desires in this passage conflict with the poetics of co-extensive authority trumpeted throughout *Paterson,* that art must be forged in the mind's co-extensive approximation of the object or event to be expressed. And given the passage's context, the literary tradition, expressed in "prejudices," is the enemy of creativity, and by extension, of life, because it insists on freezing the epiphanic moment into a predetermined form. The form's artifice and immobilization make it untrue to the moment it tries to preserve.

Since the literary tradition threatens to annihilate the imagination by either overwhelming or stifling it, the poet's only recourse is to clear consciousness of all but mind and thing, seeking the epiphanic moment of co-extensive approximation in their simultaneous and mutual remaking, to "separate the stain of sense from the inert mass." This moment of contact, which extracts what is vital and essential from consciousness of the world, is expressed sexually, removing the agency of creation from either a Logos-centered or ego-centered source.[14] And neither is the mind the source of the Beautiful Thing, first defined in Book 3 as "—a dark flame / a wind, a flood—counter to all staleness" (100). The Beautiful Thing is released at the moment of contact that allows the speaker to invest these natural phenomena with meaning, to give content to both subject and object.[15] Born of the world and the mind at the same time, it is a random, sudden, and devastating release from all restraints and closed-in spaces, forcing the intersection of the real and ideal as a way to make the distinction between the two irrelevant:

> And the guys from Paterson
>   beat up
> the guys from Newark and told
> them to stay the hell out
> of their territory and then
> socked you one
>   across the nose
>   Beautiful Thing
> for good luck and emphasis
>   cracking it
> till I must believe that all
> desired women have had each
>   in the end
>   a busted nose
> and live afterward marked up
>   Beautiful Thing
>   for memory's sake
> to be credible in their deeds.

(127)

The Beautiful Thing in this passage is both the moment of pure, unmediated expression in violence, and the conflict between desire and possession, the moment when the ideal is ravaged by contact with the real. The evidence that beauty, invoked by desire, has been made real is that it has been marred, damaged in its passage to incarnation. This stance toward beauty makes credible Williams's implicit claims for authenticity; what is lovely and inspires passion is neither a figure of idiosyncratic fantasy nor the construct of literary tradition. Rather, it is something bruised by contact, something by definition actual and incontrovertibly present, released, therefore, from either ego- or Logos-centered authority. The Beautiful Thing is the capricious catalyst that composes the mind and grants it a relationship to the world. The fact that the Beautiful Thing is so elusive enforces the sense of its transience and its freedom from the speaker's control. Obscuring the Beautiful Thing's nature obscures the speaker at the same time.

What we do see of the speaker is his situation as the expression and locus of cyclone, fire, and water. Each of these elemental forces is a figure of creative exertion, a violent dislodging from and destruction of both tradition and circumstance, simultaneously expressing the mind in motion, acting on the world, and the mind in turmoil as storms, flames, and floods pass through it. In this co-extensive approximation, the speaker is thus both subject and object: the course of cyclone, fire, and flood as well as the place they consume and pass through. This ambiguous identity strengthens the poetic statement; his voice is unfixed and thus unchallenged, but its content is apocalyptic, inflating the cultural consequences of his project. Demonstrating his participation in these elemental forces, he tries to take on their energy by blending with them in a voice of enthusiastic acceptance: "Blow! So be it. Bring down! So be it. Consume / and submerge! So be it. Cyclone, fire / and flood. So be it." (97). Still, the issue of agency remains ambiguous; "So be it," an adjuration heard throughout Book 3, can be read as either a command or a statement of acceptance. Either way, natural and personal will are at one, dissolving the distinction between Logos-centered and ego-centered authority. Instead, it is co-extensive authority that authorizes these powers, in which the mind gives voice to the world, and the world gives presence to the mind. Consequently, with the speaker's transpersonal disappearance into these elemental forces, he becomes as unfixed as the Beautiful Thing, thus thrusting into the background the fact that all of these images are merely figures for the movements of a single poet's mind.

But to see more specifically what the speaker accomplishes with these images, we must look at their particular referents. The cyclone, a force that is destructive as well as enormous, is a figure for poetic inspiration, for the mind acting on the perceived world to lift objects from their categorical ground:

> It pours
> over the roofs of Paterson, ripping,
> twisting, tortuous   :
> a wooden shingle driven half its length
> into an oak
>   (the wind must have steeled
> it, held it hard on both sides)
>   The church
> moved 8 inches through an arc, on its
> foundations—
>
> (111)

In direct homologous contrast to the breathlessness of the library, the cyclone provides an image of a force powerful enough to penetrate or puncture inflexible and obdurate traditions and to force shifts in fundamental beliefs—a natural authority potent enough to re-present the culture.

The Paterson fire, which results from inflammable elements being held in a sealed place, is a figure for the creative force exerted by the poetic mind contained in and by a nonnative literary tradition. Fanned by the wind, this fire figures as a second stage in poetic creation; though destructive, it forms and reforms what it touches, whether mind or matter:

<pre>
                                                    Papers
    (consumed) scattered to the winds. Black.
    The ink burned white, metal white. So be it.
    Come overall beauty. Come soon. So be it. . . .
                                        An iron dog, eyes
    aflame in a flame-filled corridor. A drunkenness
    of flames. So be it. A bottle, mauled
    by the flames, belly-bent with laughter:
    yellow, green. So be it—of drunkenness
    survived, in guffaws of flame. . . .
    So be it. The beauty of fire-blasted sand
    that was glass, that was a bottle: unbottled.
    Unabashed. So be it.
    An old bottle, mauled by the fire
    gets a new glaze, the glass warped
    to a new distinction, reclaiming
    the undefined . . .
</pre>

                                                    (117–18)

Describing the scope of the fire's power, the speaker makes no distinction between the mind and the world, implying that it transforms both. Sand—the aggregate of things in their unexamined banality—is blasted into coherent form, and its beauty is thereby released and made apparent. The old bottle—the poet's mind—is brought to new clarity and value under the pressure of fire. Placing the poet's mind at the same level as the world of undefined things, the speaker exalts poetic effort by severing it from human agency and transpersonalizing it into an elemental force. In this way he justifies poetic effort as the mind's primary source of vitality, as a tempered release from annihilation.

But what remains after the fire has done its work—the poem—is even more significant and problematic:

<pre>
                                        The glass
        splotched with concentric rainbows
        of cold fire that the fire has bequeathed
</pre>

> there as it cools, its flame
> defied—the flame that wrapped the glass
> deflowered, reflowered there by
> the flame: a second flame, surpassing
> heat . . .

                                                                    (118)

This passage is a more complex restatement of the conflict between the dead tradition and the living speaker, here extended to the speaker's own poetic effort and his resulting poem. The "cold fire," left on the reoriginated bottle as evidence of its creator, defies the originating fire by threatening to outlast and exceed it. This threat places the speaker in an untenable position: if he admits that the poem matters more than the effort that brought it into being, his entire polemic against the library collapses. But if he adheres to his doctrine that poetic vitality demands continued destruction of the old by the new, he must trivialize not only the results of his poetic efforts but its very idea. If the result, the poem, is without lasting value, so is the effort to create it.

The speaker tries to resolve this conflict by shifting the use of his fire image to serve as a figure of eternal generative force: "Beautiful thing / —intertwined with the fire. An identity surmounting the world, its core . . . " (120). This coupling of poetic desire and fulfillment overcomes the world's—and homologously, the mind's—fragmentation, and as its agent of union, redefines the world in that image of ecstatic generation. Here the fire, as a figure for the heat of concentration and sudden understanding, is no longer destructive or divisive but represents the mind's primary agent of coherence, focus, singleness of purpose. This new referent releases the speaker from the problem of trying to grapple with or destroy tradition, working as an *a priori* generative principle sufficiently abstract to replace the ordering function a received tradition serves. This new treatment of the fire image also lets him sidestep—temporarily—his distinction between the poem and the poetic effort needed to create it. But any emergence of the Beautiful Thing is by definition fleeting; the problem of pure consciousness vs. self-consciousness returns as the speaker realizes that unless there is knowledge of the epiphanic moment, that moment may not exist. Such moments of pure consciousness require a "voice":

>   Some boy
> who drove a bull-dozer through
> the barrage at Iwo Jima and turned it

and drove back making a path for the others—

                                        Voiceless, his

action gracing a flame

                                        —but lost, lost

because there is no way to link
the syllables anew to imprison him

                                                    (120)

Where Yeats embraced this eternal tension between embodying
truth and knowing it, Williams is disturbed by it; it seems to halt his
project. For him, poetry fails unless it can give voice to unmediated
consciousness yet do so without fixing it in the circumscribed re-
flectivity of language. Because consciousness mediated by language is inauthentic, its speaker is without authority. When the
problem is expressed in these terms, the only alternatives are the
polar ones of ego-centered solipsism and Logos-centered silence.

An alternative to the problem itself, however, is the marriage of
consciousness and language. That marriage is as momentary as the
passage of consciousness from thought to thought; it is the flash
of the mind's bringing an idea to articulation, the cataclysmic moment of knowledge when thing becomes word:[16]

> Rising, with a whirling motion, the person
> passed into the flame, becomes the flame—
> the flame taking over the person . . .
>   a shriek of fire with
> the upwind, whirling the room away—to reveal
> the awesome sight of a tin roof (1880)
> entire, half a block long, lifted like a
> skirt, held by the fire—to rise at last,
> almost with a sigh, rise and float, float
> upon the flames as upon a sweet breeze,
> and majestically drift off, riding the air,
>   sliding
> upon the air, easily and away over
> the frizzled elms that seem to bend under
> it . . .
>   The person submerged
> in wonder, the fire become the person

                                                    (121–22)

The authenticity of this voice is founded on its co-extensive authority, wherein the language approximates the event of consciousness,
re-creating it in a verbal version. The mind transpersonalizes itself

into a projected consciousness, resulting in a mutual interpenetration and the birth of a voice.

As provisional as such a union must be, it is nonetheless the most substantial plot of ground available to the speaker since his descent in Book 2. At the beginning of Book 3's third part, the prospect of this union brings him to "one answer: write carelessly so that nothing that is not green will survive" (129). Here he is acknowledging the passage of the Beautiful Thing, the moment of transpersonal union, and searching for a way to recover that moment and establish its value. He accomplishes both projects by setting up his effort as tradition's great competitor and pointing to what the word of tradition threatens:

> It is dangerous to leave written that which is badly written. A chance word, upon paper, may destroy the world. Watch carefully and erase, while the power is still yours, I say to myself, for all that is put down, once it escapes, may rot its way into a thousand minds, the corn become a black smut, and all libraries, of necessity, be burned to the ground as a consequence. (129)

Since his success at expelling tradition from the mind by fire was only momentary, he characterizes tradition in a new way, as a "sullen, leaden" flood of indistinguishable texts fetid with decay, a flood that drowns whatever creative life has taken root in his new ground:

<pre>
                                    The well that gave sweet water
    is sullied. So be it. And lilies that floated
    quiet in the shallows, anchored, tug as
    fish at a line. So be it. And are by their
    stems pulled under, drowned in the muddy flux. . . .
                                    And there rises
    a counterpart of reading, slowly, overwhelming
    the mind; anchors him in his chair. So be
    it. He turns   .   O Paradiso! The stream
    grows leaden within him, his lilies drag. So
    be it. Texts mount and complicate them-
    selves . . .
    Until the words break loose or—sadly
    hold, unshaken. Unshaken! So be it.
</pre>

                                                                (130)

The speaker acknowledges tradition's power by rendering it as an overwhelming elemental force, but unlike the other elemental forces sweeping through Paterson's brain, the flood is purely de-

structive, obscuring or ruining perception of form. More significant, though, is the fact that the flood image makes tradition its
own enemy; by its own weight it washes itself out of the mind,
returning the landscape to itself:

When the water has receded most things have lost their
form. They lean in the direction the current went. Mud
covers them
                                                    —fertile(?) mud.
If it were only fertile. Rather a sort of muck, a detritus,
in this case—a pustular scum, a decay, a choking
lifelessness—that leaves the soil clogged after it,
that glues the sandy bottom and blackens stones—so that
they have to be scoured three times when, because of
an attractive brokenness, we take them up for garden uses.

                                                              (140)

It is the grotesque excess of texts that does the damage, that destroys whatever seeds tradition might have nourished. Tradition's
excess further undermines it because texts blend into homogeneity,
allowing the speaker to compare Pound's reading list (138) to the
geological survey of the artesian well in Paterson (139). Juxtaposing the survey and Pound's letter permits the speaker to portray
the reading list as a mere accumulation of layers, with little to
distinguish one from any of the others. Concluding that the water
at the greatest depth was "altogether unfit for ordinary use," and
that the rock salt found in Europe might well be found in America,
the speaker further justifies his dismissal of the foreign past as a
source of cultural nourishment and authority.

Having demonstrated tradition's cultural failure, the speaker
counters the flood of accumulated texts with the principle of reenactment, specifically in homologous images of marriage. Union
with his bewitched wife Jane allows Mersalis Van Giesen to "see"
beyond the empirical world (133–34). An Ibibio ritual allows only
married women to recover slain warriors: only they can "extract
the spirit of fertility" from the dead men because they alone can
know the secret of life, having "felt the fertility of men in their
bodies" (143). These events are not "a skeleton of / practices, a
calcined reticulum / of the past" (142) but a natural reenactment
of practices both timeless and generative, practices dependent on
the marriage of the mind and its circumstances. Even the brutal
farmer gives his cancerous wife a song—one of marriage, growth,
and recovery (141). Reenactment, in marriage, assures continued

elemental contact, sweeping aside the layers of meta-life that would otherwise put distance between mind and reality.

Establishing the principle of marriage in place of tradition, the speaker can use it as a partial solution to the problem of how to marry the creative moment with its articulation. Approximate co-extension is itself a marriage, the mind's imaginative participation in its circumstances in the struggle to discover their meaning. For Williams, the poet's circumstances are "the roar, / the roar of the present, a speech—" (144), the unmediated language of the voices around him, from which the American culture expresses itself and from which Williams must deliver meaning in a "replica." Though not the original thing itself, a replica is a recovered version or reenactment of the original. But, like Yeats's making of the soul and Eliot's in-folding of tongues of flame into the crowned knot of fire, Williams's replica is projected and suspended between ego-centered and Logos-centered authorities:

> Not until I have made of it a replica
> will my sins be forgiven and my
> disease cured—in wax . . .
>
> No meaning. And yet, unless I find a place
>
> apart from it, I am its slave,
> its sleeper, bewildered—dazzled
> by distance   .   I cannot stay here
> to spend my life looking into the past:
>
> the future's no answer. I must
> find my meaning and lay it, white,
> beside the sliding water: myself—
> comb out the language—or succumb
> —whatever the complexion.
>
> (145)

The speaker is driven toward the present moment, away from the Logos-centered authority of the past and the ego-centered imaginings of the future. Yet living in the present provides its own Scylla and Charybdis: he must achieve a state of perception between pure consciousness and self-consciousness.[17] He must remain "beside the sliding water" and not slip into it. This uneasy situation, remaining parallel to his material, distinct from but analogous to it, is the co-extensive position. The mind exists in the context of what it purports to know, expressing itself in terms of the thing known. It is a projected marriage—but not a union—of knower and known.

The central question here is whether the speaker has accomplished anything by these characterizations of tradition and of his poetic enterprise. The answer, I think, is a qualified but definite yes. Though he slips into strident idiosyncracy, and his images seem overblown and ego-ridden, he nonetheless fulfills his mission to displace the Logos-centered authority of tradition. He begins the book newly risen from the descent, utterly without ground, and ends it with a new poetic that by definition refuses to permit silence. A poetic insisting that writing be green, be a replica of the moment of experience seized just as it crosses the threshold into mediation, does not tolerate the autotelic text. The speaker is thus under no demand to create it. Instead, the poetic of co-extensive authority requires the poet's constant participation, a relentless repositioning on the shifting ground between mind and experience to ensure contact between the two. It liberates the speaker from idealism.[18] Identifying an objective for poetry that tradition—as he has characterized it—cannot possibly achieve, the speaker leaves a vacuum for co-extensive authority to fill. His inability to fulfill its tenets ensures both his poem's textual authority and his own continued voice.

In Book 4, Williams must finally abandon his personal attempt at fulfilling the myth of rebirth with each poetic effort, instead transpersonalizing it in history and the landscape. Unlike Book 3, where the field of action is in the speaker's head, the action in Book 4 refers to the external world. The speaker must displace himself from the purely inner world for the same reason the speaker of "The Tower" does: to project a world in which his poetics outlives him. More important, he withdraws to fulfill the poetics of co-extensive authority, which demands that the ego be invested in a subjective animation of the poetic object. To do otherwise is to commit the same sin of failed love that he identifies in the romantic triangle of the first part. The failure of love is the failure of the imagination to address its object as an Other possessed of its own subjectivity, and thus a failure to animate it. A poet fails by either imposing preconceived forms or refusing to inhabit the empirically grounded forms once they have been made manifest.

The first part of Book 4 identifies this failure using the opposing poet figures, Corydon and Paterson, who in their inability to engender a child with Phyllis, express the inability to engender poetry from the raw, uprooted material of urban life. The second part counters this failure with images of generative continuity: pregnancy, the radiant gist, credit, and the father/son relationship between Williams and Ginsberg. The third part, with the acknowledgement of mortality behind it, engages in a debate between an acceptance of oblivion in the Logos and the ego's resistance to that oblivion. At the core of this debate is a descent into the past, linking birth and death, the ego and its obliteration, to recover a principle of continuity. This principle, expressed in the return of Odysseus and the terrain through which he moves, gives Williams a figure in whom he can reinvest his poetics without asserting ego-centered authority.

The fragmented love triangle in the first part dramatizes more than anywhere else in *Paterson* the interdependence of subject and object that co-extensive authority demands. Phyllis serves Williams as a figure for unmediated experience, which resists interpretation except on co-extensive terms—that is, by an acceptance of its subjectivity. Phyllis is uprooted, without father, friends, education, or heritage. She is without ground, a cut green stem, as Williams lays out the problem in Book 1:

> —unfledged desire, irresponsible, green,
> colder to the hand than stone,
> unready . . .
> a willow twig pulled from a low
> leafless bush in full bud . . .

(18–19)

She is utterly without context, her faculties limited to suspicion, disorientation, and ill-defined longing. And what makes Phyllis without focus, and thus without passion or purpose, is that she requires the mediation and the resulting self-knowledge that cultural authority can bring. In the persistence of her virginity—her unintegrated, unfertilized, and unmarried state—she cannot nourish or be nourished unless a poet is found.

As Phyllis's passports to cultural integration, and thus to meaning and purpose, Corydon and Paterson are would-be poets whose acts of love are attempts to mediate her, both to bring her into the culture and to find cultural terms for understanding her. But their acts of love fail because they refuse, finally, to mediate, to come between self and Other in co-extensive approximation. Refusing to give themselves to her, they instead try to will her into an existence on prior or self-conceived terms. Corydon's name change, for instance, derived from a Logos-centered tradition, is quite literally only a nominal effort to adapt to or place herself on Phyllis's terms. She is actually renaming them both to force Phyllis into a mythology that Corydon alone can manipulate. Phyllis, who expresses her true feelings under her breath, is as likely to prosper under such cultural authority as she is to bear Corydon's child. More clumsily, yet with equal success, Paterson at worst "mauled" her and at best "explored her body . . . courteous . persistent" (155). But whether he treats her gently or brusquely, she remains an object, unmoved and unmoving, and he is left embittered and disgusted, undone by having founded his efforts on ego-centered authority. He is unwilling to love the locust tree in bloom. Because Corydon and Paterson are unable to give in to the imagination, neither one can give Phyllis an identity that will integrate her in the urban culture. Consequently, they both give up the generative co-extensive authority that contact with her would provide. Because no cultural authority can stand unsupported by the empirical world, detachment from that world is detachment from any cultural authority. Like Phyllis, they cannot nourish or be nourished by their culture.

Though failure is the prevailing condition in the first part of Book 4, we are at least given Corydon's poem, which is both her own voice and a fourth voice in the poem, one that takes on a commentator's authority because it is disembodied, however self-conscious. As a poem within a poem, it locates poetry in the culture, making it simultaneously a subject of scorn and an authoritative voice of mediation. This dual response—the reader's and Phyllis's—places Corydon's poem both inside the dramatic triangle, where it is meaningless, and outside, where it guides our thinking about the poem *Paterson*. The implicit argument made by her poem's situation is that a society that ignores poetry ignores the chance to understand and heal itself. However, this argument on poetry's behalf is almost weighted down by self-inflicted irony in its staged, overwritten allusiveness:

> But who has been condemned . where the tunnel
> under the river starts? *Voi ch'entrate*
> revisited! Under ground, under rock, under river
> under gulls . under the insane
>
> (164)

Phyllis's reaction, "I'd like to spill the truth, on that one" (165), frames the poem in a contemptuous disregard presumably shared by the population at large. Still, three conditions give the poem textual authority. First, the absence of any other independent commentary on the society around the three characters makes it authoritative by default. Second, Corydon's particular concerns and ambitions are dispersed in transpersonal expressions of the culture's failings, thus dislocating her speaker's voice from her own voice. Third, where the poem focuses on concrete details of the everyday, the language achieves an authenticity Corydon herself lacks. And the strength of those details allows them to serve as poetic figures pointing simultaneously to concrete objects and to ideas conceived in the imagination, thus demonstrating that modern poetry can meaningfully marry ideas and things:

<pre>
                              While in the tall
          buildings (sliding up and down) is where
          the money's made
                      up and down
                                directed missiles
          in the greased shafts of the tall buildings
          They stand torpid in cages, in violent motion
          unmoved
                    but alert!
                              predatory minds, un-
          affected
                    UNINCONVENIENCED
                      unsexed, up
          and down (without wing motion) This is how
          the money's made . using such plugs.
</pre>

                                                    (165–66)

With these images of loaded but impotent phalluses, the action of the first part coheres in an unanswered demand for consummation.

The second part of Book 4 responds to this demand with the homologous images of pregnancy, the radiant gist, and the filial relationship implied in Allen Ginsberg's letters to Williams, images that project the marriage of mutually necessary antagonists, origin and continuity. Two conditions are essential for this intersection: an investment of the self in a particular time and place—the local—and an awareness of the self's situation there. Unlike the images of contact in the earlier books, these images evoke a temporal as well as physical connection with the material seized by the imagination. And unlike the first part of Book 4, characters emerge who can and do invest themselves in that contact.

Madame Curie, "an unhatched sun corroding / her mind, eating away a rind / of impermanences, through books / remorseless"

(172), invests herself in the world's material with her passionate study of radium. Curie and her world thus dwell together in mutual definition, defining a new place with their dual occupation:[19]

> Paris, a fifth floor room, bread
> milk and chocolate, a few
> apples and coal to be carried,
> *des briquettes,* their special smell,
> at dawn: Paris
> the soft coal smell, as she
> leaned upon the window before de-
> parting, for work
>
> (175)

This conscious and harmonious integration with place shows that this Paris is hers, defined—or, to use Williams's term, "colored"—by her qualities, by what she is inherently qualified to perceive and appreciate. Similarly, Paris defines, or colors, her by making available that which displays her qualities. Though as a Pole she is as uprooted in Paris as Phyllis is in Paterson, by her investment in place, time, and labor she produces that "third thing," the momentary, radiant apprehension of mutuality. In the same way only those poets married to their material can produce redemptive poetry, that which is authorized by the co-extensive imagination to absolve the mind and the world of the sins of separateness.

This same investment in the local is displayed in Ginsberg's letter, where he identifies his place in a tradition even as he implies the originality of his focus on the palpably local:

> Not only do I inscribe this missive somewhat in the style of those courteous sages of yore who recognized one another across the generations as brother children of the muses . . . but also as fellow citizenly Chinamen of the same province, whose gastanks, junkyards, fens of the alley, millways, funeral parlors, river-visions—aye! the falls itself—are images white-woven in their very beards. (173)

Using actual rather than mythical figures as authorizing models of engagement in place and time, the speaker points to and enacts the birth of originality from the belly of continuity. Incorporating Ginsberg's letter as well as his images of cloudy light, the speaker brings into the world a new poet from the belly of his poem. He transpersonalizes himself into Curie's mind and milieu, and, by not including a response to the letter, into Allen Ginsberg. This gesture lets him personify a tradition while authorizing his own implicit claims to originality. Here Williams again addresses the problem, raised in Book 3, of his relationship to tradition. The tradition on which he grounds himself is legislated not by books but by the mind's self-conscious investment in its circumstances.

To create the textual authority for this tradition, Williams forges a cultural context from a polyphonic chorus of transpersonal voices, pouring forth images of the problem requiring his particular solution. Common to the images from each voice is a conflict with the world into which they are emerging. The world's resistance to being opened or penetrated, to releasing its generative energies, is homologous with the mind's reluctance to invest imaginatively in time and place, to approximate perceived reality with a co-extensive imagination. Violence and obstruction, shown in the betrayal of striking workers and the hardships of Marie Curie, are inevitable because the world/self militates against growth, change, generation, and redistribution of financial and intellectual wealth:

> And Billy Sunday evangel
> and ex-rightfielder sets himself
> to take one off the wall . . .
> as paid for
> by the United Factory Owners' Ass'n
> .   to "break" the strike
> and put those S.O.Bs in their places, be
> Geezus, by calling them to God!
> —getting his 27 Grand in the hotel room
> after the last supper (at the *Hamilton*)
>
> (172–73)

> . . .
> —with ponderous belly, full
> of thought! stirring the cauldrons
> .   in the old shed used
> by the medical students for dissections.
> Winter. Snow through the cracks
> *Pauvre étudiant*
> *en l'an trentième de mon age*
> Item . with coarsened hands
> by the hour, the day, the week
> to get, after months of labor
>
> a stain at the bottom of the retort
> without weight, a failure, a
> nothing. And then, returning in the
> night, to find it
> LUMINOUS!
>
> (177–78)

With these passages, the speaker demonstrates the antithesis of what he protests. He invests himself in these characters and events, animating them subjectively so that they derive elements of ego, and thus of independent being, from him. Thus, by introducing Allen Ginsberg as an example of filial continuity, he submerges the speaker's voice in Ginsberg's letter. Nor does he respond to or comment on the letter; rather, he sews the letter into the textual fabric with its prevailing image, obscuring clouds:

> not half asleep
> waiting for the sun to part the labia
> of shabby clouds   .   but a man (or
> a woman) achieved

                                                                    (179)

This interpenetration of letter and poem has two related consequences. First, it shows a successful reciprocity across generations, implying that tradition—by which we mean the influence of past generations on the present—is affinitive, not canonical. Second, it enacts in language the interpenetration of mind and material, thus demonstrating the ethic of co-extensive approximation. That is, if we take Ginsberg's letter as part of the poetic speaker's raw experience, then we can see how the speaker transmutes Ginsberg's clouds for his own purposes. The images' passage between poets demonstrates their independence from the poets using them, enacting the intersection of originality and continuity: the poets awaken new meaning from preexisting images.

But as most critics of *Paterson* have noted, Williams's efforts in Book 4 collapse in the usury passages, doing so, I argue, for lack of that layer of textual authority that rises from an interplay of voices and images.[20] These passages suffer from the fallacy of imitative form: the speaker commits the same crime of usury, of withholding generative wealth, that he assaults the banking world for. The discordant voices of the usury passages, rather than being truly polyphonic, are merely echoes of a single, crank voice, a solitary sloganeer who reduces all complexities to an irritable either/or:

> I would like to have some smart economist or banker stick
>   out his neck
> and contradict one single claim I present herewith to the nation

                                                                    (181)

. . .
Take up the individual misfortune
by buffering it into the locality—not
penalize him with surgeon's fees
and accessories at an advance over the
market price for

                "hospital income"

                                (182)

. . .
What is credit?   the Parthenon
What is money?   the gold entrusted to Phideas for the
               statue of Pallas Athena, that he "put aside"
                  for private purposes
     —the gold, in short, that Phideas stole
You can't steal credit : the Parthenon.

                                (184)

The problem here is twofold. First, in none of these "voices," and in none of the images Williams uses to contrast usury and credit, is there a transpersonal extension to objects that might serve as figures for the damage usury causes, figures he used very successfully on a similar topic in Book 2. Without such figures there can be no objectively realized context where the complaint against usury could reside. Second, this context—a sense of time, place, and circumstance like those provided in the Billy Sunday and Marie Curie passages—must be supported by a polyphony of voices. The usury complaint, founded only on virulence of feeling, is itself usurious: rather than investing in the selfhood of objects, it points only to its own ego-centered anger. And neither does the speaker's own usurious failure justify an attack on usury; he does nothing to demonstrate—or even clarify—the virtues of credit. As a result, credit fails to join such homologues as the radiant gist, weakening the textual authority of the entire section. Because they are not "in things," the terms "credit" and "usury" can never take on the life or force of an idea.

With the principle of continuous origination established in the second part, the third part of Book 4 attempts to reconcile two warring urges arising from the poet's declining energies. The first is to remake the past, a source framed by the Logos, to discover a sufficiently appealing oblivion. The second is to resist the lure of oblivion, maintaining an ego in the imagination's pursuit of experience. The conflict between pursuit and surrender, ego and Logos, surfaces in the opening lines:

> Haven't you forgot your virgin purpose,
> the language?
> What language? "The past is for those who
> lived in the past," is all she told me.
> Shh! the old man's asleep
> —all but for the tides, there is no river,
> silent now, twists and turns
> in his dreams
>
> >   The ocean yawns!
> It is almost the hour
>
> > > > > > > > > (187)

This opening sets forth all that is to come. The poet is spurred to recover the "virgin purpose" of providing language that will engage the mind in its circumstances. Opposed to this effort is the claim that past projects, being past, are dead; what is more, the "old man," the poet, has surrendered to sleep. For the old man there is "no river," or ego, only the all-encompassing ocean, a figure for the ego's death by drowning in the Logos.

The initial pull to the sea comes from a sense of breakage and decline. Poets, figured by the murder victims in their marriage beds, are asleep and therefore easy prey. Corydon, too, is dead, and the "greyhaired President (of Haiti)," abandoning the local, leaves his wife and children to go with his blonde secretary. What destroys these poet figures are the inflexible, *a priori* structures of thought that the poet cannot reorder or break down:

> All the professions, all the arts,
> idiots, criminals to the greatest
> lack and deformity, the stable parts
> making up a man's mind—fly
> after him attacking ears and eyes:
>
> . . .
>
> The brain is weak. It fails mastery,
> never a fact.
>
> . . .
>
> >   Weakness,
> weakness dogs him, fulfillment only
> a dream or in a dream.
>
> . . .
>
> Scattered, the fierceness
> of knowledge comes flocking down again
>
> > > > > > > > > (191)

In this combination of the poet's fundamental inadequacy and the cultural conspiracy to compartmentalize knowledge, the speaker argues that drowning is inevitable.[21] The inevitable becomes more desirable as well, though, when sweetened by the "souvenir of childhood," which calls to mind erotic memories of various women, each at one time distinct but now collectively comprising an archetype (192). This impulse to merge them—as opposed to a simultaneous "holding together" and "scattering"—and to portray them all as lost and gone, leaving behind "a fragrance / of mown hay," shows the growing attraction of oblivion. This attraction, in turn, leads to the backward look at the labial source "In a deep-set valley between hills" (193), a gesture that is less a search for beginnings than a desire to return to its enwombed unconsciousness.

However strong the movement to the sea, the contrapuntal struggle against it is manifested throughout the third part. It is expressed most conspicuously in the horror of the various murders, evoking the ego's horror of oblivion. Also, though the phrase implies the certainty of defeat, the echo of the Poundian claim that "La Vertue est toute dans l'effort" praises the solitary efforts of the ego. The apostrophe to the river, too, expresses faith in the ego's power to prevail against the pull of the sea. By investing the river with elements of poetic imagination, the speaker displaces his own mortality into an eternal yet individuated form:

> My serpent, my river! genius of the fields,
> Kra, my adored one, unspoiled by the mind,
> observer of pigeons, rememberer of
> cataracts, voluptuary of gulls! Knower
> of tides, counter of hours, wanings and
> waxings, enumerator of snowflakes, starer
> through thin ice, whose corpuscles are
> minnows, whose drink, sand
>
> (193)

More persistent, though, is the ambiguous hope for rebirth. In the section's opening passage, the ocean's yawning could be prior to sleep or consciousness, and "the hour" could bring either death or birth.[22] And each image of death and sleep is pregnant with an image of rebirth or reawakening. Following the account of Jonathan Hopper's murder is the reference to his children's later success. After the hotel clerk and the "rather beautiful young woman" merely sleep together, they awake refreshed (188). At Corydon's funeral, Phyllis admits that she loved her (190). And the jingle "Here's to the baby, / may it thrive!" tugs against the nostalgia in the labial description of early Paterson, "In a deep-set valley between hills" (193).

In these retrospective passages, the equivocation between life and death, ego and Logos is more complicated yet equally apparent. They stress the pastness of the past, casting such an artificial sunset glow over the scene that by contrast with the prose insertions and the rest of the poem, it is richly inauthentic:[23]

> Branching trees and ample gardens gave
> the village streets a delightful charm and
> the narrow old-fashioned brick walls added
> a dignity to the shading trees. It was a fair
> resort for summer sojourners on their way
> to the Falls, the main object of interest.
>
> (195)

From the length and the dreariness of these sections emerge a speaker captivated by his own sentimentality. The images of womb-like security and the preponderance of vapid adjectives strip the passage of credibility and thus work to discredit this backward gaze. When contrasted with Book 1's account of the early settlements, which emphasizes the Dutch settlers' cruelty, the postcard hues show through plainly:

> The wigwam and the tomahawk, the Totowa tribe
> On either side lay the river-farms resting in
> the quiet of those colonial days: a hearty old
> Dutch stock, with a toughness to stick and
> hold fast, although not fast in making improvements.
>
> (194)

And where the voice does evade the mediation of sentimental longing, the language dwells on closure and decline: "In the town candle light / appears. No lighted streets. It is as dark as Egypt." This focus on darkness and the longing for the past display a disengagement from the present and thus a death wish. Moreover, because the past pictured here violates the past authorized earlier in *Paterson,* the speaker shows himself to be trying to create a past, one more worthy of nostalgia.

By simultaneously presenting and discrediting the urge to surrender to the Logos, Williams accomplishes two things. First, he demonstrates the consequences of breaking contact with received circumstances, in effect equating that breach with a longing for oblivion. This is the exertion of co-extensive authority at its subtlest: locating an idea within a thing, expressed as a voice, thus giving it a subjective, felt reality. Second, he demonstrates how the opposing urges of his dichotomy coexist and act upon each other in a single mind. As I will argue in more detail, this ambivalence within a single voice fundamentally sabotages the staged division between Logos and ego, opening a space for a textual voice.

The tension between Logos and ego finally becomes explicit in the sea debate:

> I warn you, the sea is *not* our home.
>   the sea is not our home
> The sea *is* our home whither all rivers
> (wither) run
>
>   (201)

These two voices, set in balance, both come from the mind of the river/poet heading inexorably toward the ocean. Yet intertwined with the debating voices is an indifferent voice, one that alludes to a rebirth from the oceanic chaos

>   afloat
> with weeds, bearing seeds
>   Ah!
> float wrack, float words, snaring the
> seeds
>
>   (200)

This is the voice that prevails, indifferent to both ego and Logos, engaged not in debate but in the texture and details of objective reality. It presents experience with a curiosity that defies easy conclusions:

>   What's that?
> —a duck, a hell-diver? A swimming dog?
> What, a sea-dog? There it is again.
> A porpoise, of course, following
> the mackerel . No. Must be the up-
> end of something sunk. But this is moving!
> Maybe not. Flotsam of some sort.
>
>   (202)

Because they comprehend the conflict between ego-and Logos-centered authority, this local voice, together with the landscape it rises from, neutralize that conflict. The river, "Kra," is a strong brown god for Williams just as for Eliot. It flows eternally to the ocean, which waits eternally to receive it, while the landscape eternally contains them both. In the same way, the old poet passes, yielding place to the new in a culture that, however antagonistic, cannot prevent the rise and movement of new poets.

Like Yeats in "The Tower," Williams tries to define as well as to preserve his voice by identifying his successor, but unlike the ending of "The Tower," the end of Book 4 equivocates between birth and death, ultimately comprehending both:[24]

> This is the blast
> the eternal close
> the spiral
> the final somersault
>   the end.

                                                              (204)

In this vision, as in the essential geography of the river/ocean image, birth and death are made inextricable. The co-extensive grasp of this voice lifts Williams out of reach of both Logos-and ego-centered authority. By suspending the mind's movement between death and birth, Logos and ego, he provides openness and closure at the same time. And by presenting consciousness as a cycle, the text becomes the author of that consciousness we locate in the world.

Book 5 begs the question of what in Book 4, or in *Paterson* as a whole, requires it.[25] Williams himself admits, rather whimsically, that "'When the river ended in the sea I had no place to go but back in life. I had to take the spirit of the river back in the air'" (Connaroe, 98). Indeed, the cycle of birth and death is complete at the end of Book 4; the projected continuity of consciousness demands that any voice to follow must be new, albeit one in the Williams tradition. Book 5 is a second, more personal attempt to overcome the encroachments of mortality and preserve consciousness: the speaker, Keats-like, transpersonalizes himself into the art object to take on its dynamic stasis and thus its aspect of the eternal. At base, Book 4 accommodates the death of the poet. But because the poet is not dead, he has to continue, reinterpreting his condition as a continual anticipation of death. Unlike Keats's "still unravish'd bride of quietness," Williams's virgin is continually whored and continually a virgin; it is within that contrapuntal rhythm that the poet finds his permanence.

Williams's principal strategy is to characterize art in terms of the living artistic mind, linking the action of the art object with the action of the mind in the act of creation. The mind then takes on the aspects of the eternal we associate with the art object. This mingling of art and life structures the reader's perceptions of life according to Williams's artistic criteria. The mind lives as portrayed by art, and art lives when expressed in terms of continual, cyclical creative processes. In a sense, this strategy is a reworking of the Yeatsian effort to unite soul and self, the pale eternity of the dream world and the meaty pulse of transitory mortals. While Yeats chooses the ego-centered path toward an archetypal refusal to be absorbed by dream, Williams chooses the co-extensive way: granting authority and continuity to his speaker by locating his voice in the intersection of the ideal and the real, in art. Just as the subjective animation of the object invests both subject and object with presence, the speaker of Book 5 makes art a living presence rather than a beautiful, lofty thing in opposition to life.[26] As life and art become homologous, they become mutually informing, unfixing the art object and shaping the artistic mind in an iconic pattern. Williams succeeds in this enterprise because he effects his transpersonal displacement into art, assuming a variety of roles and guises, without evading the truth of his own mortality. The text lifts the burden of agency and blends him with the art.

His speaker weaves a pattern of mind by presenting four intermingled arguments, each of which returns to the issue of death, a fate he finally escapes by incorporating it in the pattern. His first and principal argument, reinforced in each of the three sections, is that the structure of human perceptions equates the tensions of the art object with the rhythms of life. He anticipates this relationship in *Spring and All:*

> Nature is the hint to composition not because it is familiar to us and therefore the terms we apply to it have a least common denominator quality which gives them currency—but because it possesses the quality of independent existence, of reality which we feel in ourselves. It is opposed to but apposed to it. (*Imaginations,* 121)

Apposition is an equivalence in which each informs the other. For the speaker of Book 5, however, it is art's mediation that forms the categories authorizing the mind's sense of that equivalence. The second argument forges an identity between the images of virgin and whore to define both art and life as an intersection of idea and thing. The third describes the passion of heightened, epiphanic perception when images of virgin and whore are integrated, forming a homologue for the creative process. The conceit of the hunt, which incorporates that passionate movement from

ideal to actual, extends this argument by using the action of the
Unicorn tapestry to express the movement spatially. The virgin is
whored, bringing death to the subjective conception of the ideal.
The final argument names this movement between ideal and actual,
conception and execution, "contrapuntal," whereby the mind
unites the ideal and the real in an image of their dance.

Book 5 begins with the return to flight of the predatory
imagination:

> In old age
> the mind
> casts off
> rebelliously
> an eagle
> from its crag

Unlike the projections of the Yeatsian speaker from the battlements
of "The Tower," these lines express the need to return to an active
life of the imagination, which for Williams means to engage the
mind in a study of its circumstances, bidding the Muse go unpack.[27]
But now, significantly, the method of study is not contact, but the
mediation of art:

> —the angle of a forehead
> or far less
> makes him remember when he thought
> he had forgot
> —remember
> confidently
> only a moment, only for a fleeting moment—
> with a smile of recognition.
>
> (207)

Art composes the mind the way the mind composes the art object.
This memory, composed by artistic perception, restores the poet,
bringing him back to himself and to his identity with the world:

> It is early . . .
> the song of the fox sparrow
> reawakening the world
> of Paterson
> —its rocks and streams
> frail tho it is
> from their long winter sleep
> In March—

                                    the rocks
                                    the bare rocks
                    speak!

                                                            (207)

A restored Paterson, identified with eagle's flight and vision, examines his life, which he measures out in artistic milestones: "What has happened / since Soupault gave him the novel / the Dadaist novel / to translate" (209). The letter from "Josie" that follows, dense with references to flowers and to his "memories of the place," provides a homologous link between art and life, for both exist on the same terms in his retrospective mind. He forges a similar link in his account of Audubon, who followed

                    a trail through the woods
                              across three states
                                        northward of Kentucky . . .
                    He saw buffalo
                              and more
                                        a horned beast among the
                    trees
                    in the moonlight
                              following small birds
                    the chicadee
                              in a field crowded with small flowers
                         its neck
                              circled by a crown!
                                        from a regal tapestry of
                    stars!

                                                            (210–11)

This mingling of life and art accomplishes much for the speaker's co-extensive authority. For one, it brings contact with the local and the act of exploration to the archetypal level of art, making them homologues for acts of imagination. And by recalling the flowers in Josie's letter, it further blurs the line between the imagined and the real. For another, it lifts art away from its rigid, iconic height to be naturalized, brought into the world.

With art and life thus pressed in the same mold, the speaker insists that art alone can reveal the true structure of things:

                    Pollock's blobs of paint squeezed out
                    with design!
                    pure from the tube. Nothing else
                    is real . .

WALK in the world . . .
                    —a present, a "present"
world, across three states (Ben Shahn saw it
among its rails and wires,
and noted it down) walked across three states
for it
                    a secret world,
a sphere, a snake with its tail in
its mouth
                    rolls backward into the past.

                                        (213–14)

The artistic consciousness is the locus of the natural world's union
with imagination's designs. Consequently, given contact and sufficient concentration, acts of perception and composition are identical. The perceived design of things reveals the spatial
interrelationship of events in time, making them effectively simultaneous and thus within the mind's reach. This spatial arrangement
is later foregrounded in the climactic descriptions of the tapestry.
    The merging of art with the natural world is the foundation of
the speaker's co-extensive authority, which is grounded in the
imagination's subjective animation of the world. To show that desire is the fundamental energy demanding that contact, the speaker
anatomizes the apparent simultaneity of perception and composition using the images of virgin and whore. In the transformation
of virgin to whore, the ideal passes into the actual, realizing the
poet's desire. And as with the hunt of the Unicorn, the result of
desire's pursuit is death:

                    the young girl
                                        no more than a child
            leads her aged bridegroom
                            innocently enough
                                        to his downfall

                                        (208)

Portraying the poet as the aged bridegroom, the speaker shows
that desire is directed not by the poet but by natural law:

                    The whore and the virgin, an identity:
            —through its disguises
            thrash about—but will not succeed in breaking free
                        an identity

                                        (210)

This desire to make the ideal actual is a possessive one, the urge to identify two worlds in the artistic mind. Just as the ideas of virgin and whore are each inconceivable without the defining contrast of the other, so the ideal requires the form of the real, which in turn requires the meaning and purpose provided by the ideal. They both require a point of intersection, which they reach by the co-extensive authority of the imagination: "the virgin and the whore, which / most endures? the world / of the imagination most endures" (213). Importantly, the imagination is neither identified with nor the source of the ideal; rather, it structures the mind's efforts to compose the ideal with features of the natural world. To convey the nature and desperation of those efforts, the speaker uses the pursuit of whores as a homologue:

> a smooth faced girl against a door, all white . . . snow, the virgin, O bride . . . making love to a whore is funny but it is not funny as her blood beneath flesh, her fingers fragile touch yours in rhythm not funny but heat and passion bright and white, brighter-white than lights of the whorehouses, than the gin fizz white, white and deep as birth, deeper than death. (215)

The fulfillment of desire reveals the "secret world" figured by "a snake with its tail in / its mouth." It reveals the totality of things, the essential design of past and present, birth and death. As a consequence, it also frees the ego, temporarily, from the circumstances of its mortality. Thus, as the ideal is reduced to the actual, the ego, otherwise imprisoned in the actual, gets a taste of the ideal. But again, the ego is not the agent of this epiphanic experience, for "G.S." does not contrive his passion but is mastered by it.

This glimpse of the totality, or at least of its promise, is what drives the speaker. It is continually there, haunting consciousness, continually elusive even at the moment of its capture. It is thus expressed both naturalistically and mythically as a hunt. The pursuit is baldly, naturalistically expressed in the speaker's pursuit of the androgynous woman of the second section:

> Her
>   hips were narrow, her
>   legs
> thin and straight. She stopped
> me in my tracks—until I saw
> her
>   disappear in the crowd. . . .
>   if ever I see you again

> as I have sought you
> daily without success
> I'll speak to you, alas
> too late! ask,
> What are you doing on the
> streets of Paterson?
> a thousand questions:
> Are you married? Have you any
> children? And, most important,
> your NAME! . . .
>   have you read anything that I have written?
> It is all for you

(219–20)

Here the speaker does not try to raise himself from the level of the solitary voice but becomes merely one more emblem of the pursuit. She is elusive because she refuses categorization and contact, by definition unknowable.[28] In her elusiveness she represents the world's resistance to the imagination and incarnates the unknowable totality, male as well as female.[29] What the world resists is its forgery in the smithy of the soul, resists being subsumed and thus whored by ego-centered authority, to be no longer itself, no longer the object of baffled desire. This woman's inaccessibility drives the poet to keep writing—it is all for her, as a way to reach her. Like the Unicorn, she is desirable because unknowable. A look at the staging, though, shows that more is at work. His description is at once a pursuit and a capture because he proscribes her elusiveness in his characterization of her, yet by refusing to name her he withholds an ego-centered closure. The subjective animation of his description is founded on co-extensive authority, the only way she can be granted presence without destroying the unnameable totality she represents. Her elusiveness, which fuels the imagination, keeps the poet alive as well. The woman's disappearance in the crowd, like the "rabbit's rump escaping / through the thicket" (216) and the "hole / in the bottom of the bag / . . . [through which] we escape" (212) are identified with the imagination, whose exercise rescues the poet from silence. Because she is his intended audience, the moment of contact with her would remove the need for expression.

The hunt for the unnamed, the unapprehended, is fundamental to the artistic consciousness. The image of the Unicorn, portrayed both naturalistically and mythically as the center of the tapestry, shows the predatory impulses of the poetic mind and its perpetual pursuit, from moment to moment, century to century. What secures the speaker's co-extensive authority to make these claims is his transpersonality throughout the field, his pervasiveness without intrusions of ego. For instance, at the head of the third section, the poet is identified with Peter Brueghel, who customarily painted from the local, from scenes "among his own kids" (226). The poet by extension is framed as an artist grounded in eternal, mythical sources. Second, based on the pleas and prophecies of Books 1 and 2, the poet is also identified with the Christ child, promising redemptive, postlapsarian language. And if the child is also a figure for the art object, the poet is also identified, however ironically, with Joseph: "the old man in the / middle, his sagging lips / —— incredulous" (227). In this last case, the poet is more midwife than progenitor to the birth of art. Because the poet's status as agent is thereby unfixed, he is not burdened with excessive, ego-centered claims to authority. But at the same time, the totality of character-izations cannot be readily discarded. The figure of the Unicorn further colors the poet's portrait, but it characterizes the poetic act as well, uniting the two to replace poetic agency with inexorability.[30]

The Unicorn image unites the various homologues and charac-terizations as an archetypal expression of poetic sacrifice, of how much it costs "to love the locust tree / in bloom" (95). It is a sacrifice felt in both life and art in their demonstrated inextricabil-ity, held together by the tension of the movement between ideal and actual, subject and object.[31] As a Christ figure, the Unicorn must be perpetually hunted and perpetually die so that the crea-tures of the mind may be brought into the world. The ideal must be soiled with actuality, its hymen broken, for art—and life—to go on. We recall the reference in Book 3 to "A tapestry hound / with his thread teeth drawing crimson from / the throat of the unicorn" (126), and that "all / desired women have had each / in the end / a busted nose" (127). The Unicorn can be tamed, brought to heel and to its death, only by a virgin, the promise of union with the ideal. Its capture and death by the dog/poet is effected by the virgin's betrayal, a whorish act:

> The Unicorn roams the forest of all true lovers' minds.
> They hunt it down. Bow wow! sing hey the green holly!
> —every married man carries in his head
> the beloved and sacred image
> of a virgin
> whom he has whored
> but the living fiction

a tapestry
silk and wool shot with silver threads
a milk-white one-horned beast
I, Paterson, the King-self
saw the lady
through the rough woods
outside the palace walls
among the stench of sweating horses
and gored hounds
yelping with pain
the heavy breathing pack
to see the dead beast
brought in at last.

(234)

The death of the Unicorn, like the deflowering of the virgin, signals the movement from ideal to actual, from dreaming desire to the consequent reality. It thus describes the creative process—roving thoughts are assembled, composed, and then driven from subjectivity into the objective world.

The Unicorn's sacrifice bestows the Janus-faced gifts of actuality and decay in the objective world: "'Loose your love to flow' / while you are yet young" (216). Yet that very sacrifice to decay provides the poet with terms for merging art and life, unicorn and poet:

—the aging body
with the deformed great-toe nail
makes itself known
coming
to search me out—with a
rare smile
among the thronging flowers of that field
where the Unicorn
is penned by a low
wooden fence
in April!

(232)

Linking himself to the Unicorn, the speaker makes of the poetic mind not a houndlike destroyer of the ideal, but a catalyst for eternal growth and change. Like the speaker of "The Tower," he separates himself from his body to project a distinction between a mortal and an immortal part, while at the same time acknowledging that his passage is as inevitable as the Unicorn's. Consequently, his passage also becomes of equal moment and kind; the sacrifice of mind and body confers a kind of Promethean immortality. Working into the tapestry the fact of own his passing, he makes it an archetypal and thus continuous event.

The fate of the poet is a dynamic stasis, a place of calm between moments of birth and death,

> recalling the Jew
> > in the pit
> > > among his fellows
> when the indifferent chap
> > with the machine gun
> > > was spraying the heap
> he had not yet been hit
> > but smiled
> comforting his companions
> > comforting
> > > his companions
>
> (223)

Like the Jew in the pit, the poet neither longs for the past nor dreads the future, but lives engaged in the present. If consciousness of past and future are not, therefore, necessary conditions for existence, then artistic consciousness dwells in an eternal now, where "a stasis / from a chrysalis / has stretched its wings" (223). This place is expressed by the tapestries in their entirety; presenting spatially the action of the Unicorn's pursuit and death, thereby imagining its perpetuity. The artistic consciousness comprehends that action, the perpetual movement between flight and death, in a dance:

> We know nothing and can know nothing
> > but
> the dance, to dance to a measure
> contrapuntally,
> > Satyrically, the tragic foot.
>
> (239)

As "we," the speaker takes in all moments of consciousness in the moment of the contrapuntal dance between the ideal and the actual, desire and loss. Bernard Duffey's final word on the subject is close to mine:

The human condition and therefore the condition of poetry was existence within the ceaseless interplay of subjective and objective will that both together enacted. What was needed was participation in that condition as it stood, and such participation could be nothing other than action.

(Duffey, 97)

For Williams, though, being is nothing other than action. This Satyric dance is the supreme expression of co-extensive authority because the two worlds are mutually dependent: the dance and the dancers can exist only in counterpoint, in the perpetual passage of consciousness between the two. Consequently, the "I" is defined in terms of what it desires, and the object—real or ideal—of that desire takes only the form granted it by the desiring mind.

Epilogue

At the heart of this study has been the effort to reexamine what we ought to mean by the word "authority." Since the moral ascendency of Michel Foucault's analyses of cultural oppression, it has been fashionable and frequently reasonable to read the term as expressing patterns of coercion engineered by political and economic structures or institutionalized cultural bigotry. Yet such an exclusionary reading, I have argued, tends to obscure the necessary and benign attributes of cultural authority because it does not address how authority generates concepts of human identity. Moreover, and perhaps more importantly, this revised reading suggests that the pursuit of authority is not some coercive impulse inaugurated by a societal Other but is instead a ubiquitous activity fundamental to human consciousness, for the pursuit of authority is nothing more or less than the drive to integrate an audience's various interpretative structures into our own. Whatever it contains of the will to power, it contains in equal measure the will to belong.

The poetic speakers I examine in this book all begin with a perception that their culture is in disrepair, broken or enfeebled because the set of consciousnesses making up their culture is unmoored from a credible source of value and purposeful identity. In response, each speaker labors to present a mystified cultural authority capable of granting value to the individual consciousness, and to do so, each speaker's voice strives for a transpersonal departure from the finitude of individuality to a situation between a projected cultural authority and the reader. Each speaker fails, but with a paradoxical measure of triumph. The failure comes because the very fact of utterance presupposes a consciousness not at one with its authority, and the degree of distance from cultural authority is the degree to which the claims in the utterance are suspect. Yet still these poets triumph because their speakers ultimately situate themselves at the most authoritative point a mind can reach without disappearing into silence. The speakers earn these situations not by achieving some sort of cultural beatitude themselves but by dramatizing the condition of the unself-conscious mind engaged in its origin, which authorizes it and gives it meaning. Each condition is expressed in images of an integrated consciousness, one that is not mediated but enacted.

For Yeats, that condition is a union of chance and choice, the emergence of an archetypal ego so rich in satisfied imagination that death becomes a form of completion rather than closure. For Eliot, that condition is a deferred but imaginatively realized dissolution of the floating detritus of selfhood into the divine, originating pattern of the Logos. And for Williams, who collapses the tension between Logos and ego by unseating the authority of both, that condition is the emotive, generative energy released at the point of contact between subject and object. That energy, the Beautiful Thing, constitutes consciousness at its most vital and purposeful, but it too eludes the limitations of voice and thus the control of consciousness. In Williams's poetics of co-extensive authority, consciousness is not meditation, but action; to twist Yeats's marvelous line, it is to know truth *by* embodying it. This truth's authority is co-extensive because it is generated in the "dance" of mutually informing, interdependent opposites: birth and death, real and ideal, subject and object, ego and Logos.

Reading the pursuit of authority as a desired and inevitable constituent of consciousness in this way displays it as simultaneously a humbling liberation and a moral burden. Just as it is liberating to rediscover the will to authority as democratically omnipresent, it is surely humbling to see it as the simple pursuit of individual consequence, the achievement of a voice, perhaps at most the generation in an audience of a willingness to listen. Still, this humbling and humanizing of authoritative gestures does not diminish their moral burden, but merely distributes it. Because each utterance is to one degree or another in pursuit of authority, that pursuit, and the moral burden it bears, cannot be displaced onto institutional or cultural forces but must be universally shared as the cost of sentience. A culture's acceptance of a particular authority, no matter the source, inevitably comes at the expense of other voices and values being silenced.

What particular burdens, then, lie upon these speakers whose transpersonal gestures characterize the three available avenues of pursuit? First, we might argue that the Yeatsian speaker seems to push the reader out to the margins of consequence, sacrificing the Other to the stability of the Self. In apparent contrast but to similar effect, Eliot's Logos annexes the reader, thereby sacrificing the Self to the stability of the Other. And Williams's textual voice, by liberating consciousness from the shaping presence of either ego or Logos, denies it the stability and continuity of a unified culture. On the other hand, though we cannot comfortably dispute these claims, we can counter them with claims of equal validity. These poets' efforts to rescue the unmoored modern consciousness project models that, even as they seem to displace the reader—or the reader's hope for security—also point to the solution to that displacement. As the speakers' projections replace or revise cultural authority, they replace or revise identity, an act that can be protested only on the grounds that the authority and individual identity were on a secure footing prior to their displacement. Such grounds, modernism argues, are not especially solid.

The kind of salvation these poets authorize is available to all, and then all of us consequently inflict the same sacrifice—and confer the same hopes for an integrated consciousness—upon others, for the pursuit of authority is the pursuit of a self-knowledge that comes only from integration with a cultural context. The condition of the individual mind, its degree of integration and degree of loneliness, is the condition of the culture. To know oneself is therefore to re-form the culture, to establish an interpretative structure for an audience; every utterance that locates the self in its culture necessarily locates the rest of us. The burden and blessings of a cultural authority are always equally present, each an implicit challenge to the other and each set against the persistent demands of authenticity.

Notes

Chapter 1. Introduction: Temporal and Atemporal Authority

1. The link to Bloom's *Anxiety of Influence* is no doubt apparent. But while Bloom is concerned with the poet's need to assert originality in order to claim authority, this book is concerned with the inverse problem—that succession to authority inescapably requires a filial relationship with the poet's predecessors.

2. In *Myth, Rhetoric, and the Voice of Authority*, Marc Manganaro examines the anthropological influences on Eliot's rhetorical authority, observing that early twentieth-century anthropologist Lévy-Bruhl's view of the "medicine man . . . serves as a perfect example [for Eliot] of a figure uniting social power and transcendence or, more simply put, politics and religion, as his channeling of mystical participations is instrumental to the social formation and maintenance of the tribe and to the expanded authority of the medicine man himself" (93). This characterization of Eliot articulates a pattern of poetic situation that extends to all modernist speakers attempting to craft voices of cultural authority.

3. In *The Matrix of Modernism: Pound, Eliot, and Early Twentieth Century Thought*, Sanford Schwartz's formulation of the modernist enterprise as an attempt to "integrate abstraction and sensation . . . " serves as a useful way to characterize the pressure to articulate a felt authenticity (7).

4. Stead presents the relationship among poet, poem, and audience as triangular, the lengths of the lines that form the triangle expressing the closeness or distance of the poet from concerns of the poem and those of the audience. He argues that the decadents were too far from their audience while the public versifiers were too close; ideally, the triangle should be equilateral, as in his formulation Yeats and Eliot generally but not inevitably make it.

5. Perry Meisel, in *The Myth of the Modern*, argues in his discussion of *The Waste Land* that Eliot tried to "insure his own apparent originality" by coming up with the myth of the waste land, "projecting onto the world a state that really inheres largely in the history of imagination alone" (87). However, the very premises of my argument question the usefulness of this distinction between "world" and "imagination." Clearly, because the presence or absence of an "actual" waste land in any spiritual, psychological, or philosophical sense can hardly be verified independently, reading *The Waste Land* as some sort of truth claim seems a circular effort. The fact is that the poem did take root in the modern consciousness, serving as an interpretive structure through which to read experience. Its cultural authority could have sprung only from a felt authenticity. Thus, even if we dismissively conclude that Eliot simply projected this myth from his own neuroses, its phenomenal impact on Anglo-American culture suggests either that his contemporaries shared his neuroses or that they recognized them in each other. Even without an "actual" wasteland, the collective breadth of apparently

wrong-headed assumptions about its authenticity must ironically justify truth claims for this myth.

6. Among other propositions in his indispensable study, *Discovering Modernism,* Louis Menand suggests that one reason for Eliot's ascendancy is his fortuitous arrival at a time when "free-lance, journal-based literary criticism" was being supplanted by a "university-based type . . . with an interest in the condition of contemporary culture." Eliot thrived at least partly by contributing "a common set of terms and judgments, a manner—judgmental, hierarchical, but 'scientific'—perfectly suited to the needs of the modern academic critic" (155). The posture of "scientific," dispassionate, objective analysis and criticism has as its premise, clearly, the inadequacy of the solitary, intuitive individual. Gary Day's essential distinction between "individual" and "citizen" is useful in this reading on the individual's uneasy status in Britain in the first decades of this century. The subject, "no longer an active agent," came to be "perceived as a citizen, not an individual." In the "collectivist" State, "[t]he term citizen functions as a norm by which difference becomes deviancy, the term individual, by contrast, allows for and even celebrates difference." (Day, 30)

7. Michael North, in *The Political Aesthetic of Yeats, Eliot, and Pound,* defends these poets in the face of their totalitarian sympathies by illustrating their failure to sustain a "Coleridgean reconciliation of multiplicity with unity" that in turn could have projected a "resolution of social conflict through aesthetic harmony . . . [but] it is just those poetic devices that seem to represent reconciliation that instead reveal its impossibility" (16–17). This political failure is thus an aesthetic and moral triumph because it is based, North argues, on the fact that these poets never surrender their awareness of the problem's complexity to the attractiveness of authoritarian solutions.

8. This account of the polar struggle between Logos-and ego-centered authority is analogous to Yeats's description of a cyclical tendency to be pulled toward either the One or the Many. Without this tension, "all life would cease" (*Explorations,* 305).

9. Elaine Pagels's account of the debate between Augustine and John Chrysostom, essentially a dispute about whether temporal authority to mediate the divine word properly resides with the State or with the individual, serves as an archetype of the conflict between Logos-centered and ego-centered authority (98–154).

10. Michael Bernstein has an extended discussion along these same lines, defining the poet's role in shaping the "tribe's" identity (3–25). Speaking from a similarly anthropological perspective, Marc Manganaro explains Eliot's attraction to the objective correlative, which, Eliot hoped, "triggers group emotion" (78).

11. *Henry V* projects an archetypal rendering of the intersection of temporal and atemporal authority in Henry's reaction to Katherine's admonition about proper royal behavior: "O Kate, nice customs cur'sy to great kings. Dear Kate, you and I cannot be confin'd with the weak list of a country's fashion. We are the makers of manners, Kate; and the liberty that follows our places stops the mouth of all find-faults . . . " (V ii).

12. As an example of this process, Guillory describes Milton's need to evade and overcome Shakespeare's secular authority and to identify with Spenser's attempts to return the sacred to poetry (21).

13. The clearest literary example distinguishing power from authority is where Eve explicitly yields to Adam's authority in Book 4 of *Paradise Lost:*

My Author and Disposer, what thou bidd'st
Unargu'd I obey; so God ordains,
God is thy Law, thou mine; to know no more
Is woman's happiest knowledge and her praise.

(IV, 635–37)

This speech is politically disquieting to the modern reader, of course, but the suggestion remains clear that power does not exist until evil comes into the world.

14. Bell draws here from Robert Dahl's *After the Revolution* and John Kenneth Galbraith's *The New Industrial State*.

15. There is a significant distinction to be made here. Clearly, Bell's "descending" authority is roughly equivalent to Logos-centered authority, but "ascending" authority is not as close to the ego-centered version. In fact, ascending authority is equivalent to Bell's participatory stage in the individual's relation to a Logos-centered authority. The important distinction is between popular and private will; ego-centered authority claims that no temporal presence external to the ego, no system of thought presented in the objective world, is adequate to articulate and thus structure the complexity of the individual mind. If the ego cannot rely on given, traditional authority as a means of self-knowledge, then authority must lie within. This ego-centered position, however, is as untenable in the extreme as the Logos-centered. But like Logos-centered authority, it becomes interesting in the poet's discovery of its difficulties. An ego-centered poet—that is, one tending toward ego-centered claims for authority—rejects the Logos-centered position because it enforces closure, compelling the speaker to struggle to avoid disappearing in the sudden absence of external reference.

16. The logic of the hermeneutic circle authorizes his suspicions of all systems of reading, thereby removing all authority from his own, which he then proceeds to set forth, assuming the poems themselves, freed of other systems, by being read will verify his own system. Yet had he acknowledged he was contradicting himself and then proceeded insouciantly, he would in effect have been swallowing his authority or had it swallowed by his text, removing himself from a rhetorical position and thus clearing a space to be filled by immediate contact between text and reader. By not admitting his contradiction, Simpson violates his own premise dishonestly instead of to good purpose. Trying to cling to his rhetorical position, to his personal authority rather than the authority of his idea, he makes a mistake that the modernist poets discussed below see and attempt to overcome—the mistake of permitting the finite ego to intrude as a seer between text and reader. Simpson commits the very error, in fact, that he praises the Romantic poets for avoiding.

17. *No Place of Grace,* Jackson Lears' cultural history of the modernist period in the United States, examines a number of movements among the American intelligentsia and bourgeoisie, movements as disparate as medievalism, mystical Catholicism, and arts and crafts. Each of these movements represented a resistance to the dispersal of moral authority, a dispersal that threatened the general sense of individual worth. These attempts to recover, or discover, an Origin were obliquely expressed desires to find a context within which the self could be at home, a place that, in Frost's terms, he "hadn't to deserve."

18. Immediate examples are Stein's "Composition as Explanation" and Williams's introduction to *Kora in Hell*.

19. Eliot's "Tradition and the Individual Talent" and Hulme's "Romanticism and Classicism" remain the most conspicuous sources of this doctrine.

20. L. S. Dembo takes an analogous position that clearly shows the removal of

authority from the private ego: "Antipathy to personal sentiment or conventional emotion, faith in an essential or ultimate reality, a belief in language as a mode of revelation, all constitute a 'realist' poetic" (218–19).

21. Theo Hermans maintains that the prevailing characteristic of modernist poetry is the "absence of transcendental perspective," which consequently leaves perception and imagination "threatened with objective and subjective fragmentation" and so spurs the need for a "new search for unity and coherence" (235).

22. The limitations of transpersonality can be seen in the analogous tension in the avant garde's mutually exclusive needs for both integrity and legitimacy. As Michael Levenson explains: "Avant-garde movements always threaten to disappear, either shattering into a collection of individualities or ossifying into an old guard. And this is because within the avant-garde there inheres a permanent conflict: the need at once to subvert and to institutionalize. Without subversion a movement cannot justify itself; without some institutional stability it cannot survive" (218).

23. Derrida's observation that "the myth of a full presence" (atemporal authority) tends toward "the praise of silence" is applicable here; self-consciousness breaks the bond between image and atemporal presence, leaving silence as the only site for presence (140).

24. It may be useful to contrast this formulation with Albert Gelpi's division of modernist poetics into "subjective and objective epistemological poles: Symbolisme representing the mind's propensity to dissolve impressions of things into figures of its own processes, Imagism representing the mind's propensity to be shaped by its impressions of things" (6). Gelpi appropriately locates Yeats and Eliot in the symbolist camp and Williams in the imagist, but we might profitably complicate this division further. Yeats's Symbolisme is somewhat less burdened with self-consciousness than Eliot's, whose impersonality depends on explicit mistrust of the mind's Romantic impulses; thus, Eliot had to displace evidence of the creating ego, while Yeats foregrounded such evidence at every opportunity. Conversely, Williams's Imagism was based on his belief in mutually informing contact between mind and thing; the objective world moves into a field of apprehension, granting the mind both form and life.

Chapter 2. The Poles of Poetic Authority

1. John Guillory sees the essence of Milton's project to be not the establishment of a Miltonic speaker with mediating authority but the demolition of the autonomously imagining—and thus Satanic—ego as a creative force (106). I would say instead that these actions are mutually dependent, not contradictory.

2. Guillory describes this situation as a fundamental struggle for poetic authority between divine inspiration and the usurping Imagination (4–22). For Milton, Guillory says, the "messenger who usurps the authority of the message is the figure whose existence must be denied, or whose autonomy must be forfeited" (14). Kerrigan discusses the speaker's situation in the context of the Hebraic and classical prophetic traditions and the "correspondence theory of knowledge" in which the perceiver and the perceived—God and prophet—must participate in the same being.

3. Guillory refers to this movement as "accommodation," an intersection of the divine and the "upward aspiration of human vision" (152). Accommodation descends as vision rises, and "at the place of co-incidence a doubt arises" (158).

4. Kerrigan defuses the charge of arrogance by reading "assert" by way of its root, "ad serere"—"to join" (159).

5. Anne Ferry discusses this phenomenon throughout her book, explaining that this language simultaneously projects the fallen and unfallen worlds, providing evidence of the speaker's authority to mediate the divine for the fallen world. Her analysis of the line "dark with excessive bright" (III, 380) is especially apt, where she identifies "dark" as the secondary quality in the eye of the fallen beholder, and "excessive bright" as the primary quality in celestial being. The attempt to describe the primary quality is what makes the speaker's testimony credible.

6. Ferry describes this transpersonal process as a gesturing outward into figurative language instead of pointing solely at the self, thus redistributing the voice into structures of imagery and emblem (28–29).

7. In John Guillory's reading, inspiration takes place in the movement from line 37 to line 38, in the simultaneously transitive and intransitive verb "move" (126).

8. Ferry argues that the bird displaces the narrator's identity as mere fallen man, recasting it as an emblem purified by its orientation toward divinity (25).

9. I am using the 1850 edition of *The Prelude* for primarily two reasons. First, like the other four works I focus on in this study, it is the product of a later, mature vision. Second, in this edition the distinction between the present speaker and the younger self is more sharply etched.

10. Wordsworth explicitly identifies the insulating dangers of Fancy in his description of Coleridge at Cambridge, where his "self-created sustenance of a mind / Debarred from Nature's living images, / [was] Compelled to be a life unto itself" (VI, 270–318).

11. Though de Man would of course dismiss any notion of "authentic" ego-centered authority, he sharply addresses the issue of the mind's failed imperialism in the face of self-consciousness: "Critics who speak of a 'happy relationship' between matter and consciousness fail to realize that the very fact that the relationship has to be established within language indicates that it does not exist in actuality" (Bloom, 70). However, pointing out an inauthentic alternative is a rhetorical gesture that in turn points implicitly to an authentic one.

12. I am extending rather than echoing Samuel Monk's paraphrasing of Kant's definitions. Where Monk concludes that the sublime is a self-conscious sense of Reason's superiority over Nature, I am proposing that the Wordsworthian sublime, at least, is not only the perception but the sensation that the creative forces of the Imagination are analogous to those of Nature.

13. Helen Reguiero explains the presence of the Imagination in this way: "The imagination arises when the unity of self and world has been lost, and its paradoxical function is to retrieve the unity whose loss gave it birth—to enter, through consciousness, a world from which all consciousness is excluded" (24). This position is analogous to mine; the Imagination arises to compensate for the self's foundering in the absence of a directing authority. The speaker's challenge is to identify with the autonomy of this world without consciousness—ego-centered authority—yet show that presence to be perpetually deferred. Hartman identifies the apparent otherness of the Imagination as I do, in a distinction between the speaker and the younger self, specifically the child. For the latter, the mind's imaginative response to Nature seemed to have been generated by it; he "cannot separate the Nature's strength from his own." Conversely, for the "retrospective poet," the power is now seen "to have belonged to the mind" (215). With this

acknowledgement of Imagination's source comes the problematic assertion of the Imagination's ego-centered authority.

14. Richard Onorato (150), arguing against a strictly Christian interpretation of the speaker's contact with the Imagination, takes an approach similar to mine in that he identifies the speaker's "joy of increase in consciousness." In this passage, Onorato explains, "the self is trying to master the longings of the soul as it discovers them, and to assimilate the soul to the self." But while Onorato is reading *The Prelude* as the speaker's movement to identify and incorporate an "Ideal self," I see that movement as an effort to demonstrate that the Imagination's authority is authentic and that the self is its source.

15. In Reguiero's reading, the speaker is not making a choice but accepting the inevitable: "The consciousness of temporality precludes the experience the poet is trying to achieve" (84).

Chapter 3. The Archetype of Failure

1. The idea of a remade self has long been a commonplace in Yeats criticism. As far back as the *The Mysteries of Identity,* for example, Robert Langbaum claims that the individual moves to archetype "at that psychological depth where we desire to repeat mythical patterns" (160). I would amend this statement slightly by saying that we move to archetype in verse that displays the repetition of mythical patterns. Yeats himself, of course, points to the notion of the remade self in "A General Introduction for my Work," in *Essays and Introductions:* the poet "is never the bundle of accident and incoherence that sits down to breakfast; he has been reborn as an idea, something intended, complete" (509).

2. This sense of failure is the response to prevailing ideas about the modern world, notably one Karl Malkoff points to in his definition of modernism as "the abandonment of the conscious self, the traditional ego, as the inevitable perspective from which reality may be viewed." David Young characterizes the antitriumph of Yeats's diminished self at the end as a "tragedy of artistic incompleteness [that] is a resounding modernist success" achieved "by retreating, by splitting and contradicting, by sacrificing order and denying his own authority, stability, and centrality . . . " (75).

3. In "The Name and Nature of Modernism," Bradbury argues that modern art is a "distillation" of certain aesthetic features or theories claiming that "life is multiple" and "perception as plural," both of which imply the inherent inauthenticity of the view from the ego.

4. There is a series of interesting critical comments on precisely what sort of world exists in the poetic field and in what sense the speaker can be said to authorize it. Speaking of "The Tower," Stuart Hirschberg says that the poem's second section establishes a transcendant realm unifying the world of the dead and "a heaven of man's imagination" (194–201). This atemporal place, though Hirschberg does not admit it, is necessarily locked in the speaker's mind, unable to overlap into our perceptions of the objective world. Daniel Albright offers a more daring view by quoting Yeats's essay on Berkeley and concluding that Yeats believed that "human perception is a kind of creation" (36). Robert Langbaum, reading Yeats as an attempt to enact Eliot's escape from personality, asserts that Yeats was trying to move from the empirical to the archetypal self, to what Langbaum calls the "reconstructed self" (151). These qualified and thus obscure readings of the Yeatsian poetic effort can be useful if seen in the light of poetic

authority. In the expression of a world view, the speaker is attempting to exert authority over how the reader perceives the world. Gale Schricker is the rare, if not the only, critic who discusses the speaker's identity in this way, pushing the poet's need to "speak in his art as the voice of truth, or the vehicle of a more universal 'poetic I'" (27–28).

5. Jahan Ramazani, in his analyis of the "The Tower" as a "self-elegy," explains this partitioning as an "internalization" of the "cosmic trial before death [in which] Yeats delegates to himself all the judicial roles—almighty judge, prosecutor, defense attorney, and plaintiff" (167).

6. Hirschberg asserts that the speaker is doing the opposite, trying to find a way back to the physical world to seek a "revelation of reality" in the particular and concrete to avoid having to escape into the "numbing security of philosophy." He is correct to show Plato and Plotinus as an escape, but for Yeats, revealing reality is a pointless exercise incapable of redeeming the deteriorating self. It is only the ability to make something of reality that is redemptive.

7. The speaker in "The Fascination of What's Difficult" (*Variorum,* 260) has an analogous complaint and even a similar image of restraint; instead of dragging "a sort of battered kettle at the heels," the speaker has "dragged road metal." The claim that imagination has been restrained is more convincing in the earlier poem, which protests the fettering of mental energies by political matters, than in "The Tower," where the speaker has little to occupy his mind but his old age. He has no impediments but self-constructed ones.

8. Thomas Whittaker (198) uses this reference, as do Robert Langbaum (222–23), David Lynch (205), and Gale Schricker (165–68).

9. This section of *A Vision,* which explains phase 17, generally thought to be Yeats's phase, describes as its True Mask "simplification through intensity," or "Creative imagination through *antithetical emotion.*" Yeats describes the creative process in this way: "the intellect (*Creative Mind*), which in the most *antithetical* phases were better described as imagination, must substitute some new image of desire; and in the degree of its power and of its attainment of unity, relate that which is lost, that which has snatched it away, to the new image of desire, that which threatens the new image to the being's unity" (142).

10. Helen Regueiro makes this point repeatedly. Discussing "Easter 1916," she remarks that the stone image is sufficient to itself, but dead (103). Later, she explains that "self-knowledge is a reductive, not an integrative act" (110). In other words, self-knowledge—self-possession—removes the self from contact with or desire for the other. Gale Schricker describes the archetype in Yeats as "an externally stable embodiment of an internally dynamic duality" (168). Sufficiency of the self makes the self inert and therefore voiceless.

11. That Yeats creates a pattern of permanence is essentially Daniel Albright's thesis in chapter one of *Myth Against Myth.* I would extend his thesis to say that this aestheticized pattern is an effort to gain authority over cultural means of perception.

12. Albright makes a similar claim in saying that the Mary Hynes/Raftery episode is evidence of "the interdependence between poetry and the natural world" (15). Unfortunately, he sees this interdependence as only an isolated event rather than the poem's central argument. On this issue of landscapes invested with emotional force, Langbaum makes a useful distinction here between Wordsworth and Yeats. Wordsworth mythologizes landscapes "empirically" by remembering having had visions in particular places, "and thus restoring the ancient sense of holy places," but that holiness depends solely on Wordsworth's own

memories. Yeats, on the other hand, makes places "objectively sacred," that is, sacred in and of themselves, quite apart from the ego's private associations with them (173). If we accept Langbaum's distinction, we see a neat discontinuity between Romantic and modern: Wordsworth had considerably more faith in the ego's consequence and its authority to create structures of value than did Yeats.

13. John Holloway has a useful formalist account of this intersection of poetic and natural. These figures of the landscape appear by poetic "fiat," a "forming ritual, . . . the solemnized calling up of objects by the poet to people the world of his imagination." The ontology of these objects is such that they don't really have a "prior, independent existence," but Yeats's poetic form gives "incarnation" to subjective energies (97–98). To say that subjective energies are incarnated but still purely imaginative shows Holloway's difficulty, the divided sense that these figures are somehow both actual and imaginary. I try to avoid this contradiction by stressing the consequences for speaker authority when we as readers are compelled to see the imaginary and the actual in the same terms, according to the same criteria.

In "Magic," reprinted in *Essays and Introductions,* Yeats addresses this issue with his "three doctrines." In summary, these assert that individual minds are but parts of the Great mind, and consequently, that no mind ever perishes and that the borders between minds can "shift," showing that things are misperceived as objects, that all is absorbed in a comprehensive Subjectivity (28).

14. Marjorie Perloff makes an analogous claim: all the speaker's memories have "mythological timelessness . . . no reference to temporal relationships" (572). The speaker dislocates these events from their temporal positions, thus, I argue, making them subject to his authority.

15. There is a general critical uneasiness about what claims the speaker is making on behalf of the imagination. Daniel Albright waffles, saying that as a whole the poem does not assert that "man creates the universe," but that man gives value to the universe, which he says is essentially the same thing (42). Richard Ellman argues for an "affirmative capability," which asserts the right of the ego over both scepticism, which paralyzes, and "belief," which is abstraction imposed from the outside. Thus, the accuracy of any subjective projections of reality, as well as their authority, do not become an issue in Ellman's eyes because these projections are an "exposition of intellectual needs" (239–45). The subject reigns because nothing else matters.

16. Langbaum has a valuable observation in regard to a definition of tragedy: it reveals archetypes, breaking down the barriers of mere character (*Mysteries of Identity,* 220). Thus, given the difference between archetype—Yeatsian "personality"—and "character," tragedy is necessary to the Yeatsian speaker's ego-centered authority.

17. Harold Brooks discusses the idea of the "whole man" in the Protestant Irish tradition, referring to those never associated with abstract or temporal "partial causes" (14). As I argue later, that idea is analogous to madness in that both require a selfhood possessed by desire. Examining this tradition, Alex Zwerdling argues that such "wholeness" or heroism is determined by the individual's distance from conventional thinking.

18. The roots of this position come from Ellman, Albright, and Stead ("Stendhal's Mirror"), who discussed the speaker's efforts to dramatize private griefs through Hanrahan.

19. Michael North observes that "by mingling folk memories with episodes from Yeats' own work, [he] efface[s] the fact that Yeats himself has no ancestral

claim on this soil" (52). This reminder of Yeats's efforts at self-creation outside as well as inside the poem neatly underscores the claim that his anxiety is more modernist than simply post-Romantic.

20. Albright claims that the blotting out of day occurs when the mind "becomes lost in the images of its own brooding . . . the sun is eclipsed in mind's self-torture," making memory the uncreating word that blocks out day (32). This is an acceptable reading, but Albright misses the point that what is blotted out is more than the memory of failure: it is a vision of unattainable wholeness.

21. C. K. Stead points out the speaker's compounded vulnerability in the contrast between the "pride" of this passage and the one that compelled the speaker to turn aside from the "great labyrinth." The speaker's attitude toward this latter pride Stead characterizes as courageous self-criticism, unlike this later "elderly pride," a refusal to accept "the facts of life and death" ("Stendhal's Mirror and Yeats' Looking Glass," 206).

22. Albright draws a similar conclusion, explaining that Yeats saw an "ontological difference between the mind's constructs and ambient reality," but that Yeats believed that difference did not make the constructs any less valuable (41).

23. Yeats's famous admission of error appears on page 826 of the *Variorum* edition. However, he makes that admission more an apologia for his ego-centered authority than an apology: in the passage he quotes from Plotinus, he allows the uncertain distinction between "every soul" and "soul" to remain blurred so that the poetic imagination can remain the author of the perceived world.

24. Though Albright (38) asks an important question—"Why is the human soul bitter in his creating act?"—his answer trivializes it with the explanation that the creative mind has no other outlet but song, as if the mind only has the alternatives of sports or television to release it from imprisoning circumstances. I argue instead that the soul is bitter at the realization that it can never move beyond its own creations, projections of its own desire. This bitterness is ubiquitous in Yeats, typified in "Towards Break of Day": "Nothing that we love over-much / Is ponderable to our touch" (*Variorum*, 399). Objects of desire are by definition unattainable.

25. Claiming that the "loose trimetre" of Part III "has at last stiffened into clenched iambs" tells us more about Albright's response than about the verse's climactic force. He is right to "assume that the declaration of human omnipotence is made only so that the poet can make a strategic withdrawal," but he does not make it clear why or from what (42). I am arguing, on the other hand, that because true omnipotence begins with the absence of desire, this passage in Part III is the climax, the peak of desire and the beginning of that desire's dissipation.

26. Explications of the Daws passage are numerous and not in serious conflict. Langbaum (199) points us to a passage in *A Vision* (214) that is obscure for its comprehensiveness: "The bird signifies truth when it eats, evacuates, builds its nest, engenders, feeds its young; do not all intelligible truths lie in its passage from egg to dust?" Perhaps by "truth" Yeats means a grounding, authorizing pattern, a model of life's processes. Virginia Pruitt gives the standard New Critical reading, proposing correspondences between Yeats and the mother bird, the twigs and the "strata of experience," the bird's young and Yeats's poetic inheritors (154). Stuart Hirschberg explains the appositional status of the Daws section as "the work of art of our lives when it is no longer seen from a moralistic point of view but an aesthetic balance of lights and shadow" (200). M. L. Rosenthal links it to the recitation of "learned Italian things," "a symbolic gathering of cherished ideals and memories for building a warmly protective mental nest" (226). Michael

North's recent, rather daring reading presents this passage as a formal and thus emblematic discontinuity paralleling the discontinuity represented by Yeats's own presence in the "ruined" tower (53–54). With his position thus implicitly challenged, Yeats can respond as a poet to establish his own claim to the heritage based on his imaginative forces. The common ground for all of these readings finds Yeats trying to detach his poetic experience—the activity of consciousness—from the jurisdiction of the actual and temporal. But Hirschberg mars the usefulness of his position by adding that the use of daws shows the "naturalness of the poet's method," a claim that surely distorts Yeats's prevailing aesthetic of artifice. Harold Brooks proposes that the daws are assembling, nurturing, setting in order "life experience" (17). This sounds credible, but it is not in keeping with the notion of "dreaming back," that activity between lives in which the soul is driven to order its experiences of failure and remorse.

27. Suggesting an analogy between Jung's and Yeats's thoughts about self-regeneration, Brooks quotes from Jung's commentary on *The Secret of the Golden Flower: A Chinese Book of Life,* of which Yeats received a copy on 15 December 1931: "the greatest and most important problems of life . . . can never be solved, [but] they can be outgrown" (20). This parallel on the face of it seems valuable until we remember that if the speaker outgrows the limitations of mortality, he vanishes into oblivion; there is no alternative or higher form of being he could grow into. Instead, what I argue the speaker does is leave an aestheticized and thus permanent version of himself behind, much as a snake sheds its skin. Trying to describe the dynamic stasis concluding much of Yeats's late verse, Langbaum proposes that "Nature has grown intelligible because the poet, by assuming a mythical identity and walking through the paces of his own myth or phantasmagoria, has rendered the unconscious conscious; he has materialized the universal self" (*Mysteries of Identity,* 246). For my purposes, this explanation makes sense only if we assume "Nature" is equivalent to the "unconscious" or "the universal self." We can, I think, make such an assumption when we remember the three doctrines laid out in his essay "Magic" and the fact that Nature takes on fabric and meaning for him only in its fabulation, in its shaping in the unconscious.

28. Albright supposes that the speaker faces a "joyous death" because the "bird's sleepy cry" could be the "languorous contentment" of a mother bird, a daw perhaps, on an engendering nest, "incubating her species" as the speaker incubates his tradition (52). Though Albright does not do so, he might for consistency's sake have gone on to identify the last four lines as a pair of suspended alternatives distinguished from each other by "or:" one the oblivion of dusk and the other the future waiting to dawn. Brooks is more reserved in his hopes, saying that the poem ends in a "minor key," with the speaker's "contemplative detachment justified" by its penetration by the active and natural (13). But I would ask why, if the active and contemplative are unified at the end, a regeneration is not as inevitable as a death. Whittaker's reading is less ingenious and more sensible: "evil and loss no longer seem important" because they have faded with all temporality (202). The end brings neither pain nor pleasure, but the absence of desire.

Chapter 4. Speech without Self

1. It is a standard of *Four Quartets* criticism that Eliot's version of orthodox Christianity provides a way to move from a failed "romantic reliance on personal

intuition to the classical acceptance of the validity of external authority" (Weatherhead, 45).

2. We may be reminded here of Yeats's equivalent desire to escape the partiality of "partial causes" (Brooks, 199). However, Yeats did so to enlarge the self, while Eliot does so to escape the self.

3. For George Bornstein, the core struggle in Eliot's poetry is to undermine the poetic authority of the "dynamically developing consciousness" (149) so that it can be replaced with a "stillness, abstention from movement, a void in which divine presence could replace daimonic drives" (160). Though I accept the line Bornstein draws between these two sides, and he may very well be correct about Eliot's desire to abort any hint of Romantic consciousness, I don't think he properly identifies the kind of ego Eliot creates in the reader and speaker. It is precisely because the ego is not a "dynamically developing consciousness" that it must draw upon the authority of the Logos for its identity to emerge. Bornstein's presumption—that the only reason for the absence of a dynamic ego could be because Eliot had closed the lid on it—is therefore ungrounded.

4. This critical posture seems rooted in the work of George Bornstein, particularly his Eliot chapter in *Transformations of Romanticism in Yeats, Eliot, and Stevens.* Companion positions emerge in Ronald Bush's *T.S. Eliot: A Study in Character and Style,* and David Spurr's *Conflicts in Consciousness: T.S. Eliot's Poetry and Criticism.* All three divide Eliot's consciousness into a Romantic, visionary, irrational self and an abstract, neo-orthodox, rational self that must harness and contain the mind's overly creative impulse.

5. Evidence that the speaker remains on the periphery of poetic focus is clear in the diversity of critical attempts to characterize the speaker's voice. Keith Alldrit, in his study of the poem's musical form, describes *Four Quartets* in terms of a string quartet, a form that "was before all else a principle for the expression and reconciliation of opposites in experience and feeling" (28). Thus, Alldrit finds not one speaker but a series of interwoven voices in conflict—a "lecturer, prophet, conversationalist, and conjuror." On the other hand, Derek Traversi describes the speaker as a "single voice reflecting a continuous but expanding point of view" (89). More recently, Patrick Grant takes an apparently similar stance, arguing that we hear the speaker in a variety of different "modes" or "registers," for "none of them is quite distinct enough to crystallise into a separate persona" (113). Each critical perspective is useful, but none accounts wholly for the relationship between speaker and projected reader. Alldrit's characterizations, I think, demonstrate tendencies or tones rather than distinct voices; he does not or cannot fully delineate them. Traversi's claim for a single voice, however, asserts a homogeneity that does not exist. There is continuity, certainly, in the speaker's concerns, but there are too many shifts in perspective from movement to movement, quartet to quartet, for his claim to satisfy. On the other hand, while Grant's claim that the speaker is sufficiently various to remain elusive effectively articulates the speaker's situation, Traversi's notion of an "expanding" voice, though, nicely characterizes our sense of the speaker's potency. While I argue here for the opposite, in fact—that the speaker contracts rather than expands—the idea of expansion is useful to describe the scope of the speaker's vision and the indeterminacy of his location.

6. It is the generative rather than coercive sense of authority that I intend throughout, drawing on Edward Said's four-part definition: authority founds, creates a point of origin; increases and develops from that point; controls the shape of what it generates; and maintains continuity (Said, 83).

7. This analogy seems to invert the Heraclitean claim that the "creative ordering principle of the universe" is analogous to the "articulating power of the poet" (Hay, 171). However, Eliot still depends on Heraclitus's claim to justify his own claims about the situation of the modern ego.

8. Marc Manganaro's reading of Eliot's critical enterprise is relevant in this context because he makes a compelling case for Eliot's mining of anthropological methods to establish his cultural authority, suggesting that the very ambiguity of his references to iconic images and sites such as Little Gidding reinforce his hieratic influence: "The significance, sacred in the 'primitive' context, of the ritual object correlates with Eliot's postconversion figurations of sacred places, activities, or things around which the collective group gathers and generates interpretations. . . . [T]hese sites are pregnant with a significance that defies attachment to a particular meaning or interpretation . . . [each] sacred site functions as a totemic object that is simply there, utterly present, a fact in the midst of dubious, ambiguous, and conflicting motives, upright but unable to be definitively read. . . . [T]he posed inability to signify leads to the use of those sites to consolidate authority. The *absence* [emphasis his] of meaning invites the author, and he responds by filling the emptiness with power" (108–9). This reading, cynical on the face of it, perhaps, seems eminently perceptive and sound; however, in *Four Quartets,* the authority of Eliot's imagery is contingent upon his felt absence, his mediating distance from those sacred sites.

9. The view that the objective world originates and is known by way of the language referring to it inverts Williams's belief that consciousness, and thus the language it generates, can flash into life only by intimate contact with the objective world. It is because the relationship between word and thing determines the location of authority that Eliot's poetic authority is centered in the Logos, and Williams's in the coextensive contact between subject and object.

10. Harry Blamires reverently emphasizes this notion, claiming that we must read the poem in the same way we would the Still Point (16). In a logical extension of this thinking, to read the poem properly requires a submission to its authority, to the way it structures reality.

11. Derek Traversi gives a thorough account of the criticism faulting "The Dry Salvages" for ponderousness and vague thinking, and follows it with a mild but firm apology for the poem, explaining its clumsiness as an attempt to "bind his [Eliot's] experience as an individual to that of the race to which he belongs." Though this attempt brings no lasting sustenance, "not to have made it would have been to omit a link essential to the whole" (152).

12. Jonathan Culler's claims about apostrophe are relevant to the speaker's gestures here (135–54). In summary, Culler explains that the apostrophe is a gesture of self-authorization, a display of how the poets can create the worlds they seem only to refer to. This authority is amplified because the apostrophe is antinarrative and thus antitemporal, removing objects from time to a discursive "now" created by the poet. Furthermore, an apostrophe is a projection of the self in that the thing addressed—usually some form of the divine—is a stand-in for the poet orchestrating the poem's events.

13. Hay (185) reads "three districts" as "the poet's three worlds of illusion, actuality, and the higher dream." More specifically, they refer to the air and spirit of "Burnt Norton," the "earth and the Word made flesh" in "East Coker," and the "water and the baptism of desire" in "The Dry Salvages" (185). If nothing else, this reading typifies the reader's desire to integrate the vertical and horizontal, the realms of ego and Logos.

14. Describing the problem of identifying the "familiar compound ghost," Harry Blamires draws a useful analogy with harmonics, the reverberations we hear—or overhear—when a single note is sounded (146).

15. In this idea of an individual transformed by the role he occupies, we may be reminded of Max Weber's theory of charismatic authority, discussed in the first chapter. More directly, we find a source in Eliot's version of literary history, in which the individual poet absorbed into tradition alters without remaking it. Enlarging upon this theory in an effort to extend the poet's cultural authority, Eliot, in a 1933 article appearing in *Criterion,* explains that poetry breaks the "categories of thought and sensibilities of its age . . . by its speaking in the language of its time and the imagery of its own tradition, the word which belongs to no time" (Bush, 198).

16. In *A Coherent Splendor,* Albert Gelpi's unconcern with Eliot's ideological premises allows him to read this condition as a liberation from a finite perspective: "History, which otherwise would spell 'servitude' to striving factions, offers the 'freedom' to discern the field of action from the end of action" (153).

17. Michael North also reads the ending as a deferral or difference, pointing to the gap between reality and the desire expressed by Eliot's "political" aesthetic: " . . . the isolation of the individual, the tensions of class division, and the apparent separation of poetry from the world of practical politics, are all salved by a political aesthetic in which the part becomes the whole, representing it precisely because of its difference" (127).

Chapter 5. Williams's Unmade World

1. Much of my thinking on the interdependent relation of subject and object in *Paterson* is indebted to Joseph Riddel's *The Inverted Bell.* I take as a premise his explanation of the axiomatic "'Say it, no ideas but in things,'" that it does not suppose "the priority of thing over idea or thing over word. . . . [Rather], that there are no ideas unrealized and thus no thing except in the identity and difference of things" (9).

2. On the issue of "contact," Jerome Mazzaro quotes tellingly from one of Stevens's letters to Williams: "One never detects paraphrase in anything you do, either personally or in your writing, so that there really is a live contact there" (178). The effect Stevens is describing, of course, is the absence of a mediating ego.

3. In his rather reserved apologia for the term, Williams writes that "contact always implies a local definition of effort with a consequent taking on of certain colors from the locality by the experience, and these colors or sensual values of whatever sort are the only realities in writing or, as may be said, the essential quality in literature." (*Selected Essays,* 32).

4. Mazzaro quotes from Williams's "Letter to an Australian Editor," *Briarcliff Quarterly,* III, October, (1946): 208.

5. Though Miller uses it to present his theory of immanence, his phrase, "a system of reciprocal motions," might also describe the effect of mutual animation of subject and object (289).

6. Both Joel Connaroe (111) and Bernard Duffey (74–77) describe the movement of the poem as a movement from the inner self to the outside world.

7. Margaret Lloyd glances at the issue of a textual voice with her discussion of *Paterson*'s structure, which "may be engaged on several levels [that] share a

common dependency upon nonlinear patterning and upon a process that is open and dialectical and which occurs only with the active participation of the reader" (146).

8. Inserting the poem in the Romantic tradition, Joel Connaroe contends that in the Sunday in the park, the "external events serve mainly to trigger his [the poet's] thought processes; the focus never shifts from his receptive, inventing sensibility" (69). This view, though, is misleading; it presumes a circumscribed, neo-Wordsworthian presence examining his own situation in the landscape and its effects on him. Instead, Williams is concerned with altering that very distinction between mind and world—not in Miller's sense of a union of subject and object, but rather, a transpersonal investigation into experience that intersects the homologous worlds of perceiver and perceived. The worlds of self and Other remain separate; poetic expression enacts the scenes where the two rub against each other. This contact is geometric and mutually creative, just as a plane is formed when two lines intersect.

Kinreth Meyer updates the claims about Williams's Romanticism in an ideological assault on his use of the American landscape. Principally, she asserts that "the language of *Paterson* also suggests that Williams may be guilty of the same 'crime' [as Hamilton]—the remaking of the city in his own image, through an economy of appropriation" (161). Unfortunately, Meyer can demonstrate Williams's "guilt" only by association with Whitman, whom she quotes as a synecdoche for the nineteenth-century American tradition of masculinist appropriation. Consequently, she overlooks the intricate means Williams employs to display the antigenerative evil of the ego's phallic intrusiveness into the objective world. By contrast, in her admirable dissertation, "Networks of Empowerment: Feminist Poetics and Tradition in the Works of William Carlos Williams, Denise Levertov, and Kathleen Fraser," Linda Taylor argues persuasively that Williams "resists" the Poundian aesthetic that "perceived of poetic authority and creative power in explicit terms of masculine mastery . . . by valorizing what he himself defines as a feminine attribute—to make contact . . . " (80). Both his implicit poetics and explicit language fight at every turn the "appropriation" Meyer describes.

9. Sayre describes what is essentially a co-extensive relationship between mind and grasshoppers, both stone and actual: "the concrete weight . . . finds a 'counter buoyancy' in the 'mind's wings'" (101).

10. Henri Sayre, for instance, claims that it is not until the end of Book 2, when Cress's letter overwhelms the poem, that Williams abandons his "ameliorative" intentions and has to stand back to watch his material "asserting itself as itself" (Sayre, 101). This complaint is especially interesting in the light of Theodora Graham's seminal examination of Williams's revisions of Marcia Nardi's "Cress" letters ("'Her Heigh Compleynte': The Cress Letters of William Carlos Williams' *Paterson*"). Graham convincingly argues that the consequence—and thus perhaps the intention—of the revisions was to diminish perceptions of Williams's culpability and augment perceptions of Nardi's neurosis. The fact that, first, Williams felt a need to shield himself from her accusations and second, that Cress nonetheless emerges as such a potent accusing figure, testifies at the very least to a consistent commitment to his co-extensive poetics. Considering how tempted he must have been to reduce "Cress" to mere emblem, it is ultimately to his credit—personally and aesthetically—that he made no *apparent* interference with her enactment of autonomous re-creation.

11. Sayre makes a related point when discussing *Paterson* as a new genre: "the work of art is now dynamic, never fully knowable in and of itself because it refers

beyond itself, both as a mimetic structure, a tool of reference, and as a structure which invites interpretation, the operation of producing meaning" (134). His final phrasing here is particularly useful: it is through the demand to interpret the world of the poem that the mind is redeemed.

12. For a provocative discussion of the Dadaist influence on Book 3, see Peter Schmidt's *William Carlos Williams, the Arts, and Literary Tradition,* 173–205.

13. It is perhaps ironic that the library image could be used equally well as an emblem of circulation and distribution, permitting a continuity with the past.

14. Mazzaro treats this process allegorically, as a wedding of "the male language of thought and art and the female language of life to produce the complex eye-ear idiom" (127).

15. Miller's elaborate definition is most instructive in the relationship of the Beautiful Thing to subjective animation. He describes the Beautiful Thing as a "nameless presence," or, in Williams's terms, a "hidden flame" circulating between the formless, chaotic ground and the formed, defined thing, holding them together in a mutually in-forming process (328–35).

16. To describe this phenomenon, Riddel uses the Heideggerian idea of the poet's *"place"* of "inaugural naming," which is "where language breaks out, where we are brought into the presence of its first appearing, its beginning to take 'shape,' its flowering" (60).

17. We may again be reminded of a parallel in Yeats's lines from "To the Rose upon the Rood of Time": "Come near, come near, come near—Ah, leave me still / A little space for the rose-breath to fill!"

18. Carl Rapp challenges this anti-idealist view rather oddly, claiming Williams "was constantly striving *within his art* [emphasis his] to express the nature of his own spiritual preeminence, not only with respect to the world of natural phenomena, but also with respect to art itself" (30). Even if we accept the premise that he was preoccupied with his spiritual status, the multitude of Williams's explicit statements of artistic failure clearly contradict any idea that he was presuming a preeminence. More important, Williams is concerned only with the status of the poet as a medium of articulation, a voice through which the subject and object could meet. What he strove to do was to identify and express that place and act of meeting.

19. Riddel's description of "marriage" articulates this process very cleanly: "the two partners do not become one, as in some ideal union, but they join in their separateness and therefore incorporate a third" (26).

20. Connaroe, typical of those critics who fault Williams here, dismisses the passage because the "ideas are unconvincing, the tone often offensive, and the treatment of themes distractingly repetitious" (127–28). I am arguing that the cause of these flaws is Williams's failure to subscribe to his own tenets.

21. To understand the apparently derogatory meaning of "knowledge" here, we must turn to *The Embodiment of Knowledge,* where it permits "the escape of man from domination by his own engines" (62–63). If knowledge is instead treated as a fetish, it creates barriers to experience rather than a means to fuller understanding (44–45).

22. My readings here are indebted to Connaroe's (81–98).

23. Randall Jarrell, whose early condemnation of these lines still expresses the critical consensus, remarked that they "sound like the stuff you produce when you are demonstrating to a class that any prose whatsoever can be converted into four-stress accentual verse simply by inserting line-endings every four stresses" (Connaroe, 36).

24. Though the last line of Book 4 is "the end," the consensus, regardless of the critical premises, has become that the end projects a beginning. Pearce concludes that "Johnson's death, or our learning of it, blasts us spiralling and somersaulting back toward that beginning which is our end" (130). For Connaroe, the "image of the spiral . . . suggests a beginning as much as an end" (98), and Lloyd claims that the man walking out of the water indicates "that at least a key to a redeeming language has been found through the enactment of the four books of Paterson" (224–25). Drawing on the Derridean term, Riddel explains the end as a commitment to a "'*seminal* [emphasis his] adventure' in which the end is a 'blast' of dissemination of the seed-words that insure the continuation of the game [of invention]" (251–52).

25. Since the 1950s, the relationship between books 4 and 5 has not interested many critics. Martz explains that this book "served to recapitulate and bind together all the foregoing poem" (155). Lloyd says simply that the later book is "a new beginning which accommodates the changes that have occurred in Williams and the world" (276). Duffey explains that at the end of Book 4 the poet escapes the "abrupt dismissal" of "'the final somersault / the end'" by going inland, "to an interior that will emerge in its time as his work's true close—insofar as closure is possible" (90–91). If we read this as a movement to the subjective world, it can be argued that Book 5 follows in a natural sequence.

26. In "Beautiful Lofty Things," Yeats transfers an iconic rigidity to the men and women he has most deeply admired. Conversely, Williams transfers the energies of life to the faculties of art.

27. Sayre takes a similar view of the eagle's descent: "The drift of the imagination, its dream, is always toward the eternal and divine. But if the imagination is to survive, if it is to escape death 'intact,' it must quit its flight . . . and descend into the material reality of its art" (122). The imagination, however, is no more prone to flee the actual than an eagle is to flee his prey. Rather, the eagle, like the imagination, must constantly move between earth and sky to stay alive.

28. In reference to the Sappho passage, Riddel provides a useful description of the same effect: "Beauty defies authority, escapes subordination to a mediation that stands outside it, and reveals the enigma at its center" (169).

29. In an important sense, the androgynous female can be read as Williams's answer to Melville's "whiteness of the whale." Liberated from nineteenth-century sublimity, the woman attracts Williams for the same reason the whiteness horrified Melville: "in essence whiteness is not so much a color as the visible absence of color, and at the same time the concrete of all colors; is it for these reasons that there is such a dumb blankness, full of meaning, in a wide landscape of snows— a colorless, all-color of atheism from which we shrink?" (163).

30. Attempting to minimize the disturbing "ideological and ethical questions of masculinist aggression against the female" in *Paterson,* Albert Gelpi points to the androgyny of the Unicorn, which "presents—and reconciles—both the submissive feminine and the potent male. . . . It is the androgynous character of the Unicorn, at once victim and victor in the sequence of tapestries, that makes him-her Paterson/Williams's totem animal" (363). Gelpi is right to come to Williams's defense in this regard, but he does so by implicitly reinforcing the image of women as potential or actual victims. By contrast, Williams's use of the Unicorn's female qualities tends to emphasize the generative; in fact, it is quite arguably the female in the Unicorn that constitutes the image of the poet.

31. Though his interest is primarily in the parallel between art and religion,

Mazzaro explains the hunt in similar terms, calling it "an allegory for secular incarnation, a making of the word flesh. It is the 'thinging' of ideas . . . secularizing and aestheticizing the myth of the Incarnation. . . . The courting of the virgin becomes a myth for writing and perhaps also . . . a way of making writing into a religion and the writer's living on a substitute for Everlasting Life" (154).

Works Cited

Abrams, M. H. *Natural Supernaturalism: Tradition and Revolution in Romantic Literature.* New York: W.W. Norton & Company, 1971.

Albright, Daniel. *Myth against Myth: A Study of Yeats's Imagination in Old Age.* London: Oxford University Press, 1972.

Alldrit, Keith. *Eliot's* Four Quartets*: Poetry as Chamber Music.* London: The Woburn Press, 1978.

Altieri, Charles. *Enlarging the Temple: New Directions in American Poetry during the 1960s.* Lewisburg: Bucknell University Press, 1979.

Alvarez, A. *The Shaping Spirit.* London: Chatto & Windus, Ltd., 1958.

Arendt, Hannah. *Between Past and Future: Eight Exercises in Political Thought.* New York: The Viking Press, Inc., 1971.

Bell, David. *Power, Influence, and Authority: An Essay in Political Linguistics.* New York: Oxford University Press, 1975.

Bernstein, Michael. *The Tale of the Tribe.* Princeton: Princeton University Press, 1980.

Blamires, Harry. *Word Unheard: A Guide Through Eliot's Four Quartets.* London: Methuen, 1969. New York: Barnes and Noble, 1970.

Bloom, Harold. *The Anxiety of Influence.* New York: Oxford University Press, 1979.

Bornstein, George. *Transformations of Romanticism in Yeats, Eliot, and Stevens.* Chicago: University of Chicago Press, 1975.

Bradbury, Malcolm, and James MacFarlane, ed. *Modernism.* Middlesex: Penguin Books, Ltd., 1976.

Brooks, Harold. "W.B. Yeats: 'The Tower.'" *Durham University Journal,* 73, 1980.

Bush, Ronald. *T. S. Eliot: A Study in Character and Style.* New York: Oxford University Press, 1983.

Connaroe, Joel. *William Carlos Williams'* Paterson: *Language and Landscape.* Philadelphia: University of Pennsylvania Press, 1970.

Culler, Jonathan. *The Pursuit of Signs.* Ithaca: Cornell University Press, 1981.

Day, Gary. "The Poets: Georgians, Imagists and Others," in *Literature and Culture in Modern Britain: Volume One: 1900–1929,* Clive Bloom, ed. Harlow, Essex: Longman Group UK Limited, 1993.

de Man, Paul. "Romanticism and Anti-Self-Consciousness," in *Romanticism and Consciousness,* Harold Bloom, ed. New York: W.W. Norton & Company, Inc., 1970.

Dembo, L. S. *Conceptions of Reality in Modern American Poetry.* Berkeley and Los Angeles: University of California Press, 1966.

Derrida, Jacques. *Of Grammatology,* trans. Gayatri Spivak. Baltimore: Johns Hopkins University Press, 1976.

Duffey, Bernard. *A Poetry of Presence: The Writing of William Carlos Williams.* Madison: University of Wisconsin Press, 1986.

Eliot, Thomas Stearns. *Collected Poems: 1909–1962.* New York: Harcourt, Brace, & World, 1963.

————*On Poetry and Poets.* New York: Farrar, Straus, & Cudahy, 1961.

————*Selected Essays.* New York: Harcourt, Brace, & Company, 1950.

Ellis, Peter G. "T.S. Eliot, F.H. Bradley, and *Four Quartets,*" *Research Studies: Washington State University,* 37, No. 2 (June, 1969).

Ellmann, Richard. *The Identity of Yeats.* New York: Oxford University Press, 1954.

Ferry, Anne Davidson. *Milton's Epic Voice: The Narrator in* Paradise Lost. Cambridge: Harvard University Press, 1963.

Fish, Stanley. *Surprised by Sin: The Reader in* Paradise Lost. Berkeley: University of California Press, 1971.

Gardner, Helen. *The Art of T.S. Eliot.* New York: E.P. Dutton & Co., 1959.

Gelpi, Albert. *A Coherent Splendor: The American Poetic Renaissance, 1910–1950.* New York: Cambridge University Press, 1987.

Gilbert, Jack. *Monolithos: Poems, 1962 and 1982.* Port Townsend: Graywolf Press, 1982.

Graham, Theodora R. "Her Heigh Compleynte: The Cress Letters of William Carlos Williams' *Paterson,*" in *Ezra Pound and William Carlos Williams: The University of Pennsylvania Conference Papers.* Daniel Hoffman, ed. Philadelphia: University of Pennsylvania Press, 1983.

Grant, Patrick. "Knowing Reality: A Reading of Four Quartets." Bagchee, Shyamal, ed., in *T. S. Eliot: A Voice Descanting: Centenary Essays.* London: Macmillan, 1990.

Guillory, John. *Poetic Authority: Spenser, Milton, and Literary History.* New York: Columbia University Press, 1983.

Hartman, Geoffrey. *Wordsworth's Poetry, 1787–1814.* New Haven: Yale University Press, 1965.

Hay, Eloise Knapp. *T.S. Eliot's Negative Way.* Cambridge: Harvard University Press, 1982.

Hermans, Theo. *The Structure of Modernist Poetry.* London: Croom Helm, Ltd., 1982.

Hirschberg, Stuart. "The Visionary Landscape of Yeats's 'The Tower.'" *Literature in Wissenschaft und Unterricht.* 10, 1977.

Holloway, John. "Style and the World in *The Tower,*" in *An Honoured Guest.* London: Edward Arnold Publishers, Ltd., 1965.

Hulme, T. E. "Romanticism and Classicism," in *Critical Theory Since Plato,* Hazard Adams, ed. New York: Harcourt, Brace Jovanovich, Inc., 1971.

Jeffers, A. Norman. *A Commentary on the Collected Poems of W.B. Yeats.* Stanford: Stanford University Press, 1965.

Kenner, Hugh. "Into Our First World," in *T.S. Eliot's* Four Quartets, *A Casebook.* Bernard Bergonzi, ed. London: Macmillan, 1969.

Kerrigan, Richard. *The Prophetic Milton.* Charlottesville: University of Virginia Press, 1974.

Langbaum, Robert. *The Mysteries of Identity.* New York: Oxford University Press, 1977.

Lears, T. J. Jackson. *No Place of Grace: Antimodernism and the Transformation of American Culture 1880–1920.* New York: Pantheon Books, 1981.

Levenson, Michael. *A Genealogy of Modernism: A Study of English Literary Doctrine: 1908–1922.* Cambridge: Cambridge University Press, 1984.

Lloyd, Margaret. *William Carlos Williams' Paterson: A Critical Reappraisal.* Rutherford: Fairleigh Dickinson University Press, 1980.

Lynch, David. *The Poetics of the Self.* Chicago: University of Chicago Press, 1979.

Malkoff, Karl. *Escape from the Self.* New York: Columbia University Press, 1977.

Manganaro, Marc. *Myth, Rhetoric, and the Voice of Authority: A Critique of Eliot, Frye, and Campbell.* New Haven: Yale University Press, 1992.

Martz, Louis, ed. *The Meditative Poem: An Anthology of 17th Century Verse.* New York: Doubleday & Co., 1963.

Mathiessen, Francis Otto. *The Achievement of T.S. Eliot.* New York: Oxford University Press, 1959.

Mazzaro, Jerome. *William Carlos Williams: The Later Poems.* Ithaca and London: Cornell University Press, 1973.

Meisel, Perry. *The Myth of the Modern.* New Haven: Yale University Press, 1987.

Menand, Louis. *Discovering Modernism: T.S. Eliot and His Context.* New York: Oxford University Press, 1987.

Meyer, Kinereth. "Possessing America: William Carlos Williams' *Paterson* and the Poetics of Appropriation." Franklin, Wayne and Michael Steiner, eds., in *Mapping American Culture.* Iowa City: University of Iowa Press, 1992.

Miller, J. Hillis. *The Poets of Reality.* Cambridge, Mass.: Harvard University Press, 1965.

Milton, John. *John Milton: The Complete Poems and Major Prose,* Merrit Y. Hughes, ed. Indianapolis: The Bobbs-Merrill Company, Inc., 1976.

Monk, Samuel H. *The Sublime: A Study of Critical Theories in XVIII-Century England.* Ann Arbor: University of Michigan Press, 1960.

North, Michael. *The Political Aesthetic of Yeats, Eliot, and Pound.* Cambridge: Cambridge University Press, 1991.

Onorato, Richard J. *The Character of the Poet: Wordsworth in* The Prelude. Princeton: Princeton University Press, 1971.

Pagels, Elaine. *Adam, Eve, and the Serpent.* New York: Random House, 1988.

Pearce, Roy Harvey. *The Continuity of American Poetry.* Princeton: Princeton University Press, 1961.

Perloff, Marjorie. "'The Tradition of Myself': The Autobiographical Mode of Yeats." *Journal of Modern Literature,* 4, 1974

Pruitt, Virginia. "Return from Byzantium: W.B. Yeats and 'The Tower.'" *Journal of Modern Literature.* 4, 1974.

Ramazani, Jahan. *Yeats and the Poetry of Death: Elegy, Self-Elegy, and the Sublime.* New Haven: Yale University Press, 1990.

Ransom, John Crowe. *God without Thunder.* New York: Harcourt, Brace and Co., 1930.

Rapp, Carl. *William Carlos Williams and Romantic Idealism*. Hanover and London: University of New England Press, 1984.

Regueiro, Helen. *The Limits of Imagination*. Ithaca: Cornell University Press, 1976.

Riddel, Joseph. *The Inverted Bell: Modernism and the Counterpoetics of William Carlos Williams*. Baton Rouge: Louisiana State University Press, 1974.

Rosenthal, M. L. *Running to Paradise*. New York: Oxford University Press, 1994.

Said, Edward. *Beginnings*. New York: Basic Books, 1975.

Sayre, Henri. *The Visual Text of William Carlos Williams*. Chicago: University of Illinois Press, 1983.

Schmidt, Peter. *William Carlos Williams, the Arts, and Literary Tradition*. Baton Rouge: Louisiana State University Press, 1988.

Schricker, Gale. *A New Species of Man*. Lewisburg: Bucknell University Press, 1982.

Schwartz, Sanford. *Matrix of Modernism: Pound, Eliot, and Early Twentieth Century Thought*. Princeton: Princeton University Press, 1985.

Sennett, Richard. *Authority*. New York: Alfred A. Knopf, 1980.

Simpson, David. *Irony and Authority in Romantic Poetry*. London: MacMillan, 1979.

Spanos, William V. "Hermeneutics and Memory: Destroying T.S. Eliot's *Four Quartets*." *Genre XI*, Winter 1978.

Spender, Stephen. "Moderns and Contemporaries." *The Idea of the Modern in Literature and the Arts*. Irving Howe, ed. New York: Horizon Press, 1967.

Spurr, David. *Conflicts in Consciousness: T.S. Eliot's Poetry and Criticism*. Chicago: University of Illinois Press, 1984.

Stead, C. K. *The New Poetic: Yeats to Eliot*. London: Hutchinson & Co. Ltd., 1964.

————"Stendhal's Mirror and Yeats' Looking Glass," in *On Modern Poetry: Essays Presented to Donald Davie*. Nashville, Vanderbilt University Press, 1988.

Taylor, Linda A. "Networks of Empowerment: Feminist Poetics and Tradition in the Works of William Carlos Williams, Denise Levertov, and Kathleen Fraser." *Dissertation Abstracts International*, 1990.

Traversi, Derek. *T.S. Eliot: The Longer Poems*. New York: Harcourt Brace Jovanovich, 1976.

Ward, David. *T.S. Eliot Between Two Worlds*. London: Routledge and Kegan Paul, 1973.

Weatherhead, A. Kingsley. "*Four Quartets:* Setting Love in Order." *Wisconsin Studies in Contemporary Literature*. 3, No. 2, 1962.

Whittaker, Thomas. *Swan and Shadow*. Chapel Hill: University of North Carolina Press, 1964.

Williams, William Carlos. *The Autobiography of William Carlos Williams*. New York: New Directions, 1967.

————*The Embodiment of Knowledge*. New York: New Directions, 1974.

————*Imaginations*. New York: New Directions, 1970.

————*Paterson*. New York: New Directions, 1963.

————*Selected Essays*. New York: Random House, 1954.

Wordsworth, William. *William Wordsworth: The Prelude,* J.C. Maxwell, ed. New Haven and London: Yale University Press, 1971.

Yeats, William Butler. *The Variorum Edition of the Poems of W.B. Yeats,* Peter Allt and Russell K. Alspach, ed. New York: Macmillan Publishing Co., 1977.

————*A Vision.* New York: Macmillan, 1965.

————*Essays and Introductions.* New York: Macmillan, 1961.

————*Explorations.* New York: Macmillan, 1962.

————*Mythologies.* New York: Macmillan, 1959.

Young, David. "High Talk: The Voice from *The Tower.*" *The Kenyon Review.* 11: 4, 1989.

Zwerdling, Alex. *Yeats and the Heroic Ideal.* New York: New York University Press, 1965.

Index